WHAT HAPPENED, MISS SIMONE?

A veteran music journalist, **Alan Light** is the author of *The Holy or the Broken: Leonard Cohen, Jeff Buckley and the Unlikely Ascent of "Hallelujah"* and *Let's Go Crazy: Prince and the Making of Purple Rain*. Light was previously the editor-in-chief of *Vibe* and *Spin* and a senior writer for *Rolling Stone*. He is also a frequent contributor to the *New York Times*.

WHAT HAPPENED, MISS SIMONE?

A BIOGRAPHY

ALAN LIGHT

CANONGATE

But what happened, Miss Simone? Specifically, what happened to your big eyes that quickly veil to hide the loneliness? To your voice that has so little tenderness, yet flows with your commitment to the battle of Life? What happened to you?

—MAYA ANGELOU, 1970

WHAT HAPPENED, MISS SIMONE?

INTRODUCTION

"**A**re you ready, black people?"

In the summer of 1969—before, during, and after the "three days of peace and music" being held at Max Yasgur's farm in Bethel, New York—another all-star outdoor music festival was taking place in Mount Morris Park, northeast of Manhattan's Central Park. The Harlem Cultural Festival, also sometimes called the "Black Woodstock," happened over the course of six Sunday afternoons from June 29 to August 24, with legends like B.B. King, the Staple Singers, and Sly & the Family Stone playing to an estimated one hundred thousand concert-goers.

Tony Lawrence, a New York nightclub singer and sometime movie actor, was the producer, promoter, and host of the events. On campuses and in black neighborhoods throughout the country, unrest and upheaval were at a fever pitch, so while the city's mayor John Lindsay spoke at the event (and was introduced as a "blue-eyed soul brother"), the New York Police Department refused to provide security for the concerts. In their stead, a delegation of Black Panthers managed the crowds.

At one of the July shows, Jesse Jackson addressed the throngs of people. "As I look out at us rejoice today," he said, "I was hoping it would be in preparation for the major fight we as a people have on our hands here in this nation. Some of you are laughing because you don't know any better, and others laughing because you are too mean to cry. But you need to know that some mean stuff is going down. A lot of you can't read newspapers. A lot of you can't read books, because our schools have been mean and left us illiterate or semiliterate. But you have the mental capacity to read the signs of the times."

It was a time of joy and danger, of liberation and fear, testing the opportunities and the limits of empowerment. And no performance over those six summer Sundays would capture the moment, in all its contrasts, more than the appearance of Nina Simone.

>*Are you ready to smash white things? Burn buildings?*
>　　*Are you ready?*
>*Are you ready to build black things?*

Simone's concert came near the end of the series, on August 17. Just a few weeks earlier, she had recorded "To Be Young, Gifted and Black," inspired by the memory of her friend and mentor Lorraine Hansberry, an anthem of hope for the future of a civil rights movement that had already been battered and ripped apart by murders, philosophical and tactical divisions, and government interference; still, the song would be named the "Black National Anthem" by the Congress of Racial Equality and covered by Aretha Franklin and Donny Hathaway.

When she took the stage at Mount Morris Park—in a long yellow-and-black-print dress, her hair teased into a sort of Afro-bouffant, massive silver earrings dangling to her neck—she made explicit the tensions and the possibilities of an event celebrating black culture and black pride in the aftermath of the riots that had erupted in urban areas during the previous summers.

Backed by a loose but propulsive and earnest-looking group of musicians wearing dashikis, she dug into a set focused on protest material of various moods: the brand-new "To Be Young,

Gifted and Black"; "Four Women," her controversial examination of the black female experience, and the insidious power held by varying black skin tones, in America; a fiery new song titled "Revolution," with the refrain "Don't you know it's going to be all right," borrowed from the Beatles' hit of the same name; the joyous "Ain't Got No—I Got Life" medley, from the "American Tribal Love-Rock Musical" *Hair,* which had opened on Broadway the previous year and was still running, about seventy blocks south of the Harlem stage.

But it was the final number of her performance, a recitation of "Are You Ready, Black People?," the battle cry written by David Nelson of the proto-rap group the Last Poets, that would define Simone's performance for history. "I did not memorize enough, so I have to read it," she told the crowd. "It's for you." And as her band banged out a rhythm on the congas and chanted, "Yes, I'm ready," in response to the poem's questions, she bit down on Nelson's words.

> *Are you ready to change yourself?—You know what I'm talking about.*
> *Are you ready to go inside yourself and change yourself?*

The Harlem audience yelled its approval. They shouted affirmations at the challenge to "smash white things," to "go inside yourself and change yourself." Simone built the poem to a climax, then said quietly, "See you later." She left the stage as the band kept the groove going.

But once again, on that day and the days that followed, true revolutionary action failed to materialize; the chaos the crowd chanted about did not ensue. And whether or not she still literally believed in her music's power to inspire social or political change, soon thereafter, Nina Simone—who often referred to herself as "the only singer in the civil rights movement"—would reach a breaking point in her frustration with America and with what she saw as the dwindling potential of true black progress.

"We had no leaders," she would say in 1989. "Lorraine Hansberry was dead, Langston Hughes was dead, Eldridge Cleaver was in jail. Paul Robeson was long since been dead, Stokely Carmichael was gone, Malcolm X was dead, and Martin Luther King was dead. We had nobody left."

On top of the scarcity of true visionaries, Simone was also disappointed with the men in the Student Non-violent Coordinating Committee, who she had been hoping would take up arms and lead a real revolution. "I became very disillusioned about it all," she recalled. "I felt that there was no more movement anymore, and that I wasn't part of anything." Earlier in her life, she had invested years into the dream of becoming America's first great black classical pianist; after the disappointment of abandoning that aspiration, she was losing hope in her second grand ambition—the struggle for racial equality that had dominated her recent work.

Only a few years after the Harlem Cultural Festival, Nina Simone would renounce her country, living out most of her final decades drifting in exile through the Caribbean, Africa, and Europe. Although she had steadily produced albums between *Little Girl Blue*—the 1958 debut that made her a sensation—and (the presciently titled) *It Is Finished* in 1974, she released just three more studio albums before her death on April 21, 2003.

After her reign as one of the culture's most influential artists—as a singer and an activist—Simone's later life began as a sad, disturbing saga. She spent years struggling against managers and record labels, trying to wrest control of her work from them. She frequently fought with those closest to her. She found and lost various loves, real and imagined, and her sometimes-obsessive quest for another husband dominated her thoughts until her last days. ("Most of my love affairs were too blind and too desperate," she said. "That's how I lost them.") But her final act also had its triumphs. Following many inconsistent years, she would ultimately emerge—against all odds—as a financially solvent, beloved icon. She would appear on stages until the last year of her life, often entertaining lengthy standing ovations after a show.

"What I hear about Nina is either 'Her music is fantastic' or 'Oh, she was a difficult person,'" said Gerrit De Bruin, her close and trusted companion throughout the tumultuous 1980s and '90s. "But she was a very lovely person as well, a very loving person. If she hadn't been such a genius, nothing would have happened. She would have been in the gutter, a bag lady or whatever. But the world accepted a lot because it was the genius artist Nina."

Most of this troubled existence, of course, had to do with her specific circumstances: being a piano prodigy who grew up in the rural and segregated South, with complicated relationships to her family, her music, and her sexuality. Her mother was a traveling minister who, Simone always felt, cared more about her parishioners than her daughter, while her beloved father eventually (inevitably?) disappointed her late in his life, causing her to disown him before his death. Her letters and diaries reveal a woman who feared her own husband, questioned her sexual preference, battled depression.

But it's hard not to look at Nina Simone's triumphant, tortured life as, in some ways, a reflection of her time, her race, her gender. If she was both brilliant and unstable, did she not live through a moment in history that was also brilliant and unstable?

Attallah Shabazz, one of Malcolm X's daughters—whose family lived next door to Simone's family for several years in Mount Vernon, New York—put it another way. Simone "was not at odds with the times," she said. "The times were at odds with her. When a person moves to their own kind of clock, spirit, flow, you're always in congress with yourself. The challenge is, how does the congress around you accept you? How do we fit in in the world that we're around, but be exactly who we are? Was Nina Simone allowed to be exactly who she was? No. So she had to seek places to be at one with her congress—to Africa, to Paris. But then she was away from other comforts, people, family, roots.

"How does royalty stomp around in the mud and still walk with grace? Most people are afraid to be as honest as she lived."

"She is loved or feared, adored or disliked, but few who have met her music or glimpsed her soul react with moderation. She is an extremist, extremely realized." This was Maya Angelou's description of Nina Simone in a 1970 profile for *Redbook* magazine. If it feels a bit overstated now, it seems to be an accurate representation of Simone's standing at the height of her powers. Her commercial success may have been slight next to that of the pop giants who emerged during the same era ("I've only got four very famous songs," she would later say), but her impact was profound.

Simone's music was singular, inimitable, uncategorizable. "In many ways," wrote Princeton professor Daphne Brooks in an essay examining several different performances by Simone of "Four Women," "Nina Simone would shape the bulk of her career in response to an aesthetic conundrum: what should a black female artist sound like?"

Trained as a classical pianist, she was often called a jazz singer, but it was a label she deeply resented, seeing in it only a racial classification. She grudgingly accepted the popular nickname "the High Priestess of Soul" but gave it little significance.

If anything, she claimed, she was a folk singer, and her dazzling, unpredictable repertoire—Israeli folk tunes, compositions by Bertolt Brecht and Kurt Weill, songs by the Bee Gees and Leonard Cohen and George Harrison, traditional ballads, jazz standards, spirituals, children's songs—is perhaps unmatched in its range.

Her piano playing, the blazing focus of her early life, was accomplished and sophisticated well beyond that of her peers. And her delivery, on her best days, was unparalleled in its intensity and force. Her voice, a husky contralto, was untrained and, for some, a bit of an acquired taste but was incomparably equipped to express certain emotions, and *Rolling Stone* ranked her number 29 in its list of the 100 Greatest Singers of All Time. "I heard her sing a song in French—I didn't even know what she was saying, and I started crying," Mary J. Blige told the magazine. "Then she goes from that to 'Mississippi Goddam,' singing it like a church record, but she's cursing out the system. Nina could sing anything, period."

"She was hip-hop twenty years before the beats arrived," writer/musician David Was, best known as part of the band Was (Not Was), told NPR in 2005. "In the 1960s, no black woman was any more 'gangsta' than Nina Simone. . . . Nina Simone may have been embittered by racism and social injustice, but that gave shape to her persona as a kind of female black Bob Dylan, albeit with a bit more swing than twang and an unmistakable passion and intensity that remain unrivaled to this day."

Simone herself would not allow her work to be reduced simply to a product of anger, a push-button reaction to white racism that could be dismissed without an acknowledgment of the music's layers. "I sing from intelligence," she said. "I sing from letting them know that I know who they are, and what they have done to my people around the world. That's not anger—anger has its place, and fire moves things. But I sing from intelligence."

That intellect was noticed by many of the leading black thinkers and writers of her time, including Langston Hughes and LeRoi Jones (later Amiri Baraka), who became her fans and champions. Simone's good friend James Baldwin spoke of her artistic role in a 1973 interview. He addressed the concept of the artist as lover and offered that Simone and Billie Holiday (a singer with whom Simone was often linked, in a comparison that she would always be sensitive about) were at once poets and lovers because they "gave you back your experience . . . and you recognized it for the first time because [they were] in and out of it . . . and made it possible for you to bear it."

From her earliest days onstage, Simone's live performances were their own kind of drama. She was always quick to cut a concert short or scold an audience if they were not giving her their full attention, and those tendencies were exacerbated in the latter half of her career; her shows could be scattershot, and she sometimes didn't bother to show up. "White people had Judy Garland," Richard Pryor once said. "We had Nina."

But witnesses agree that when she was at her best her power onstage could be astonishing, transformative. "When you saw her in person, she could make you believe whatever it was she wanted to make you believe," said jazz writer and cultural critic Stanley Crouch.

Simone seems to have been better suited for recording in front of an audience rather than in a studio; though of course live settings ran the risk of disaster, they also offered the chance to capture her at her most passionate and intense, displaying the playfulness and engagement that proved harder for her to reveal in the colder confines of a studio. She was well aware of her power as a performer, her gift for transmuting raw energy into a message. She once described her own reactions to music as a child in terms that were vibrantly physical: "Anything musical made me quiver ecstatically, as if my body were a violin and somebody was drawing a bow across it." Early in her career, she would prepare for a show the way an athlete scopes out a stadium before a big game—pacing the theater to get a sense of the sound and sightlines from different seats, feeling out the vibe of the city, the day, the crowd. It was an exercise in mapping out the best way into her audience's heads.

"Actually, what I do when I'm at my best is mass hypnosis," she said. "You can hypnotize an entire audience and make them feel a certain way. I think about what they're feeling, because I'm making sure they feel a certain way. And I know when I've got them.

"It's a spell that you cast. You start with a certain song and you build the mood with it. Another song that's related to the first song, and the third song is related to the second song, and so forth and so on, until you reach a certain climax in feeling. And by that time you've got them hypnotized. I always know that they're with me when I hear nothing but silence—then you've got them."

George Wein, the legendary promoter of the Newport Jazz and Newport Folk Festivals, booked some of Simone's most triumphant shows (her 1960 Newport debut) and some of her most disastrous (a 1977 Carnegie Hall appearance, when she canceled just a few hours before the doors opened and left town without telling anyone). "She didn't copy anybody, she was an original artist—and there are very few that are original artists," he said. "When you have that unique talent, that talent that is only yours, that only belongs to you, you are creating and giving something that people have never heard before. And that's why she was great—and I use the word 'great' advisedly, 'cause she was great."

Even after her best performing days had passed, though, Simone's influence endured. "To me, she was the quintessential woman: strong, unafraid, brutally honest, genuine, vulnerable,

soulful and passionate," Alicia Keys wrote. "She made me want
to practice the piano twenty hours a day until my skill was as
great as hers. She made me want to live life, learn and experience
it earnestly and use my voice to say SOMETHING!! Say something that could ring true in the spirit of the people."

Other wildly successful artists also took cues from Simone.
At 1994's American Music Awards, on the heels of her performance in *The Bodyguard,* Whitney Houston—then arguably
the biggest pop star in the world—constructed a medley that
cemented her own place within American musical history's lin-
eage, while paying homage to the honored position Nina held
there. For the performance's opening, Houston chose Simone's
very first single and highest-charting song in the United States,
"I Loves You, Porgy," belting the George and Ira Gershwin song
Nina had made famous before launching into "And I Am Telling
You I'm Not Going," the show-stopping climax from the musical *Dreamgirls*. Houston concluded the appearance by tearing
into a wrenching version of *The Bodyguard*'s "I Have Nothing,"
seamlessly fusing multiple decades of black female passion and
strength in ten minutes. And when the night ended, Whitney
walked away with eight AMAs, the most trophies ever awarded
to a female performer in a single night.

That same year, Jeff Buckley included his achingly emotional
version of "Lilac Wine"—a song Simone recorded in 1966—on
Grace, the one and only album he released in his short lifetime,
a record that influenced everyone from Radiohead to Coldplay
to Miley Cyrus, who released her own cover of "Lilac Wine" in
2014. In 1996, Lauryn Hill name-checked Simone on "Ready or
Not," the first single from the Fugees' Grammy-winning, six-
times platinum album *The Score*. ("While you're imitating Al
Capone / I'll be Nina Simone / Defecating on your microphone,"
L. Boogie rhymed.)

Simone's own music maintained a steady cultural presence. Her brassy "Feeling Good" continues to pop up in numerous TV shows (including the cultural sensation *Sex and the City*) and singing competitions, a swaggering jolt of old-school girl power. It's a Nina standard that's been covered by George Michael, Michael Bublé, and the rock band Muse. In 2008, during his historic presidential campaign, Barack Obama revealed that he too was a Nina Simone fan. On a list of his top ten songs, he put her 1965 recording of "Sinnerman"—a song she had learned in her childhood at revival meetings led by her mother—at number 5, in between the Rolling Stones' "Gimme Shelter" and "Touch the Sky" by rapper Kanye West. (Toward the end of his tenure, Obama may have signaled a change in his own mood by including "Feeling Good" as his Simone selection on a playlist for Spotify.)

West, in fact, introduced Simone's work to still more listeners, sampling her recordings numerous times on productions for other artists and on his own albums—most controversially, using a segment of her chillingly matter-of-fact version of "Strange Fruit" for his 2013 "Blood on the Leaves," an appropriation leading many to question the incorporation of a groundbreaking composition written to protest the lynching of southern black men into a song that most listeners assumed was only about a breakup, groupies, and drugs.

More recently, though, interest in Simone has escalated dramatically. A feature film project has spent years in limbo; though Mary J. Blige was initially cast in the starring role, the part eventually went to Zoe Saldana, sparking ongoing protest that Nina Simone, writer of "Four Women," should not be portrayed by a lighter-skinned actress. After lengthy delays, the movie was scheduled for release in December 2015.

In the meantime, the spirit of Simone figured prominently in

2014's acclaimed *Beyond the Lights,* which starred Gugu Mbatha-Raw as the rising, ambitious R&B star Noni Jean. "Nina Simone, she's sort of like the ghost throughout the movie," said Mbatha-Raw. "Artists like Nina Simone and India.Arie represented the more soulful side of where Noni wants to be, even though she is in this sort of packaged persona."

By February 2015, mentions of Simone were spiking in connection with major events in music. In the week leading up to the Grammy Awards in Los Angeles, Bob Dylan was honored by the MusiCares charity. Following performances of his songs by the likes of Bruce Springsteen, Neil Young, and Jack White, Dylan unexpectedly stole the show with a lengthy, freewheeling speech looking back over his own history, influences, and inspirations.

"Nina Simone, I used to cross paths with her in New York City in the Village Gate nightclub," said Dylan. "She was an artist I definitely looked up to. She recorded some of my songs that she learned directly from me, sitting in a dressing room. She was an overwhelming artist, piano player, and singer. Very strong woman, very outspoken and dynamite to see perform. That she was recording my songs validated everything that I was about. Nina was the kind of artist that I loved and admired."

Also in February, John Legend and Common won the Academy Award for Best Original Song for "Glory," their theme to Ava DuVernay's film *Selma,* a retelling of the 1965 voting rights march led by Martin Luther King Jr. Legend—who had included "I Wish I Knew How It Would Feel to Be Free," written by Dr. Billy Taylor but popularized by Simone, on his 2008 collaboration with the Roots, *Wake Up!*—began his acceptance speech by stating that "Nina Simone said it's an artist's duty to reflect the times in which we live. We wrote this song for a film that was based on events that were fifty years ago, but we say Selma is now, because the struggle for justice is right now."

And that same month, Grammy-winning singer/bass player Meshell Ndegeocello, who has worked with such artists as Madonna, John Mellencamp, and the Rolling Stones, played a tribute show to Simone as part of the Lincoln Center American Songbook series; she had previously released an album in 2012 titled *Pour une Âme Souveraine: A Dedication to Nina Simone*. Asked about her ability to inhabit the songs of another artist, Ndegeocello noted that this was precisely the inspiration she took from Simone.

"Nina [was] great at that," she said. "Look at her version of 'Don't Let Me Be Misunderstood.' I think [the Animals] have sold more records, but hers is the quintessential version. Her ability to take a Leonard Cohen song ('Suzanne') and make it her own is a testament of her improvisational ability and greatness, and that's definitely the one thing I try to celebrate with her, is that she's the one who inspired me to look at songs just as songs and try to put your own character inside of them."

Why was there such a sudden burst of attention for an artist who had been dead for a dozen years? How had public consciousness remained so high for someone who had only grazed the pop charts a few times and who had no songs that had penetrated mass nostalgia sufficiently to stay in circulation on oldies radio?

"Fifty years after her prominence, Nina Simone is now reaching her peak," wrote Salamishah Tillet in the *New York Times*. "Today Simone's multitudinous identity captures the mood of young people yearning to bring together our modern movements for racial, gender and sexual equality."

Maybe in the months of Ferguson and Baltimore (following the death of Freddie Gray, her 1978 recording of Randy Newman's song "Baltimore"—"Oh, Baltimore / Ain't it hard just to live"—was being widely shared on social media), and the resurgence of protest by and for black Americans, Nina Simone's music, image, and history had a new resonance. Writing in *The*

Nation, Syreeta McFadden asserted that "at this critical moment in our national life, Simone's voice has once again reached an urgent pitch, her music and activism has captured our cultural imagination again." Or maybe the majesty, purity, and distinctiveness of her work mean that it's always there, waiting for those who will discover and appreciate its power on its own terms.

Simone presumably would have welcomed the ongoing vitality of her music; she was certainly never shy about expressing her disappointment that she was underappreciated. "I really thought that this planet automatically rewarded you for excellence," she said. "I really thought that, because I felt that the planet knew its own deficit, its own lack of music. I thought it appreciated its artists. We work, they give us money or they give us food, whatever."

Her fight for acceptance had to do with her race, no question, but also with her uncompromising aesthetic and personality. And though it may not have served her purposes to say so, she was apparently aware of these nuances. "For films or interviews, she's always said, 'They didn't accept me because I was black,'" recalled De Bruin. "But she told me, 'Gerrit, they couldn't accept my freedom in music, and that's why they didn't want me.' But that was not for the outside world."

But Nina Simone found other rewards in her complex, thorny life and was continually striving for more. She claimed that she had tried virtually all the world's religions at some point to see what they each had to offer. In one interview—for one of the numerous false starts at a memoir, which eventually resulted in 1991's often fascinating, wildly inaccurate, maddeningly uneven *I Put a Spell on You*—she was asked whether she could find God in her own music.

"Of course, all the time," she replied. "How do you explain what it feels like to get on the stage and make poetry that you know sinks into the hearts and souls of people who are unable to express it? How do you talk about that? There aren't many words, but in some way you know that tonight was a good thing. You got to them. That's God.

"I am very aware that I am an instrument," she continued. "I have fights with God every day. I tell him, 'Unless you do such and such a thing, I'm not going to play anymore. I'm not going to sing anymore. I'm not going to let anybody know I'm around.' I've been given the gift of being able to play by ear, having perfect pitch, having things that ordinary people do not have. When you have this gift, you must give it back to the world. That's the only way you're going to get it off your back. I don't know if I can explain any better than that what God is."

CHAPTER 1

I was born a child prodigy, darling. I was born a genius.

Nina Simone was born Eunice Kathleen Waymon in Tryon, North Carolina, on February 21, 1933, the sixth of eight children. The Waymon family was rounded out by sisters Lucille, Dorothy, and Frances and brothers John Irvin, Carrol, Harold, and Sam. Perhaps foreshadowing the instability that would go on to define much of her life, her father, John Divine Waymon, worked various odd jobs, never sticking with one craft for too long; mother Mary Kate was the granddaughter of slaves and came from a family of preachers (fifteen of them in all, according to Simone). She carried on that storied tradition and became a traveling Methodist minister, supplementing the spare income with cleaning and domestic work.

Tryon was a resort town, which created—superficially, at least—a more liberal racial atmosphere than in most of the South. "It was not as rigidly segregated as other towns," said Carrol Waymon, who would later become an educator and activist, forming the Africana Studies Program at San Diego State University. Black neighborhoods scattered through Tryon. This also meant that black people interacted more frequently with white people than they might in other places, playing sports together and working at the resort.

Still, there was only so far such contact could go. "One of my brothers' friends who must have been, I don't know, nineteen, seventeen, something, it was found that he was going with one of the white girls," said Carrol. "It was hush-hush, I didn't know about it. He had to get out of town one night, so we went, 'Why did he leave so soon?' I began to understand he was not supposed to be going with whites."

By Carrol's count, the Waymons lived in about seven different houses in the area. Frances, the youngest, described one of the residences as "a wooden house that was not much to be desired"—very old, with a brick stove, an outhouse, no insulation, and a porch that had been enclosed to serve as an extra bedroom.

"You went out and you brought in buckets of water," she said. "We had big round tin tubs, they call them. You heated the water on the wooden stove, that's how you took your Saturday night bath. It was such an ordeal that everybody took baths on Saturday night. And we had a garden, we had pigs and cows and chickens. We were very poor."

Despite the family's poverty, Nina Simone's earliest images of her childhood were pleasant enough. "My first conscious memory of my mother is her singing while she cooks, while she washed clothes," she said. "She was always cheerful. We had a farm, a little bitsy one. Momma used to churn buttermilk on an old-fashioned churn and she showed me how to do it.

"Most of all I remember being with the other kids. Momma would cook for us, and sometimes she would say, 'I don't know where I'm going to get dinner.' Sometimes we didn't have much to eat and she would pray, and then by the time evening came on, we'd have enough food."

To stretch the rations and feed her family of ten, Mary Kate would make what she called "Waymon Specials"—dumplings or a concoction called vinegar pie. She canned fruits and vegetables to eat during the winter. "Momma never seemed to worry about being poor or hungry," Simone said. "We weren't ever hungry 'cause Momma knew how to not do that. It is true we were very poor, but we didn't feel the poverty because of the way she did things."

The singer's first recollections of her father were also charmingly bucolic. More approachable than her mother, he was lighthearted, even mischievous, and he and Eunice had a genuine intimacy, a special bond. "My daddy putting me on his knee, rocking me to patty-cake, my dad playing with me—I was his pet," she said. "He had an old jalopy, a Model A Ford, and that thing used to make all kinds of noises; I could hear him clear across town coming home and I would run up the hill, through the woods, to be there when he crossed that particular spot, to jump on the running board and go home with him. I would do this every day."

"His whole life was playing," she said in another instance. "He played at everything. He didn't tell us any jokes, we were too young. But he was playful, always."

John Waymon's flair for entertaining—including his distinctive "double whistle"—was more than just a way to amuse his family and keep their spirits light. In fact, he and Mary Kate had started out performing onstage together. "Daddy loved the 'St. Louis Blues,' had his spats, he could dance and sing," said Carrol. "He'd play his guitar, and he also played the harmonica, he was excellent at that. Had he not met Mother, he would have probably gone on to be on the stage."

But when Mary Kate started preaching, after they were married, it put an end to his performing career. John worked as a barber, a truck driver; he even started a dry-cleaning business. He had what his daughter Frances described as an entrepreneurial spirit and was a pillar of the church community. As a business owner, he could proudly call himself middle class.

But when the Depression hit, John's options dwindled.

Around 1931, he closed his businesses down and lost his trucks. He took work as a handyman, a caretaker for white families, a cook at a lakeside Boy Scout camp. But by the time Eunice was born, he was mostly working in the garden for sustenance and anything he might sell or trade.

Some of this slowdown, though, might have had more to do with his health than with the country's dire economic straits. He had a blockage in his small intestine, and in 1936 he had an operation. After the surgery, a rubber tube was inserted into the stomach so it could drain, and the wound needed to be exposed in order to be washed and bathed. And this condition meant that the sole responsibility of supporting the family fell on Mary Kate.

Eunice, age three, was tasked with nursing her father back to health. "I would take him for a walk every day and fix his meals, and I was so happy," she said. "He loved the heat, and he had these raw eggs that had to be beaten up with a little vanilla and a little sugar, and it tasted so good I used to get a little bit for myself. But I had to feed him this every day and take him for a walk."

There were additional upheavals during this time, too. During his recovery, the Waymon house burned down in the middle of the night. They moved once, then again to a town called Lynn, where their house was so primitive that not only did it not have indoor plumbing, it didn't even have an outhouse; the family had to use the woods as the bathroom.

The conditions were so poor that the Waymons left and stayed with a relative back in Tryon, then finally resettled in a house of their own again. Despite this, John hadn't fully lost his political spirit—serving on the town council, he led a protest against a poll tax and had the law changed—but a decade of illness and financial insecurity was weighing on him.

"He was energetic, active, well accepted, well respected,"

said Carrol, "and had to go from being on his way to great things to the bottom economically, and it just knocked him for a loop."

Whether John's own problems were a cause or merely an effect, the Waymon family was fracturing. Eldest brother John Irvin fought with his father and left home at sixteen, completely vanishing from the Waymons' lives for more than ten years. With the advent of World War II, Carrol enlisted in the army.

"There was a lot of conflict between my mother and father, and there was a lot of conflict between Dad and the children," said Frances. "I never met my oldest brother until some thirty-one years of my life, because he left home because of Dad. My mother was very independent, very strong-willed, very determined. Very strongly committed, very, very religious. She is a pillar of strength, and highly respected.

"I felt like some of the frustration came from the fact that maybe Mom was more dominant. I feel that that added to that frustration, with Dad constantly trying to be respected as the head of the household."

Simone felt that her father resented his wife's autonomy and her prominence. "He had more blues than anything," she said, "because my dad did not like my mother preaching. It was always a rivalry for him. Something that takes her away—he didn't like it, he never liked it. He finally started preaching himself, became an ordained minister. I think now I look back, he did it to spite Momma." Not that Simone took his preaching too seriously. "The fact is, I thought it was a joke," she said.

At the time, though, Simone didn't feel there was significant strain in her parents' marriage. They may not have shown much affection for each other, but they didn't fight, so as far as she was concerned they seemed happy enough.

As a girl, Eunice was proud of her mother's role as a leader in Tryon. "I loved the way she looked, I loved the way she preached, I loved the way she cooked dinner, when she sang, when she walked," she said. "I was interested in everything to do with my mother—everything.

"They called her 'Mother Waymon' in the community. They'd come to her with their problems and things, and my mom always has someone around who needs her for something. She loves that role. It doesn't complete her life, but I've never heard her complain. Me, I complain all the time."

But as much as she admired her mother, there was a distance between them, and it would bother her for the rest of her life. Eunice never felt the same kind of intimacy from her mother that she had with her father. "I didn't get enough love from my mom, did not have no affection," she said. "I needed to touch. I needed someone to play with me. And everything in the house was serious. There were never any jokes. There were never any games. My mom didn't allow Chinese checkers, she didn't allow cards. No dancing, no boogie-woogie playing. Everything was 'no.'"

It was primarily Lucille Waymon, the oldest sister, who took care of the children. She stood in as a sort of surrogate mother while Mary Kate was out on the preaching circuit and provided the maternal affection they were missing.

"My mother never kissed me, she never held me," Simone said in another interview. "I got that from Lucille. When Lucille got married I cried, 'cause he was taking her away from me. My mother wasn't my mother—Lucille is my mother, she brought me up."

There was also constant pressure on the Waymon children. Given their mother's status and their father's ambition, it was assumed that they would be high achievers, shining examples who were active in the community. "We were expected to be model kids, because we were preachers' kids," said Carrol. "We were supposedly the very epitome of good kids, living lives publicly, real bright. It was expected that we be the brightest in the school and we had that kind of reputation."

Eunice's behavior certainly lived up to this high bar, and she was desperate to please her mother. "I never got into any trouble," she said. "If I got in trouble at all, I'd go downstairs in the basement and cry. All my mother would have to say to me is 'You did something wrong.' She never spanked me or anything, all she had to do was say that I did something wrong and I would cry myself to death. If my mother told me to jump in the river, I would have jumped in the river because she said so. I never disobeyed at all. Never."

All the time she was navigating the complexities of her family life, though, Eunice Waymon had already found the thing that would offer her solace and give her direction. She had, in fact, already begun the path that would determine the rest of her life. From her very first days, the girl who would become Nina Simone had discovered music.

When Eunice was a baby, she saw a page in a magazine. It was an advertisement, with some musical notes on a staff. She looked at the notes and started to sing.

At six months old, she knew what notes on paper actually were. When she was three, a piano arrived at the Waymon household; she recalled playing the spiritual "God Be with You Till We Meet Again," in the key of F—though she didn't quite know about keys yet. "I didn't get interested in music," she once said. "It was a gift from God and I know that." She would later tell an interviewer, "Music is a gift and a burden I've had since I can remember who I was. I was born into music. The decision was how to make the best of it."

Carrol said that as a baby Eunice would clap and sing along

in church and that she would turn toward music whenever she heard it. And in the Waymon household, with the onetime musical performer John Divine at the head, there was no shortage of opportunities to listen.

"There was music every day," Carrol said. "Music going to bed, music waking up. I remember first we had an organ, and after Nina was born and discovered she had a musical talent, we eventually got a piano, and the piano was the center of the family."

The entire clan was so musical that they would jostle to play the piano each night: at the end of supper, whoever called it first got the coveted seat in front of the keys. "We all liked to play," Simone said. "Everybody knew I was the best in the family, but I wasn't that special."

Even though the Waymons were allowed to listen only to religious music, Eunice was still exposed to other styles. "I was and still am influenced by everything I hear that is musical," she would say, mentioning Ella Fitzgerald and Louis Armstrong, the blues singer Ivory Joe Hunter, and celebrated contralto Marian Anderson as voices she recalled from her childhood.

Simone's dad would let her play "worldly music" on the piano—boogie-woogie was her favorite—and he would serve as the lookout when her mother was due home. "He would come running down and say, 'Baby, you can't do that now, your momma is on her way home now.' And then he would grin in my face and hers like nothing was wrong at all."

Although she was secretly playing secular music at home, Eunice's talents were almost immediately put to use in her mother's church services. "My mom christened me in the church," she said, "and she used to always say, 'I'm giving all of you back to God, you're in his hands now.' She took [me] with her at her Bible meeting when my feet didn't even hit the pedal. She was preaching in many cities and many towns, and she'd always take me to start the service."

"On Sunday morning, she'd play for the morning service," said Mary Kate. "And people would come just to hear her play. 'Cause when she struck the piano, people said something went all over the church." The rise and fall of the service, the control a masterful preacher had over a congregation—church is a performance, of course, and the lessons learned on these Sunday mornings would forever inform Nina Simone's approach to being onstage.

She later described the sheer intensity of the church rites. "They were some of the most exciting times that I've ever had. In many ways, what the kids are doing now when they dance for hours, listening to rock and roll music until their minds are blown and they're in a trancelike state, this is what revival meetings were like. The music was so intense, the rhythms were so intense, that you just sort of went out of yourself. I would start to play a spiritual at precisely the moment in my mother's preaching when it was needed, and this would spark everybody in the room. And then the rhythms would get more intense, and it's just like anything that starts and gets more exciting, and everybody gets involved in it."

As she got older, Eunice's schedule of services became increasingly grueling. She went to church in the morning and played for Sunday school, then at eleven o'clock for the choir, and then for two sessions of programs in the afternoon. There was prayer meeting every Wednesday night, choir practice on Fridays. But after a while, though she loved music in her bones, she began to grow bored with all of this church work.

Nor was she entirely at ease with the zeal of the revival environment. The visceral pleasures of the music were a reflection of an all-encompassing faith she hadn't fully embraced. "My early joys were mixed with fear," Simone said later. "The church where I spent most of my time spilled over with music and revival. Joy danced around the walls as lively as children, and music was the air we breathed and the water we drank. To watch the people in church meet and greet their God was like watching a reunion between old friends.

"But at the same time, I felt left out. Included in the general happiness, but left out from the deeper secrets. I was afraid when my mother spoke in tongues. Or when she became silent. Especially when she became silent and went into her private place. I feared that the very thing that provided me with joy could also bring about my alienation."

Playing constantly in church may have been dull at times, intimidating at others, but the rigorous discipline she developed there laid the foundation that informed her playing for the rest of her life. "Whatever she did, I would trace it back to her house, that black Baptist church," comedian and activist Dick Gregory would say. "She was overqualified for the blues—she had a good sense of the whole piece, she wasn't somebody just there yelling a song. She had something to go on, and you trace that back to the mother, and to church involvement, and the aspirations she had for her."

The music of her mother's church may not have been her ideal outlet, but it was evident that Eunice Waymon had exceptional ability and that she had a structure in which she could develop it. Soon she would find music that would touch her own soul the way the Gospel reached her mother, and she would be ready to give all that it required.

CHAPTER 2

"There was a white woman who had money, she heard about me. There was another white woman who was a music teacher. The two of them got together and did a job for me." Her even teeth show in a half-grin. "And on me."

—IN AN INTERVIEW WITH MAYA ANGELOU, 1970

If church music was constricting Eunice, it did also provide opportunities she had never dreamed of. When she was six years old, in 1939, the community choir performed at the Tryon Theater, with Eunice accompanying the group and playing some solos. She later described it as the day that saved her life.

Two women in the audience took notice of her. One, Mrs. Miller, employed Eunice's mother as a housecleaner, while the other, Muriel Mazzanovich, was a local piano teacher. When they heard her play, it was immediately clear to both that this young girl had a gift and should be taking formal lessons. They approached Mary Kate after the concert and convinced her that her daughter should have formal weekly instruction to nurture her talent.

Fifty years later, Nina Simone still remembered showing up for her first lesson with "Miss Mazzy," a British woman who had moved to Tryon with her husband, a Russian painter. The house was set back from the road, and the studio was made out of local cement, with a fireplace and a high ceiling. If it sounds like an intimidating space, it made a strong impression on Eunice when she first arrived.

"It was on a Saturday afternoon at three o'clock," she said. "I'll never forget it, scared me half to death. I remember how she looked, how she smelled, it all registered at one time. She frightened me. It was a huge studio, at least twenty to twenty-five feet high, and her husband was painting when I got there."

By this time, Mrs. Mazzanovich was already a middle-aged woman, and although she was tiny she had a formidable presence. "She was so elegant," Simone said. "She was from England, and you know how the English are. She wasn't an old white woman. She was petite. She looked like a bird, she ate like a bird, she talked very fast like that—'Eunice, you must do it this way. Bach would like it this way. Now you do it. You try again. All right?'"

Miss Mazzy always wore her silver hair in a bun. Eunice thought she was very pretty and remembered that she always rewarded her with candy at the end of a lesson.

"I thought all white people was like that," she said. "That's one of the shocks I got when I found out about prejudice. I just thought they were hard to get to know and somewhat standoffish, but all elegant. I had no way of knowing they weren't." Maintaining her own sense of elegance, and trying to create a truly black version of sophistication and pride, would be crucial to Simone's identity—and it was initially inspired by this childhood mentor.

Simone's relationship with Muriel Mazzanovich would become one of the most purely warm, positive relationships in her life. "Mrs. Mazzanovich used to hold out her arms to me every time I came," she said, "and hug me, and kiss me, and say, 'You're home.' She always said that I was her child—that my mother birthed me, but that I was actually spiritually her child. Because she loved me, and she took more care of me than my mother."

Though her teacher's affection was welcome, even necessary, it wasn't a perfect relationship. Eunice felt ashamed when Miss Mazzy would call her pupil her "little colored child." And Mrs. Mazzanovich had a temper, a quick fuse that Simone felt she inherited.

Her teacher introduced Eunice to the music of Johann Sebastian Bach, the composer who would be her greatest influence. Bach's work not only became her ideal of how she wanted to play but also served as a model for the ways she would structure her own music later in her career.

"Bach is technically perfect," she said. "He's a mathematician, and all the notes make sense mathematically. They add up to something, and they always add up to climaxes, like waves of the ocean gathering momentum as they get bigger and bigger and bigger. And then, after a while, after so many waves have gathered, you will see a tornado or you will see the ocean come up and destroy land.

"When you play Bach, every note is executed flawlessly. It has to be. And every note is connected to the next note. And when you get thirty-two or sixty-four notes, they all make sense with your left hand, and then you have a second voice with your right hand, you've got two voices going on. And when that happens, my actual voice came in as a third voice. It wasn't as strong as my right and left hand, but it added enough weight to climax.

"Mozart was close to Bach," she continued, "but he wasn't half as deep. Beethoven was a very forceful composer who composed things in waves and in storms. But he didn't have what Bach had. Bach did it in a technical way, Beethoven did it in an emotional way."

The precision of Eunice's training would later be obvious to the musicians who played with her as Nina Simone. "The band suffered because of Mrs. Mazzanovich," said Al Schackman, the guitarist who would become Simone's most lasting collaborator, "because when Nina made a mistake studying with Mazzano-vich, she had to repeat the phrase ten times. So we would go to practice and if anyone made a mistake we would have to play the piece ten times."

Eunice walked three miles every Saturday to take her hour-long lessons. Mrs. Mazzanovich also instructed her in posture, proper placement of the piano stool, how to bow; she taught her how to be a performer and an artist. At the end of the session, they would play duets together.

Her life was highly regimented. She was waking up at three o'clock in the morning, studying and doing her chores before she went to school, then practicing piano for hours. Studying Bach, singing gospel in church, playing blues for her father, being both a preacher's daughter and a prodigy supported by the community, young Eunice Waymon had to perform a balancing act that involved managing complicated ideas about race, various cultures, and shifting priorities.

"Without willingness and probably consciousness, I traversed two worlds, two cities, two customs, two states of mind, each week," she said. "The mannerisms of my piano teacher and her values had to influence me. I was a baby and bombarded by a weight heavier than most children bear, and more than I could analyze at the time."

When Eunice first completed her Saturday lessons at Mrs. Mazzy's, she would go to Mrs. Miller's and play with the Millers' son David while she waited for her mother to finish the house-work. As the children grew older, though, she was no longer allowed to hang out with her friend, a sudden slap in the face that she said was her "first introduction to being black."

After that shock, she adopted another postlesson ritual and stopped every week at Owen's Drug Store for a grilled cheese sandwich and an orange soda. In retrospect, that tradition was also tainted by racism and segregation, as she wasn't permitted to sit at the store's counter for her snack. "I ate it outside, standing," she said. "I knew I couldn't go in because I was black. But it was my reward for a good lesson, and then I walked home."

Following four years of lessons, Mrs. Mazzanovich organized the Eunice Waymon Fund to raise money for the young pianist to continue her training after she left for high school. Mrs. Mazzy put an ad in the *Time Bulletin* newspaper and took up collection at church. As a thank-you for backers, she also put together ten-year-old Eunice's debut recital, on a Sunday afternoon in the spring of 1943 at the Tryon Library.

The whole town was invited, and about two hundred people attended. "My mother had bought me a white dress for that day," she recalled. "It had short little cap sleeves and a fitted waist." Eunice was old enough to be nervous and self-conscious: "I was scared. I was trembling in my boots."

Even before she started playing for her first audience, though, something profound happened that forever changed how Eunice Waymon understood the world. Her parents, who were seated in the front row, were asked to move to the back of the room to make space for other, white audience members.

"They were fixing the seats so that people could watch her fingers," her mother said. "And that meant I would have to sit over there and not watch my daughter's hands. And when she went over there and saw it, she came back and says, 'I will not be playing. My mother is a black woman. And if she can't sit where she can watch my hands, then I won't be playing.' She said, 'Daddy, you can hit me, you can beat me, you can kick me, you can do anything you want to me, I will not.'"

Nervous as she was, Eunice Waymon took her stand. She couldn't understand why her parents were being displaced, but she knew that it wasn't right. And so she waited to start

her performance until she felt that the situation had been cor-
rected—a pattern that would become very familiar during her
career onstage.

The Waymons were returned—somewhat awkwardly—to
their original seats, and the recital went on as planned. Eunice
was especially proud that she was allowed to improvise her last
number; five audience members were asked to each choose a
note, and then she created a piece using their selections. The
juxtaposition of Bach-inspired structure and the freedom of improvisation, a thrilling tension that sat at the heart of Nina Simone's artistry, was taking shape even at her very first concert.

Despite the slights—with the Millers, at Owen's Drug
Store—that she had already experienced in her young life, this
recital was the first time that Eunice ran up against the full sting
of racism. After confronting it directly, Eunice started to resent
that racism was an issue her family never discussed. To her, that
silence was irresponsible. "Of course I wish they had admitted
that it existed and told me all about it, so that I wouldn't have
been so shocked when it happened," she reflected. The Waymons may have been trying to shield their children from the full
effects of prejudice, but of course there was no real escape. Even
after taking on the mantle of an activist, though, Nina Simone
focused on conditions larger than just her own experience.

"When [my mother] talked about Jim Crow and segregation,
she rarely referred to it at that stage in her life, even though it
did touch her," said Nina's daughter, Lisa Simone Kelly. "She did
tell me about times when she was told her nose was too big, her
lips were too full, and her skin was too dark. I assume she was
told that there are only certain things you'll be good for in your
life."

⟨∞⟩

As she prepared for high school, despite her time on the road with her mother, Eunice remained especially close to her father, who continued to offer the tenderness that her mother held back. "He is the first person who showed me what to do when I had my period," she said. "My father told me how to destroy the cotton and where to do it, because we had a wood stove and we had an outdoor toilet. My momma didn't tell me anything."

Her maturing body coincided with the arrival of her first boyfriend. When Edney Whiteside and his family moved into the Waymons' neighborhood in Tryon, Eunice immediately took notice of the handsome boy, two years older than she was. Soon they were meeting every Sunday afternoon at four o'clock for a ritual drive, with no chaperones, to the town of Edneyville, from which he got his name. The parents all liked one another, and despite Mary Kate's strict sense of decorum the young couple received everyone's full approval.

"I had no boyfriend," Simone recalled. "I was hanging around with a little gang of five girls, but most of them had been taken, and I felt so left out of things. I was alone most of the time. I tried to fit in, but I couldn't. But when Edney came, something did fit, he was the perfect person to be with. He was quiet, sensitive as all hell. What I liked about him the most was how well he dressed and how much in order he kept. And we obeyed the rules, that American dream where you go together a long time and get married." It was the first of many times that she believed a relationship could help her "fit in" and solve deeper problems.

Despite this new romance, however, her family and teachers decided that in order to continue with an education that would challenge her talents, Eunice would be sent to a girls' boarding school, Allen High School in Asheville, North Carolina. The first thing to do, naturally, was to set her up with a piano teacher there. Mrs. Mazzanovich contacted a former music professor at Columbia University to look after Eunice in Asheville. That professor, in turn, arranged for weekly lessons with Clemens Sandresky, a Polish-born instructor, to be paid for by the still-active Eunice Waymon Fund.

Eunice arrived in Asheville in the fall of 1945 and was thrown into a far more rigorous educational environment than the one in Tryon. "It was a black boarding school for girls, with white teachers," she said. "I like to say that I've been international all my life, because those teachers came from Redwood, California, from France. They had three black teachers, the superintendent was black, and the rest of them were white. Unbeknownst to me, these women were preparing me to be the world's first great black classical pianist. That's what they were preparing me to do."

As it had been in Tryon, her schedule was demanding, the discipline of going from classes to homework to piano practice unrelenting. She would wake up at four o'clock in the morning to play the piano before the school day started. "In high school, all I did, sweetheart, was study," she would tell Kiilu Nyasha in 1986. "If it was not the piano, it was studies in science and French and the regular studies that you have in high school. I studied all the damn time."

This intense focus, however, probably had as much to do with discomfort in her new setting as it did with the school's strict approach. Though only about sixty miles from Tryon, Asheville had a very different vibe, and the cultural shock may have propelled the teenager to take solace in the familiarity of her strict piano routine. She described the contrast to Maya Angelou—"from the Black town with its easy rhythms, its smiling and familiar faces, its well-known sights and scents, to the bordered and tight, frightened and frightening ash-pale face of white Asheville."

While at Allen, Eunice kept up a frequent correspondence

with her mentor, Mrs. Mazzanovich. "She constantly, constantly in her letters assured me of her love," Simone said. "I mean, it got to the place where she knew how much I needed to hear it. But she would underline sentences—'Of course I love you child, you know I love you.' And she'd send me poems, the most beautiful poems that she would read, if they were applicable to the situation, 'cause I used to write her a lot."

According to some people in Simone's circle, she had some same-sex affairs at the all-girls school. "I met her girlfriend, who was by then a middle-aged woman in her early fifties," said Nina's longtime friend Al Schackman. "When Nina and I did a tribute to Paul McCartney with the Boston Pops, she was invited and she came to the performance at Symphony Hall. She came backstage and we had a chance to talk. I said, 'How was Nina back then?' And she said, 'Nina was always a little odd.' To me, that said a lot. She was always remote, removed."

In Asheville, then, Eunice Waymon was searching for affection where she could get it. But what she claimed was really happening at the time was that she was being kept from Edney, whom she would regard as perhaps the great love of her life.

When Eunice left for Allen, her beloved Edney would write her letters every week; acutely aware of the social pressures of an academically competitive high school, she hid these from her friends because his spelling was so bad. He would drive up to visit her most Sundays. After a while, though, the letters' frequency dipped, and Eunice began to feel as if something was off between them. Her gut was right. Not long after Edney's correspondence became more sporadic, she discovered that he had started seeing Annie May, her best friend back in Tryon.

"I cried and I cried," Nina said later, "and one day I confronted him, and he said, 'Yes, I'm going with Annie May—you're not home and I miss you too much.' And I got really worried, my love was leaving me."

As graduation approached, she was working feverishly, practicing longer, and hearing from Edney less often. Mrs. Mazzanovich was encouraging her to go to New York's Juilliard School of Music, but Edney had issued her an ultimatum. "He told me, 'If we don't get married in June, it's not gonna happen. If you go to New York, you're never coming back and I know it.'"

Eunice and Edney never slept together. "We petted all the time and we waited for our parents to approve our going to bed," she said. "I was deeply in love with him—he could look at me and I'd get hot.

"I never got over the fact that Edney and I never went to bed. We should have done it years before. I had those feelings from the time I was twelve."

It soon became clear, though, that even her strong attraction to her childhood sweetheart wasn't enough to stop her from pursuing a career as a classical pianist, and she decided to move to New York. In a last-ditch effort to keep Eunice from leaving, Edney made an attempt at overpowering her sexually, an attack made more bizarre by the cavalier way she brushed it off in later retellings. "He tried to rape me, but he didn't know what to do," she said. "Somebody had talked about raping; he didn't know what to do and it was pitiful. He was just trying to keep me there any way he could."

Eunice was offered a scholarship to the world-renowned music school at the liberal arts college Oberlin. Mrs. Miller advised Mary Kate Waymon that she should accept the offer so that she could be around kids her own age with different interests, perhaps the closest thing to a normal college experience that someone with Eunice's talent could have. But the Eunice Waymon Fund benefactors and Mrs. Mazzy continued to insist that she pursue the conservatory focus of Juilliard, so the teenager had a big decision to make.

Edney attended her Allen High graduation—at which she

spoke as the class valedictorian—but because he knew that he was losing her to her musical aspirations he decided to marry Annie May after all. The demise of this relationship would stay with Simone forever and, in some ways, shape the person she would become. Years later, after she had become famous, she even came back to Tryon to declare that now she was ready to be with him, but by then Edney Whiteside was a broken-down, middle-aged man, in no way suited for the life she was leading.

The way that things played out with Edney would become familiar to Nina over the years, with a string of different lovers; she would fall deeply in love, then hesitate or sabotage the situation, propelled out of those relationships by the emotional explosion. Sometimes she was afraid to get hurt; other times she was unwilling to compromise her own desires. But always, she would later second-guess herself and her heart and attempt to rekindle the flame, only to find that her efforts left her even more shattered, wounded, or angry.

Nina's failure to make Edney her own would haunt her well into her adult life. "How did Eunice Waymon, protected by the customs and comforts of the Black South, emerge as today's brilliant, obsidian gem, Nina Simone?" asked Maya Angelou in 1970.

"'I found a youthful love and lost it,' Nina said. 'That was the turning point. I lost love and found a career. . . . [But] I'm a long way from compensating for what I gave up.'"

CHAPTER 3

I had been looked down all my life, being colored. Now I had the
added stigma of show business.

Despite Mrs. Miller's case for Oberlin, following her graduation Eunice opted to move to New York City. She would
spend the summer of 1950 there, studying intensely prior to
the auditions for music conservatories. The plan was to attend
Juilliard for six weeks, with her primary focus on preparing for
the examination for a scholarship at Philadelphia's Curtis Institute.

She moved in with a friend of her mother's, another female
preacher named Mrs. Steinermayer, who lived in Harlem on
145th Street. Shy and overwhelmed by the city, Eunice didn't
stray far from the Steinermayer apartment and didn't make
many friends. She did apparently meet a few men during this
time, though—including a boyfriend named Chico. He was the
first to call her by the nickname "Niña," using its Spanish pro-
nunciation, as a term of endearment.

Mostly, though, her time was occupied by work at Juilliard.
She studied with a teacher named Carl Friedberg, whom she
held in the highest esteem, working on repertoire by Beethoven,
Bach, and Handel and perfecting her finger placement and posture. She had a lesson with Friedberg once a week but spent four
or five hours a day practicing.

A month after she moved north, the rest of the Waymon family relocated to Philadelphia in order to be closer to her, operating under the assumption (or at least the hope) that she would land the invitation to attend Curtis. After a long summer of preparation and dedication, she sat for her exam in August.

Though she was pleased with the performance she delivered, Eunice Waymon was denied the scholarship. For the rest of her life, she maintained that she didn't know the reason for her rejection but that eventually those around her made it clear that it was because she was black and female. Her brother Carrol was particularly vocal about this theory.

"There was some talk about they were not going to accept an unknown black for Curtis, and [that] even if they had accepted a black, it would have been a male," said Carrol. "But not a little black girl, unknown, and more than that, a very poor black unknown. The people in the know suspected it was simply because she was black. It was a double, race and poverty . . . had she been a rich kid and black, it might have been different, but not a little poor black girl."

In retellings of the story, Simone would sometimes alter key details depending on the point she was trying to make. "I went to Curtis and I passed the test," she said in 1984. "I know it was good—I was, at that time, kind of humble. Not too much these days. I was playing Czerny and Liszt and Rachmaninoff and Bach, and I knew it was good.

"I didn't understand why I didn't get that scholarship for anything. And there were people around me who knew about my talent as well, and they said, 'Nina, it's because you are black.' And that shocked me."

Sometimes she placed the focus of her rejection from Curtis not on the institute but on Juilliard, implying that it was a failure of the program she completed to prepare for the exam. In 1970, she presented the situation this way:

" 'When I was seventeen, I left my love to go north and study. I had gone to the Juilliard School, in New York City, for a summer's course, and at seventeen I went back to compete for a scholarship.' Pause. 'I was not accepted.' "

And while sometimes she made a point of saying that she had received a scholarship for her summer studies at Juilliard, she also claimed the opposite. In 1967 she said on Dick Hubert's *Celebrity's Choice* that after her high school graduation she came to New York hoping for a Juilliard scholarship but that she wasn't "good enough." She continued: "So the [Eunice Waymon Fund] money that had been saved during those years sent me to Juilliard for a year and a half as a special student."

Regardless of the particulars—which schools rejected her and for what reasons—Eunice Waymon's dream of becoming the first great black American classical pianist, the goal she had fiercely been working toward for most of her life, had now essentially collapsed. The racism she had encountered at that first recital back in Tryon had now solidified in her mind as an institutional issue in classical music and, by extension, mainstream America.

But according to Vladimir Sokoloff, the piano teacher in Philadelphia who subsequently accepted her as a student, it was not so cut-and-dried. "It had nothing to do with her color or background," he insisted. "She wasn't accepted because there were others that were better."

"Whatever the truth is," said Roger Nupie, a Nina Simone fan and collector who would become a friend and adviser, "we should realize in those days there were no black students of classical music in Curtis Institute, and certainly no black women. Was she not accepted because of her color, was there another reason? We will never know."

With an acceptance rate of less than 5 percent, Curtis was extremely difficult for anyone to get into, much less a black applicant. In fact, Curtis had admitted African American students as far back as 1928, including the future Pulitzer Prize winner George Walker. Even as Simone sat for her audition, a young black woman named Blanche Burton-Lyles was studying in the piano department.

More important than the actual outcome, though, was how it affected Nina and shaped her future, her career, her understanding of her place in the world. "The thing is that it was a kind of trauma for Nina, and it never really disappeared," Nupie said.

After being denied admittance to Curtis, Eunice had no real reason to remain in New York. Her Waymon Fund money was running out, and her family, still stationed in Philadelphia, needed financial support. So she moved down to Philadelphia and took a job as a photographer's assistant, assuming that her musical days were behind her. But, of course, the piano was too much a part of her identity for her to really abandon it. Soon enough, with the encouragement of Carrol, she started lessons with Vladimir Sokoloff.

"[She was] not a genius, but she had great talent," he said. "I accepted her on the basis of her talent, and with the understanding that I would prepare her for [another] audition at Curtis. It was during that early period that she demonstrated, at one lesson, her ability to play jazz. I remember distinctly telling her, 'Why don't you pursue this as your profession?' And she said, 'Oh, no, my first love is classical music and I want to be a pianist.'"

Simone would claim that Sokoloff's instruction didn't measure up to the instruction she had been getting from Carl Friedberg. ("Friedberg was much more gifted and much more learned than Vladimir Sokoloff," she said. "He [Sokoloff] was a great teacher, but Carl Friedberg was from Juilliard and Juilliard was the best school, so naturally I preferred him.") But she stayed as diligent as ever about her training, continuing to practice four or five hours a day.

She also found a job at Arlene Smith's vocal studio working as an accompanist. It wasn't concert work, but it did allow her to make money playing the piano—enough to cover her lessons, pay her own expenses, and have some left over to contribute to her family. "I accompanied students who studied popular singing," she said. "I used to hear them talk about agents and things. I didn't know what agents were, but I knew that I was gifted. I knew that I could play anything I heard."

Eventually, Eunice was ready to move into a place of her own and also decided—in a further fit of independence—that she could increase her income by giving private lessons. The most efficient setup, she felt, would be to find a space that could double as a work studio and an apartment, a requirement that led her to a storefront at Fifty-seventh Street and Master—a big room, with a kitchen and a toilet, that looked directly out on the street. There she taught young students, ages seven to fifteen, for $2.50 an hour. Eight kids left Arlene Smith's studio to work directly with her, leading to some tension, though Smith would continue to offer Eunice some part-time work when she was in need of some quick cash.

This period also saw her begin her first lengthy relationship since Edney Whiteside, with a man she met in church. "I was near my family. I was studying music. I had a boyfriend, and I had a storefront. So that was a pretty normal existence."

Her day-to-day circumstances may have seemed stable, but Eunice was still in the process of recalibrating her life's plan. She felt unsettled, troubled. She began seeing a psychiatrist named Gerry Weiss and visited his offices every Thursday afternoon for about a year. "I didn't feel like I belonged anywhere," she said. "I did not understand the people in Philadelphia, I didn't understand what I was doing with them. And so I went to a psychiatrist, not because anything was particularly wrong with me, but I didn't fit anywhere."

These feelings of alienation would stay with her, in one form or another, for much of her life. She did have a few close friends, though presumably not the sort of folks her mother would have chosen—in fact, she was drawn to women who displayed an independence and a sexuality in sharp contrast to her church upbringing. Her best girlfriend was a prostitute named Kevin Mathias, also known as Faith Jackson; after allegedly meeting at a brothel where Nina played the piano, they saw each other practically every day. There was also Faye Anderson, a blond woman who "took care of me and dressed me at that time."

For some time, Eunice had been overhearing some of her vocal students talk about the work they were getting over the summers in seaside resorts and supper clubs. Most took jobs as waiters or bellhops, but one of them—and not, to her mind, the most talented—told her he had gotten a job as a pianist. The students bragged about the money that they could make, up to $90 a week; the success of these moderately gifted students gave Nina an idea. She thought maybe she could pick up that kind of work for the season.

She called the agent of the boy who had scored the piano job, and the agent soon got back to her with the news that she had an offer to spend the summer of 1954 as the house entertainment for the Midtown Bar and Grill in Atlantic City. Eunice quickly realized, though, that pious preacher Mary Kate Waymon would never stand for her daughter playing secular music in a nightclub. In an effort to avoid discovery, Eunice came up with the solution of adopting a pseudonym—at least until she could break the news to her mother.

Recalling her first taste of freedom that summer in New

York, she chose "Nina" in reference to her old boyfriend Chico's pet name, flattening the Spanish accent. "Simone" she took from the French actress Simone Signoret, inspired by the foreign art films she had become a fan of since moving to Philadelphia. So "Nina Simone" was how her name would appear in newspaper ads and all billing at the Midtown. (Of course, in classic Nina style, competing versions of how and why she settled on this moniker abound. A press bio for the Philips record company, her label during the mid-1960s, opted for a more general, awkward explanation: "The name derived from her childhood when she sometimes had been called 'Nina,' meaning little one. Simone was euphonic and just happened to sound well with it.")

She showed up at the Midtown—"a very crummy bar" a few blocks in from the beach—in an evening gown. Asked what she wanted to drink, she requested a glass of milk. She had never been in a bar before.

She played classical numbers and instrumental improvisations for her first set. "I played everything that I could think of," she said. "Classical, spirituals, all kinds of things. It was very strange." The cigar-chomping owner, Harry Steward, told her that her piano sounded nice but she should also be singing. She replied that she was only a piano player, that she had never sung in her life. He told her that here she was either a singer or out of a job.

So she started to sing. Early on, she still kept the focus on her piano playing—she would play for most of her set and sing a few standards, like "My Funny Valentine" or "In the Evening by the Moonlight," to fill out the time remaining. It was a tentative shift, but after unleashing a vocal power even she was unaware of, Nina noticed a change in the Midtown's clientele.

"It was a joint, but it became quite well behaved after about five nights when the students started coming," she said. "The first two nights was just these Irish drunks. I closed my eyes and played on, anyway. I played for five hours without stopping."

According to Carrol, it didn't take long for Nina Simone's audience to find her. "They knew she was a star," he said. "It was not a pop place. It was an intimate place. And immediately, word got out of this tremendously talented pianist and singer. And from then on, every night we went there, the place was crowded. Couldn't get in. Everybody heard about Midtown. For the serious music lovers, Midtown became the spot. No talk and no whispering, just music."

"A cult was developed right then," said Simone in 1986. "Kids who were working as waiters in Atlantic City, in these hotels and things, heard me playing like this at the nightclub and they filled it up every night and made everybody be quiet."

From her very earliest performances, Nina was apparently able to hold a crowd's interest fully—much more like a classical or sophisticated jazz artist, playing for people who are there to listen, than a conventional pop or lounge act, happy to provide background music for the drinking, socializing, and flirting that are the priorities for most bar patrons. The fact that she was able to establish this hierarchy so quickly would lead to an expectation that it was how all audiences behaved, which of course was soon followed by her disappointment and frustration that it wasn't always so.

Though she was playing from 9:00 p.m. to 4:00 a.m. every night, with fifteen-minute breaks each hour, Nina discovered that she was having no trouble filling the time. In fact, having the opportunity to explore these songs so freely was unlocking for her new ways of thinking about music.

"All the time I was practicing, I'd practice Bach and Beethoven and Handel and Debussy and Prokofiev," she said. "Man, all the talent that I had inside me, that was created from me, songs that I should have been composing, I didn't know anything about those songs until I first started playing in a nightclub. Then, all of a sudden, the fact that I had to play five hours, I started improvising—but I didn't know I could improvise like that. I was repressed to the point where I hadn't played any songs of my own for fourteen years, and I didn't even know I had them down there. I didn't know until I first started at the Midtown Bar, and it came out."

But even though she was finding some interesting possibilities in her nightclub work, Simone still felt that the environment was a waste of her gift. "I felt dirtied by going into the bars," she said. "That made me feel dirty. To me, it was so inferior to classical music that it was like water falling off a duck's back to play 'Little Girl Blue.' That was just nothing. That's why I infused it with 'Good King Wenceslas,' to give it some Bach in the background.

"The popular world was nothing compared to the classical world. You didn't have to work as hard, and it was easier to please an audience. All they wanted to get was the words. It was just another world."

After the summer in Atlantic City, she returned to her routine in Philadelphia, teaching in her storefront and studying with Vladimir Sokoloff. But the next year she returned to the Midtown nightclub, where she found a cluster of fans waiting for her, including a college student named Ted Axelrod, who was working as a waiter for the summer. Axelrod, who was gay, had become her first dedicated fan, and at her late sets much of the room was filled with his friends after they got off their dinner shifts. These were the aesthetes and outsiders of the Jersey Shore scene, the community who would make up the core of Nina's following for years to come. (One of the other outcasts who became a fan at this time was a young Jewish man named Shlomo Carlebach; he went on to become a Hasidic rabbi, and a highly fictionalized version of his friendship with Simone was the basis for 2007's Off-Broadway production *Soul Doctor*.)

One night Axelrod, a record collector, brought in a Billie Holiday album for Simone and suggested that she learn one of the songs, "I Loves You, Porgy," from the Gershwins' pioneering opera *Porgy and Bess*. Ever the dutiful student, she practiced it the next day and added the song to her set that night. She'd included it mostly as a favor to her friend (she was never a big fan of Holiday's), but when she saw how well the audience responded she kept it in.

After her second summer at the Midtown, Simone had become so comfortable as a performer that she asked the agent who had first gotten her the gig if he might find her some work in and around Philadelphia during the year. He booked her into the Pooquesin club, which led to more work at local supper clubs like the High-Thigh Club. The audiences were older and wealthier than the Atlantic City crowd but not as attentive as her devoted collegiate following—they were just looking for some simple dinner entertainment to impress their dates, and they often chatted through Simone's sets.

This kind of behavior was something that she wouldn't tolerate for long, but it was more lucrative and more rewarding than accompanying young vocal students. She even thought about reapplying to Curtis, now that she had some more funds to pay her way and wouldn't be dependent on a scholarship offer. The major drawback, though, was coming clean with her parents. Since she was now playing in public more than just seasonally, and much closer to home, Simone finally had to stop hiding behind her stage name and tell them what she was really doing for work.

"It had been our secret that she was playing at a nightclub," said Carrol. "And we discussed who was gonna tell Mom. I said, 'Well, eventually I'm just gonna tell her, get over the shock. This is crazy.' I had been the one who always said, 'Forget all that other mess. Do what you've gotta do. You're an artist. Mother would have to change or not change, but do it anyway.'"

As had been the case when Nina was growing up, former aspiring musician John Divine Waymon—her more lenient and tolerant parent—was immediately supportive of her new direction. "Our father was real pleased," said Carrol. "That's why they had that secret bond. He thought it was great, and he knew what the life was about. It's dangerous but also okay. Mom didn't know anything about all that. If you don't know about it, it's dangerous until you know what it is."

Though Simone explained that she was performing mostly classical music and spirituals, and that she never drank anything stronger than milk in the clubs, Mary Kate Waymon didn't spare her daughter from her disapproval. Simone felt that her mother never accepted the fact that she was playing the devil's music in dens of iniquity.

"Mom always said that my grandmother [hid] her albums under the mattress," said Lisa Simone. "I don't know if that was true, but the message was that Grandma did not approve of what she was doing. And that even though the whole world revered Nina Simone, she still could not have the blessing of the one person whose blessing meant the most."

Simone had started to make some progress with her career. She made some demo recordings and played in more upscale venues like the Queen Mary Room in the Rittenhouse Hotel. Despite such professional advances, though, she felt alone and adrift. But just as she was most lonely, she found some new company; there was now a man in her life.

Simone met Don Ross—a white self-styled beatnik, aspiring painter, and drummer—at the Midtown in Atlantic City. "He was one of the people who came and befriended me," she said. "He was at the bar every night and I was lonely and drinking milk. I was very shy. And he befriended me and got rid of my loneliness."

Ross worked as a salesman, a "pitch man," selling trinkets to fairs and boardwalks. It's difficult to get a sense of Simone's attraction to the man; those around her were asked about Ross only many years later, and no one seems to have a good thing to say. Carrol Waymon called him a "charlatan," and Simone's sister Frances said, "I couldn't stand him. Don was a leech."

If this courtship with Ross seemed to be leading nowhere good, in August of 1957 Nina Simone was introduced to someone who would go on to be perhaps the most consistent and stable relationship she ever had. Al Schackman was a guitarist who had recently returned from the army and was living in New Hope, Pennsylvania. He was working as a session musician in New York, playing with R&B acts like the Drifters, the Isley Brothers, and Solomon Burke, as well as performing with his own jazz group in the Village. He had worked with Billie Holiday and Burt Bacharach, and with comedians like Mike Nichols and Lenny Bruce.

That summer, he was playing at the Canal House restaurant with his trio. One night after his set, a few audience members suggested that he meet another musician who was in town, performing at the Playhouse Inn. On a Sunday evening, he went over to see this woman named Nina Simone, bringing his guitar and amp in case she was amenable to letting him play with her. She was between sets when he arrived, but their mutual friends asked her if it would be okay for him to sit in on the rest of the performance; she agreed, and before they had even exchanged pleasantries he set up onstage.

Simone finished her break and came up to the piano. She didn't look at the guitarist, said nothing, and started playing the

Christmas carol "Good King Wenceslas," which she used as an introduction to "Little Girl Blue."

"After about eight bars I came in, and before you knew it we were just weaving in and out, we were off and running," said Schackman. "Right at the height of this—you couldn't get more intense—she brings in her vocal, this love ballad with all of this going around, impossible."

Simone's long hours of work at the Midtown had helped hone her artistry, and she was now able to incorporate the use of multiple, independent musical lines that she had learned from Bach into pop songs and improvisation. This intricacy would allow her to stake out truly distinctive creative territory. "Years later," Schackman said, "Miles Davis asked me, 'How does she do it?'

"I have no idea how anybody could isolate so many parts of music at one time. And that was my introduction to Nina Simone."

When she finished her set, the pianist and the guitarist were formally introduced. Simone asked Schackman if he would join her for tea the next Saturday. She gave him her address and as she was leaving said to him, "By the way, please bring your guitar."

That weekend he went to her place—now she had a bright, sunny, third-floor apartment, a considerable upgrade from her old storefront residence—and they played for hours. It cemented a connection that was truly remarkable, that went beyond sympathetic accompaniment and into a blending of two uncommon, unlikely, uncanny styles. The relationship built by the music was so strong, in fact, that it would sustain them through decades often marked by Nina's challenging personality.

"I had never felt such freedom in knowing that someone knew exactly where I was going, and that she knew that I knew exactly where she was going," Schackman said. "In other words, we couldn't lose each other. It was like telepathy.

"I think we saw, in each other's playing, a reflection of the way we approached music, which was to tell a story beyond the notes and with color. Nina had a way of taking a piece of music and not interpreting it but . . . morphing it into her experience, and that's what I always liked to do myself. I wanted the freedom of playing my guitar like a saxophone, more like a horn player, rather than the more angular lines of a guitar player. That allowed me to travel all over the fingerboard and harmonics and everything. And that's what Nina did."

It took a certain adaptability and a keen ear to accompany Simone's inventive, virtuosic flights, but Schackman easily kept up with her. Beyond their own musical camaraderie, he also quickly realized that he was dealing with an extraordinary talent, a player whom he rated next to the true giants, regardless of genre. "The closest person that had a sound that was not Nina but similar was Thelonious Monk. The way he used chord clusters and it sounded like dissonance or like somebody slamming an elbow, but it was a real musical experience, like Jackson Pollock throwing a can of paint on a canvas. I put her in a place with Ravi Shankar or Glenn Gould."

Schackman wasn't the only person taking notice of Simone's exceptional playing. Someone at Bethlehem Records in New York had apparently heard the demo recordings she'd made in Philadelphia and was interested in signing her to the label.

In December 1957, she went to New York and recorded thirteen songs backed by bassist Jimmy Bond and drummer Tootie Heath (Schackman was touring and unable to make the session). The selections were essentially the songs she played as her set at the time but, given the time restraints of a studio recording, without her extended improvisations. "I had sung all these songs in 1952," she said, "so when I recorded them it was just like doing them again."

The opening track was a stunning, surprisingly upbeat version of Duke Ellington's "Mood Indigo." She also included, of

course, "I Loves You, Porgy," the crowd-pleasing song Ted Axelrod had brought to her; her reading was magnificent, yearning
but still strong, clear and deep but restrained, with none of the
simpering or histrionics that other singers ladled onto the song.
The thirty-second piano solo was a marvel of fleet concision.
(She pointedly left out the "s" on "loves" in the title phrase, a
remnant of the Gershwins' effort at "Negro dialect.") Simone
also cut a one-take instrumental titled "Central Park Blues" because the album's cover photograph had been taken earlier that
day in the park.

The tone of the album was melancholy—"I didn't know any
happier love songs," she said, "I only knew wistful love songs,
things about unrequited love"—so near the end of the session
the label requested an up-tempo song to lighten the mood. She
quickly tossed off a breezy shuffle called "My Baby Just Cares
for Me," including a memorable, elegant piano solo. (Though
Simone would often identify the song with Frank Sinatra, he
didn't actually record it until 1965; when she pulled it out for
this album, the tune was relatively obscure, first written as a
feature for Eddie Cantor to sing in the musical *Whoopee!*) The
album took its title from "Little Girl Blue," the first song she had
played onstage with Schackman that featured the Bachlike em-
bellishment; once the session was finished, she sold the rights to
Bethlehem for a reported $3,000 and went home the next day.

Little Girl Blue was released in June 1958, and Simone was getting more and more calls to perform outside the Philadelphia
area. Though she was still studying classical piano with Vladimir Sokoloff (such was her distaste for popular music that she
said she played Beethoven for three days after the Bethlehem
session to cleanse her system), she was considering making the
move back to New York City, which had more professional opportunities for her, despite the sting of her youthful experiences.

"I had an agent named Jerry Fields," she said. "He came and

heard me and he said, 'My name is Jerry Fields and I'm going to make you a star.' I didn't know what a star was." Fields remained her agent until he died a few years later. He also introduced her to an attorney named Maxwell Cohen. "Max was very good for her," said Schackman. "He was very strict, which was very good, because Nina was already showing her diva temperament and she couldn't put it over on Max, he was too old guard."

There was one thing she wanted to take care of, though, before relocating. Two years later, out of habit or a fear of facing solitude, she was still dating Don Ross. And still, no one in Simone's life approved of him.

"I met him when I visited Nina for tea, but he pretty much stayed out of the way," said Schackman. "I think that he hovered around her and took care of some things, paid attention to her.

"I didn't care for him myself. To me, he always had some kind of scheme going and he needed money for it. He was insipid, inconsequential, a hanger-on who somehow captured Nina for a moment."

According to her sister Frances, Simone was drinking heavily, abetted by the freebies offered to her at clubs. In addition, Simone had started taking LSD—she said that it was prescribed medication, but her sister wasn't buying it. Decades later, Frances recalled seeing Simone "just out of it" back in these early days and felt that her intake had a long-term negative effect.

"I think she was very innocent, very gullible," said Frances. "She was not exposed to a lot of stuff because of family, what we came from. In a small town, they didn't have a lot of sophistication."

Whatever the basis of their relationship—and even Simone seemed baffled by what had kept them together—in late 1958, following the release of *Little Girl Blue,* she and Don Ross were married at the county clerk's office. Nobody attended, and she later wrote that she couldn't even remember the wedding date.

As for her family's reaction, it was a moot point—in addition to struggling to recall the day, she was unsure she had ever even bothered to tell them that the wedding had happened.

Simone would look back on the decision to tie herself to Ross with clear-eyed regret. "I married him because I was so lonely," she said. "Nothing happened with Don Ross. There was no sex with Don Ross. He just was no good. He was a creep."

CHAPTER 4

My music had such power, I was so good at it, that [club owners] were scared of me. People believed me when I told them things.

T hough Simone was unhappy with the support she was getting from Bethlehem Records, something strange was happening. Sid Mark, a disc jockey at WHAT in Philadelphia with whom Simone was friendly, had started playing her recording of "I Loves You, Porgy" on air, sometimes multiple times in a row. Ironically, part of Simone's frustration with Bethlehem came from their resistance to issuing a single. Eventually, prompted by Mark's support, they put out this one, which was becoming a local and then a regional hit.

In June of 1959 the song entered the national charts, and as the year wore on "Porgy" kept gaining steam. It peaked at number 18 on the pop charts, number 2 on the R&B list. At age twenty-six, Nina Simone had arrived as a recording star. The song she had learned overnight to humor Ted Axelrod would remain her signature number for the rest of her life, and the biggest hit she would ever have in the United States. In 2000, forty-one years after it was first cut, the recording was inducted into the Grammy Hall of Fame.

"Porgy" was an ideal introduction to Simone's approach, a distillation of her strengths—emotional but not overwrought, a familiar standard given a new mood, occupying an indefinable space between pop and jazz, with a hint of the direct impact that would come to be called "soul." In addition to the single's surprising commercial appeal, it was also immediately clear to the music cognoscenti that Simone's was a talent both unique and special.

"When I heard the real version of 'I Loves You, Porgy' after hearing hers, I was like, 'They need to throw that version away and go study her version,'" said critic Stanley Crouch. "She makes the lyrics extremely important. Oftentimes, singers who sing songs written by George and Ira Gershwin, they're perhaps overly impressed by the melodies. Nina Simone doesn't ignore the melody, but her idea is that she's going to sing every one of these words with ultimate value emotionally. So she lifts the song up in the air that way.

"She may have discovered how to solve the problem of aviation in music. What makes an aviator what he is? An aviator is a person who deals with getting heavier-than-air objects off the ground. She could do that, musically and emotionally. She could take a feeling and actually lift it off the ground, and it would stay there. That's what she does with 'I Loves You, Porgy.'"

She had signed with a new manager, a literary agent in New York named Bertha Case who had initially contacted Simone when a young writer submitted a potential musical project to Case's office. The singer on the demos he gave her was Nina, and Case reacted immediately to her voice. Under this new management, and with the success of "Porgy," Simone was approached by Colpix Records, the music division of Columbia Pictures. Joyce Selznick (niece of the legendary movie producer David O. Selznick) made the initial contact, and in April 1959 Simone and Case inked a new deal with Colpix.

As her bookings in New York grew following the release of *Little Girl Blue,* Simone and Ross moved to the city, initially staying in the East Village apartment of a friend of ever-loyal

Ted Axelrod's. As she started playing the club circuit, word quickly started to spread about Simone's mysterious alchemy of showmanship, technical prowess, and husky vocals.

"She did One Fifth Avenue, and that was prestigious for that level of playing," said Al Schackman. "Suddenly, the jazz aficionados discovered her, and she really became the darling of the upper crust of the music. People were awestruck by her ability, and also by her presence and her formality. You just didn't get close to Nina. She was extremely cautious and protective of her space."

From her very first shows, Simone was frequently showing up late, sometimes in a prickly mood. This hard line had been her attitude from before she came to New York, even before she had made a record. On the very first night Schackman met her in New Hope, people in the audience were talking and she just sat at the piano and waited them out, refusing to start playing until they had quieted down and given her their full attention.

"My first piano teacher taught me, you do not touch that piano until you are ready and until they are ready to listen to you," she said, referring to her beloved Mrs. Mazzy. "You just make them wait."

Schackman asserted that audiences truly weren't prepared for what Simone was offering them. "What Nina was doing in her performances was a far higher level than people might assume a so-called jazz artist was going to do," he said. "When Nina did a concert, it was truly, in a classical sense, a concert. I think people are uplifted when they identify with something that's truly unique, that's with us only for a very limited time. There are some people in the world [who] know it when they see it. Nina has been touched with that gift of transmitting, and people want to be in its presence."

Promoter (and sometime pianist) George Wein pointed out that Simone was part of a new generation of singers that were emerging in the 1950s, following the "four reigning queens"—Ella Fitzgerald, Sarah Vaughan, Billie Holiday, and Dinah Washington. She was coming up alongside such vocalists as Betty Carter, Abbey Lincoln, and Dakota Staton. Wein liked Simone and was impressed by her musicianship and the range of her repertoire, but he hadn't singled her out.

"But I had a partner at that time whose name was Albert Grossman," said Wein. "He ended up managing Bob Dylan and Peter, Paul and Mary and Odetta and many important artists. He saw Nina at my club and he said, 'She's the one.'"

Crouch felt that Simone's actual approach lifted her into a category above her peers, creating music that was genuinely unique—a talent that would serve as both a great strength and a challenge. "She could bring deeper meanings to songs, that was her gift," said Crouch. "She didn't sing jazz, because in jazz you have to submit to the force of the band—it's a collective experience, and I don't think Nina liked to play like that. I think she liked it to be about her.

"Her sound is freer than many sounds, because she doesn't imitate an instrument," he continued. "She actually wants her sound to be a *human* sound. Many jazz singers miss the boat by trying to sound like a horn, and that's a mistake, because the human voice actually has greater freedom than any horn has. But Nina Simone knew that—different registers, different inflections, she knew all that. And so nobody sounded like her."

In May 1959, Simone had made enough of a name for herself to play at the Village Gate, a club run by Art D'Lugoff that would become a consistent and important venue for her for many years. The Gate was a nexus of the creative explosion happening in Greenwich Village at the time: Woody Allen opened for her there, and she shared bills with Richard Pryor, Lightnin' Hopkins, Richie Havens, Yusef Lateef.

Even as a new artist at this vibrant club, Simone had an uncompromising, often challenging onstage personality. During her first stand at the Gate, she noticed a piano string that had a buzz in it. She apologized to the capacity crowd for the condition of the instrument and then made it her night's mission to destroy the faulty string. She used it as a pedal tone through the evening, and in the last set, toward the end, the string finally broke. "There!" she exclaimed triumphantly.

But more exciting for music buffs than her onstage antics was her sheer inventiveness as a performer. "It was almost always electric, exciting," Art D'Lugoff would say in 1991, looking back on Simone's early appearances on his stage. "You never knew what she would do. She would start playing a Bach riff, and she had the most unusual musical arrangements. I don't think anyone in the world could get people as excited as she did, and for me, her greatness was what kept me going with her, because she was a very difficult person."

She often arrived at the Gate so late that the first set started at the time announced for the second set. She also had bodyguards with her—though, according to at least one bouncer at the club, not for the usual reasons that a celebrity would hire security. They were "to protect the public from her, not to protect her from the public," as on at least one occasion she got into a fight with a fan who wasn't sufficiently grateful for an autograph.

Having won over the Atlantic City bar crowd in her first nights as a performer, she never learned to accept anything less than an audience's full attention. Sometimes this was now becoming more openly confrontational, even to a room of customers who might seem like her most sympathetic fans—as on the occasion of another eventful night at the Gate.

"There were lines around the corner, the people were energetic and there was talking and laughter and glasses and stuff like that," Al Schackman recounted, "and she belts out, 'Wait a minute, what's going on, don't you know how to behave yourselves?' She said, 'You people want equal rights'—black crowd, yuppyish, New York—'You want civil rights? You don't *deserve* civil rights, you don't know how to behave yourself. How were you brought up? Don't you have any manners? I'm here trying to tell you things and let you know where things are at and you're just rude. I'm gonna tell you right now how to get civil rights. Go home, take a bath, use underarm deodorant, and that's how you get civil rights.' Boy, did that shut them up."

Part of the excitement of a Nina Simone concert was seeing whether or not it was actually going to happen—if she would make it to the stage, and then, if she would be able to get through a full set without incident.

"I had my music and if you didn't want to listen to it, go the hell home," she said. "I wasn't making that much money that I had to compromise. I felt that I could always go back to classics. When the students came to see me, they would tell each other, 'You got to be quiet or I'm going to throw you out of here.' They protected me themselves, and because they did that early, I had that same attitude when I played bigger places. I had gotten that from being a classical pianist. You're supposed to sit down and be quiet. If you couldn't be quiet, then leave.

"I regarded myself as one of the most gifted people out there. As far as I was concerned, I condescended to play for them. If they couldn't listen, fuck it. I thought they needed teaching, because they didn't know how to listen."

In certain ways, artists—as opposed to entertainers—need to be arrogant. They have to feel confident that what they're doing is important, that it needs to be heard, that it's taking their form to a new place or level. So Simone's sense of her own artistry isn't necessarily that far from what those she considered her peers also believed. But there were a few crucial differences in Nina Simone's relationship to her listeners.

First, she was working in the context of popular music, playing bars and nightclubs and signed to record companies who needed to see her songs embraced by radio—a far different sphere from the world of "high art," where difficult temperaments and noncommercial work are excused in service of creative breakthroughs. And Simone may have simply lacked (or been indifferent to) the filter that defines polite, "acceptable" behavior from a performer—the displays of modesty and gratitude that we expect from our celebrities as our compensation for buying tickets and records; of course, it would also later be discovered that this impulsive, volatile style was likely something more than simple rudeness—it may have been related to Simone's periodic chemical imbalances and the emotional turmoil that resulted from her troubled relationship with her second husband.

In August, *The Amazing Nina Simone,* her Colpix debut, was released. The album was a mix of standards ("Willow Weep for Me," "It Might as Well Be Spring") and gospel songs. An even bigger milestone came the following month, when she made her concert debut at New York's Town Hall, a performance that would be recorded for the first of her many live albums.

Despite the show's visibility, she had not rehearsed with, or even met, the musicians who would accompany her on that stage until the curtain rose. Fortunately, she had Wilbur Ware, a veteran who had often played with Thelonious Monk, backing her on bass. "If I had had a choice in the matter, I wouldn't have done it that way," she said. "Jazz musicians like Wilbur Ware are rare. Most of the youngsters don't know beans about music, and I would never trust myself to do anything cold with them."

Some of the material would have to be rerecorded in the

studio a few weeks later. When it was released in December, though, *Nina Simone at Town Hall* gave a fuller sense of the range of her material, introducing several songs that would become staples of her performances and would appear on later albums— "Black Is the Color of My True Love's Hair," "Wild Is the Wind," the traditional country song "Cotton Eyed Joe"—mixed with several instrumentals that showcased her piano virtuosity.

Though she was still making weekly trips to Philadelphia to continue her studies with Vladimir Sokoloff, Simone was developing her own distinct style and was fast outgrowing those lessons. She was now a critics' darling, a marquee name, a signifier of downtown hip. She claimed, though, that this burst of success didn't sink in immediately. Although she always believed in her talent, the way that she arrived on the scene was such a surprise that it didn't seem real.

"It didn't hit me that I was sensational," she said. "Town Hall, the press was so good, I felt like it was a dream. When people came around, famous people, I wouldn't take their names and numbers and call them. You know that song by Janis Ian called 'Stars'—'They come and go, they come fast, they come slow/ They go like the last light of the sun, all in a blaze?' I felt very much like that. All the men who say they love you, you never can believe they really love you. Everybody be kissing on me and asking for autographs, but I never went home with them or anything, because I didn't believe them. I thought it was a dream."

But she certainly didn't question her right to look like a star in public. When she received her first big royalty check from the success of "Porgy," the first thing she did was buy a fancy car. Al Schackman found her a gray Mercedes 200 SCE convertible with a red top and matching red leather luggage. They would drive down the West Side Highway to the Village; Nina liked to wear a long scarf, and when they had the top down it would blow in the wind and she'd turn to Schackman and dramatically say, "Grace Kelly."

Beyond the glamorous clothes and the car, the most significant purchase she made with her new money was her first real apartment on West 103rd Street, across the street from Central Park. It was a seven-room unit on the building's twelfth floor, complete with two furnished bedrooms, wall-to-wall carpeting, a $700 couch, and a live-in maid named Mary.

Although she was still married to Don Ross, he was more of a shadow in her life than a real presence. She described herself as "very much alone," hanging out in Village coffeehouses, befriending the folk singer Odetta but few others. "I missed my parents first of all," she said, "and I missed being home, the feeling of home."

Some of these feelings of rootlessness might also have emerged from the touring Simone had undertaken for the first time. Backed by an extraordinary trio—Schackman, bass legend Ron Carter, and frequent Monk drummer Ben Riley—she played a number of the country's leading black nightclubs in the second half of 1959, including the Showboat in Philadelphia, the Casino Royal in Washington, and the Town House in Pittsburgh. These dates culminated in five nights, including New Year's Eve, at New York's celebrated Copacabana.

She was on her best behavior for these shows. "It was great," Schackman said. "In the clubs, there was never really a problem—there was noise and talking, and she would put up with it. I think a lot of it was the scene. There was so much energy, but different than a concert."

When Simone was booked into the Blue Note in Chicago, she received an additional, surprising offer. She was invited onto Hugh Hefner's new talk/variety television show, *Playboy's Penthouse*. Hefner introduced her as "a star who came out of nowhere

last year," and Simone—in a white gown, and surrounded by
tuxedo-clad Playboy wannabes and their dates—performed
three songs: "The Other Woman," "Where Do the Children
Go," and, of course, "Porgy."

"I couldn't believe what I was seeing, with all of these hip
white people sitting around on sofas smoking their cigarettes,"
said Schackman. "It was a riot. We left there and we're in the car
going to the hotel. And she turns, she said, quiet, 'Do you believe where we just were? Do you believe what we just did?' She's
grabbing my hand, 'Do you believe what we just did?'"

It would be the first of several high-profile TV appearances
over the next few months. She performed on the *Today* show
and on May 8, 1960, paid her first visit to the *Ed Sullivan Show*—
the crown jewel of the small screen for entertainers of the time.
Eager to capitalize on Simone's success and visibility, Bethlehem
Records issued the few extra songs she had recorded for *Little
Girl Blue* but had never released on an album titled *Nina Simone
and Her Friends*. The label also put out "Little Girl Blue" itself
as a single, followed by "Don't Smoke in Bed." None of these
legal but unauthorized releases met with much success, but they
helped solidify in Simone an intense distrust of record companies that would escalate as the years went on.

She was equally suspicious of the club and theater owners
who were booking her. Though her television performances all
went well enough and upped the buzz around Simone, exposure
on this kind of national platform didn't smooth out the rough
edges of her stage conduct. At her concerts, she insisted on receiving her performance fee up front, in cash, which sometimes
resulted in near comic situations.

One night at the Apollo Theater, she refused to go on until
she had her money in hand. Honi Coles, the great tap dancer
who served as the Apollo's house manager, informed her that
her fee was in an envelope on the piano.

She went onto the stage and the audience began applauding. Without acknowledging them, she sat down, opened the envelope, and counted the money by carefully spreading the bills out on the piano. Satisfied that every dollar was accounted for, she put it back in the envelope and stood to take the cash backstage—but as she made her way from the piano, she tripped over the stool and wiped out. The audience laughed at the absurdity of it all, and Simone sat on the stage telling them off, insisting that none of them cheer. Someone called out, "We love you, Nina," and she yelled back, "No, you don't," then they went at each other for a while.

Finally, she got up, walked off, stashed the envelope, and came back onstage. She repositioned herself at the piano, said, "Good evening," and started the show, as if none of the earlier slapstick had ever happened.

Still, she continued to rise as a concert draw, and in June another prestigious booking came with the invitation to perform at the Newport Jazz Festival. "We paid attention to her, and in 1960 I put her on at Newport and she was a hit," said George Wein. "That was a very tumultuous year, 'cause there was a riot in the town and the festival was closed down. But Nina became part of our life, part of our professional life, and remained so over the years."

Her Newport set was recorded for a live album. It was the first document of the trio that would be her backing group for a number of years—the ever-present Schackman, bassist Chris White, and drummer Bobby Hamilton.

A highlight of the show was a fired-up rendition of the traditional "southern dialect" song "Little Liza Jane," which would become a staple of her concerts. It's a different sort of performance for her; rather than sitting at the piano, Nina sat on a high stool, with a tambourine. Schackman said that she had second thoughts about doing the song and asked him for encouragement. "We'll get some rhythm started here and see what happens," she said, before starting in with an arrangement more spare and propulsive than her usual intricate piano backing. (There's footage of the performance on YouTube, and Schackman says that when he watches it "she has that little smile from time to time, and it was really cute.")

Against the backdrop of this excitement and success, and despite a glowing article in *Sepia* magazine about her home life, Simone had finally reached the end of the line with Don Ross. The couple was divorced in late 1960. To her friends and family, it was as if the marriage had never happened—and there were even some questions among them about whether it really had. "I don't remember very much about it," said Carrol Waymon. "I know it was a tumultuous thing, didn't work out too well. If she did marry Don, it was like an error and it seems to me she got out of it."

As Ross was exiting her life, though, there was another community that offered her companionship. The gay following that she had begun to develop during her early nights in Atlantic City, when Ted Axelrod was spreading the word, was playing a bigger role in her offstage hours, centered on the Village lesbian club Trude Heller's. With her unconventional, stylized sound and image, Nina's appeal to those marginalized by society—and, in turn, her own interest in such people—was solidifying.

"When she would leave the club where we were playing, she'd be going to a gay club," said Schackman. "They would be taking her to Trude Heller's or another one, below the [Village] Vanguard on Seventh Avenue. And it was real dyke stuff. They were all white. They would dress like men, and some of them wore jackets. They wore loose kind of dress shirts with ties, and pants and men's shoes. They were all tough. They were formidable."

Simone later recounted that she felt uncomfortable with her

popularity in the gay community. "I attracted a lot of gays, a lot of them," she said. "They always thought I was gay, so it was very difficult being with them."

Speaking to Stephen Cleary in 1989, she said, "Have I been approached by women? Yes, I have. Trude Heller, who owned a discotheque in New York City. She used to say she went with Sarah Vaughan, and she tried to make me for about five years. I never would do anything with her.

"I've started liking gay people when so many of them were attracted to my music," she continued, "and there's so many still attracted to my music, so I had to change my view of them."

Her relationship to the gay community, reaching back to her high school days, was even more complicated than her often contradictory statements indicate. People close to Simone claimed that in the early days in New York Simone had several physical relationships with women. Schackman and others said that her close friendship with the prostitute Kevin Mathias had developed a sexual component. Mathias was a downtown "party girl," and she and Simone spent much of their time together. Simone apparently helped Mathias financially, telling her, "You're costing me $50 a week"—not an insignificant amount at the time.

"Kevin was a very light-skinned black woman, long black hair," said Schackman. "She had her schedules in different cities, different towns—she had a route. Nina was going with her. They'd go shopping, sometimes she'd have this scarf and she'd drive this thing and she was gorgeous. Sometimes she'd stay down there, whatever she was doing."

It's hard to know how much credence to put in these accounts. Was a friendship with a highly sexual woman like Kevin definitely the basis for a physical relationship? Were close friends at an all-girls school necessarily sexual partners (as some speculated), and if so, would that be explained as adolescent experimentation? Was her own stated "difficulty" being around gay people an example of homophobia or bad experiences or overcompensating?

She did, however, express her admiration for the independence that someone like Kevin represented. "I have envied other women and their freedom," she said. "For example, the whore that was my close friend. Kevin Mathias, I always wanted to be like her. She was free, and she could get men all the time. She was pretty and she had beautiful clothes and beautiful shoes. And she never had to worry about men, and I envied that. She would whip them—she would actually come to my house, make them fix Christmas dinner, and take a whip to them when they wouldn't do it."

Yet all of Nina Simone's relationships would change in March of 1961 when, while playing a midtown supper club, she was introduced to a larger-than-life New York City police officer.

CHAPTER 5

> She had her own mind. She didn't give a fuck about anybody or anything. She said at one point that I represented strength, and that this is what she liked. And this was her MO. She always looked for security. She was looking for protection.

> —ANDREW STROUD

"My dad was the fifth son of a fifth son," said Lisa Simone Kelly, née Lisa Stroud. "He was born in Virginia. His father was Dutch, his mother was dark as night. A mulatto child in Virginia, and the youngest son—so that sets our stage right there.

"I believe something happened to my dad early in his life that made him so hard that he swore he would never be a victim again."

When he met Nina Simone, Andrew Stroud was a thirty-five-year-old Harlem-based detective who had served in the navy. It was said that he was so feared on the streets near his precinct that when he stepped out of his squad car everyone would scatter—guilty, innocent, passersby, it didn't matter; they just wanted to stay out of Andy's way.

"And that's what attracted my mom to him, because she had this love affair with fire," said Lisa. "On top of being charismatic, he was not afraid, and he could be a bully—he could be very mean. I think they were both nuts, because that's like invit-ing the bull with the red cape, 'Just come on into my kitchen and let's see what we can do.'"

Stroud could often be found at a Harlem bar called the Lenox Lounge, where he was friendly with the manager and his wife, a sometime nightclub entertainer named Becky Harding. One night while Stroud was drinking at the Lenox, Harding told him that she had just seen a fantastic singer named Nina Simone at a midtown supper club called the Round Table and that she was going to go back and he should join her.

Stroud drove them down to the venue. Harding had intro-duced herself to the singer on her first visit, so after her set Simone came to their table to say hello. Stroud was eating a ham-burger next to Harding. Simone playfully snatched up some of his French fries and, as he said later, "We got cute and whatnot."

Stroud was driving his friends home, so following her final set Simone joined them and they headed up to Harlem. She hung out for a few drinks at the Lenox Lounge, and then he dropped her off at her Central Park West apartment, just a few blocks from his police station. Before getting out of the car, she handed him the Round Table business card, which had a note on the back saying, "Nice to have met you—Nina," and her phone number.

They started seeing each other immediately; she claimed at one point that when she said goodnight to Stroud after their second or third date, he broke into her apartment with skeleton keys, just to show that he could (Stroud denied this story). Not that this kind of aggression frightened her off. "By this time," she said, "I was quite hot for him."

"He scared me to death," she said in 1967. "He knew what he wanted and he was gentle with me. It was like he just took over, and I'm glad of that."

"I had met a lot of women in show business," Stroud said.

"These women are a little stronger than the ordinary women that you meet. They have a lot of character, spunk. She stood out as a person, strong character, and could really turn on the charm when she wanted to. She was very unusual, and a chemistry just set in."

Stroud had been married three times already, and he had two sons in addition to a daughter who had died. "His first wife was from the West Indies," Simone said. "His second wife was a high-yellow woman, and his third wife was Puerto Rican. Obviously you can see what he was trying to do with me, trying to find himself. He knew about his problem with the race, and he didn't know where he belonged. So he wanted a woman who he knew would accept that and understand that."

As her personal life was undergoing this thrilling, dramatic transformation, Simone's career was continuing to thrive. Her single "Trouble in Mind" / "Cotton Eyed Joe" had been a Top 10 R&B hit, and the *At Newport* album—documenting her high-energy festival appearance—peaked at number 23 on the pop charts, the highest spot any of her LPs would reach. She went back into the studio for the first time in almost two years, and an April performance at the Village Gate was recorded for another live album (a show that was also notable because her opening act was a young and terrified Richard Pryor, in one of his first-ever public appearances).

On weekends, Stroud would sprint out at the end of his shift and race to meet her at out-of-town gigs. "I'd catch an eleven or twelve o'clock p.m. plane out of LaGuardia, fly to Boston, or one time to Chicago," he said. "Another time I drove down to Philly. I used to go meet her on the last day of the engagement, and we'd hang out, then come back together."

Even the early days of their relationship, though, came with some obstacles. As he was getting involved with Nina, Stroud was actually still in the process of breaking up with his previous wife. It wasn't necessarily a clean break: once his wife saw some lipstick on his shirt and, he claims, threw a pot of hot lye at him.

Meanwhile, he was insisting that Nina abandon the downtown lesbian scene. Stroud, who described Simone's high school days as the time she "got contaminated" with "gay associations," was clearly uncomfortable with gay men and lesbians around his woman. "I got rid of that," he said. "I made that as part of the deal—'Hey, you want to be serious, you want to be steady, you got to be straight.' I said, 'I'm not going to be involved with all of these people. That's not a part of my life.'"

He felt that Simone was testing him, not just with the women in her life, but sometimes with men, too. Once she kept him waiting forty-five minutes for a date, then pulled up in a car with one of her other suitors. "I don't know what their relationship was," Stroud said, "but he was one of the guys that I beat out, you might say." As they went up to her apartment, he slapped her—hard—in the elevator. It was the first time Stroud hit her.

"I felt that I had been insulted," he said. "I just slapped her and I said, 'Look, forget it, I don't need this bullshit. You want to play games? I don't have time. Bye.' And I left."

Simone tried downplaying the situation, telling Stroud that nothing was going on with the other man and that it was no big deal. But after he left she immediately sent an apologetic telegram to the police station.

That July—on the heels of the release of the *Forbidden Fruit* album, her second studio record for Colpix—Simone was scheduled to perform in Philadelphia. She drove the short distance south from New York, but by the time she arrived she was in agonizing pain. "I couldn't see, there were hammers in my head," she said. She called her former psychiatrist, Gerry Weiss, who sent for an ambulance.

They placed her in an isolation ward and did multiple spinal taps. At different times she claimed that she had been diagnosed with nonparalytic polio, with spinal meningitis, or with some mystery illness that the doctors couldn't identify. She also wasn't sure who had first contacted Stroud, or if she had called him herself, but he was there within a few hours.

"He came and he saw me in this room eating oatmeal with a spoon," she said. "Andrew stood over me and it was so much love in the air. It was like a dream. The tenderness and affection that he held the spoon with, to feed me."

She was institutionalized for seventeen days, and Andy drove from New York to Philadelphia each day. When he wasn't there, Simone wrote to him, clearly in the absolute thrall of new love (and lust), in a note from July 1961:

Darling Andy—

. . . I feel like you are a bottomless well that I can pour water into endlessly and it would never be all you needed or wanted. . . .

As I told you—you're the most pleasant thing to think of when I want to go to sleep or not think of anything disturbing . . . then I imagine all sorts of places we haven't been, and what we'll do when we get there—besides that! We'd go dancing and dance and dance—can you ballroom? We must sometimes—I don't do it very well and its so beautiful to watch. You know something? As much as we both like to dance, we've only been to one! That's typical of me—not to do the things I most enjoy—Maybe when we are not so "hungry" and don't have to go to bed the minute we see each other, then we'll go dancing or do something else, huh! Meanwhile, I enjoy you so much and there's so much more there that I'm actually in no rush to do anything but stay in bed with you—to hold you, to feel you so heavy beside me—to feel so terribly protected when I go to sleep beside you—I've never felt that way, particularly that way, with a man before—it's so hard for me to trust, you know . . . and you're so gentle—you're my gentle

lion, my Saint Bernard and sometimes my Stud Bull! and some-
times Bully.

Standing over her hospital bed, with a surgical mask covering his face, Stroud proposed to Simone, almost exactly four
months after they had first met. She said that she laughed and
cried at the same time, and nodded her answer. When the hospital dismissed her, he announced their engagement to his family.

"He had five brothers and sisters, and he did it right," Simone
said. "That's the biggest thing—Andrew dotted every I and
crossed every T, the way the system said it should be done. Everyone thought he was strange, and he *was* strange, 'cause being
a cop ain't funny. It ain't easy."

Simone made no secret that she was attracted to Stroud's
macho, aggressive style. But soon after the engagement he revealed that he was capable of brutality that she never imagined.
Nina Simone would come to understand, very acutely, the temper that caused people to scatter when they saw Andy Stroud on
the street.

As Nina had suggested in her letter from the hospital, she and
Andy went to the Palladium Ballroom to celebrate their engagement. Stroud seldom drank, but on this night he was downing
white rum. They stayed late into the evening, until it was almost closing time. During the course of the evening, a fan came
over to Simone and handed her a note, which she slipped in her
pocket. This exchange—its meaning presumably amplified by
the alcohol—upset Andy, and when the newly engaged couple
left the club, he started pummeling her.

"He started raining blows on me," she said. "In the cab, he
beat me all the way home, up the stairs, in the elevator, in my
room. He put a gun to my head, made me take out all the letters

that Edney had written to me, and he examined them with my hands tied behind my head. He thought that I was having some affair going on with some of these men that I'd been dancing with at the discotheque where I was celebrating my engagement to him. Then he tied me up and raped me."

In different accounts of the incident, the details Simone offered would vary in their severity—though the incident was clearly terrifying regardless of the specifics. "My husband beat me nineteen hours, or perhaps it was nine," she said in another interview. "With a gun at my head after the beating was finished, and laughing, saying, 'You thought I was gonna kill you, didn't you?'"

"I had a gun," Stroud said. "I took the bullets out of the gun, and I was telling her, 'If you don't do this, that, or the other, I'll shoot you, whatever.'"

He grabbed her again, leading her down in the elevator and through the building's courtyard; a bellman on duty turned his head away. Simone saw some policemen, but Stroud said, "You think they're gonna help you? As far as they're concerned, we're just two niggers on a Saturday night." Stroud later said that he knew the cop who saw them and that (especially since Stroud outranked him) he wouldn't help.

He took her, bleeding in the street, up to his apartment, and continued to beat her until his hands and knuckles were bloody. "After he was exhausted, he tied my legs and my hands to a bed and struck me, and raped me, and fell asleep," she said.

Eventually, she freed herself from the ropes while he slept. First she ran to the nearby apartment of Becky Harding, the woman who had introduced her to Stroud, but Harding didn't want to get involved.

She then called Schackman, in the middle of the night, and fled to his apartment on the Upper West Side. "She needed to hide out, and she came to my place, and she was beat up. I put her to bed, and she rested for a couple of days." Stroud figured out where she was and called, expressing remorse and asking if he could see her. "Nina was lying down, and I told her that Andy was on the phone, wanted to see her, and wanted to apologize. And she said okay. He came over, and they talked and patched it up."

According to Simone, when Stroud tracked her down at Schackman's home he had no memory of the assault. "He asked me who had done that to me," she said, "that he had gone to the apartment, seen it ransacked, seen all the blood, and he thought I was dead."

Stroud said that he remembered going to sleep and that Simone was gone when he woke up. It took him four or five days to locate her at Schackman's apartment. When he arrived, her face was still swollen. "I said, 'Who the hell beat you up?' I didn't remember."

"I told him that he had done it," Nina said. "He says, 'I couldn't have.' He felt he had gone temporarily insane. I said, 'Will it happen again?' He said, 'I'm not sure, you have to take your chances.'"

Speaking about the incident years later, though, Stroud didn't deny the assault—in fact his own account of the evening mostly aligns with Simone's version. He said that he had gotten annoyed because she disappeared at the Palladium, keeping him waiting for a long time after the club had emptied out. He yelled at her—"What have you been doing? Where were you at?"—on the drive home, before launching into the brutal beating.

Stroud maintained, though, that his actions did not come out of nowhere and that it wasn't an isolated event that set off his rage. "This beating, it was provoked," he said. "It was a culmination of maybe five or ten different incidents that ticked me off. Her being unfaithful, disrespectful, and everything else, several months of what I suspected to be infidelity and fooling around with guys and girls and the whole bit. And then she pulled this on me, and that's what happened."

Asked directly by Joe Hagan whether he regretted his violence that night, Stroud said that he didn't, showing no remorse or shame. "This is retaliation—when you chastise a child if he did something wrong, you don't regret having done it, because what you're trying to do is a correction. I had several run-ins with her where I had told her, 'Hey, you play the game, you play it straight. Don't fuck with me.'"

Now Simone needed to decide whether or not she would go forward with the wedding. Confused about how to proceed, she insisted that Stroud see two psychiatrists for evaluation. One told her not to marry him. (Her Philadelphia psychiatrist, Gerry Weiss, also advised her against the marriage.) The other doctor concluded that Stroud's fury might have been a temporary state that might or might not appear again, so she'd have to make her own judgment call.

Willfully vetoing the doctors' opinions, she ruled that her wedding to Stroud would go on. "I married him because I needed desperately to love somebody," she said. "I had lost complete self-respect for myself and knew it. I determined the only way to get it was to stay with him long enough to absorb what made him violent in the first place."

"She was lost," her brother Carrol said. "She didn't know which way to go and Andy came along and gave her some direction. She didn't know what to do, and he was the one that saw that she had big potential. Therefore, when she married Andy, he took over her life completely."

Al Schackman could certainly confirm this kind of domination, but even after seeing firsthand the kind of explosive violence that Stroud was capable of he ultimately viewed him favorably. "I knew Andy as a decent friend, and always fair and honest. You treat him fair, and he treats you fair."

On December 4—Andy's birthday, and nine months after they met—Simone and Stroud were married in her apartment. She dressed all in white and carried fifteen white roses. His five brothers attended, as did her sister, her two psychiatrists, Schackman, and the ever-faithful Teddy Axelrod.

Notably absent were Simone's parents; having spent time with Stroud while she was hospitalized, they had mixed feelings about her new husband. "My father didn't like him," she said. "He didn't think he was good for me. My mother liked him."

There was little time to celebrate the wedding, though, because two weeks later Simone and Schackman left on a historic trip. Since her move to New York, the city's black intelligentsia had discovered Simone, responding to her independent spirit and unconventional sound; Langston Hughes (whom she had actually met when he came to speak at Allen High School) and the young literary sensation James Baldwin in particular had sought out her friendship.

Hughes invited her on an excursion to Africa organized by the American Society of African Culture (AMSAC). She joined a group of musicians, artists, and writers including Baldwin, Lionel Hampton, Randy Weston, and many more. "It was like a black who's who," said Schackman. "It was unbelievable."

The plane carrying these luminaries landed in Lagos, Nigeria, in the middle of the night, more than ten hours behind schedule. When the doors opened, they were greeted by hundreds of people, including tribal drummers who had come to pay tribute to the visitors. At the Federal Palace Hotel, the country's prime minister met them and the group was feted with an enormous banquet.

"Everybody on the plane—not Langston, Langston's too cool for that—everybody thought they were going home, back to their motherland," said Schackman. "And that wasn't Nina. She was like Langston, she's a tourist in a way, she wasn't going back to her homeland—not at that time." It wouldn't be until years later that Simone would feel that Africa offered the truest sense of home that she would ever find.

Still, she had a great time. She and Schackman walked around the grounds of the hotel one night, holding hands, on the perimeter of a forest. "Suddenly we realized that there was somebody standing there behind us in the dark," he recounted. "I said, 'There's a man back there.' 'Is he handsome?' 'I don't know, Nina, it's dark.' I turned around, and I see he's got a uniform on. It turned out to be a Federal Palace guard, one of the guards that stand all night and protect the grounds."

Schackman went over to say hello, and Simone walked up to him and said, "Good evening. You're very beautiful."

"Thank you very much, ma'am," the guard replied.

"He was very formal and he had a very big gun," said the guitarist, still tickled by this silly, playful side of Nina. "It was just fun to see how she was acting, having a ball and being flirtatious."

A letter she sent to Stroud from Lagos indicated her excitement about the trip and a fondness for the people of Africa that would stick with her and help introduce the idea of her return to the continent.

i didn't want to write until I finally knew I was here—it has taken me this long, too. I don't know how to start talking about this experience—it is so so fantastic—like leaving the security of a womb where you've been all your life and running head long into a volcano—about to erupt! Can you imagine??

they are exceptionally warm and friendly and uninhibited (needless to say) although they are bashful and shy at times—in this category I feel quite at home—the southern negro is very much like that.

FEDERAL PALACE HOTEL
P.O. BOX 1000 · VICTORIA ISLAND · LAGOS · NIGERIA

TELEPHONE 26691 (10 Lines)
TELEGRAMS: PALACE-LAGOS

December — '61

My Dearest Andy —

It's 1:25 A.M. and the whole group has gone night clubbing — I wanted to go, but was much too tired (as usual) after having spent all afternoon riding around town, taking pictures, and shopping . . . Right now — this moment — I miss you terribly — all of a sudden it's come down on me — maybe because I'm finally writing to you . . . . . . I don't know what day it is there, sweetheart, but here it's Saturday — we've been here only two days counting today. I didn't want to write until I finally knew I was here — it has taken me this long, too.

I don't know how to start talking about this experience — it is so so fantastic — like leaving the security of a womb where you've been all your life and running headlong into a volcano — about to erupt! can you imagine?? It started the minute we got off the plane. There was a reception committee of approximately fifty women, men + children dancing, beating drums + singing — this in addition to a receiving line and another 200 people standing around to greet

The trip to Africa was brief—"Such a short introduction was cruel," she would say—but it planted some important seeds in her thinking about the world. For one thing, it had an impact on her personal style and image. Rather than continue wearing the usual formal wear or cocktail attire that signaled success and sophistication, she had the designers Joe Fouts and Louise Gilkes make African-style gowns, shoes, and accessories for her at their studio on the Bowery, an early example of her interest in the idea of a specifically black sense of beauty.

After Simone returned, the newlyweds began to discuss

their plan moving forward. They both had professional aspirations; Simone's career was unsteady—although she was growing as a concert draw (largely thanks to her television appearances), she hadn't come close to duplicating the commercial success of "I Loves You, Porgy"—while Stroud was moving ahead in the police department, up for promotion to lieutenant, and was talking about starting law school.

"It was a gamble," said Stroud. "At first it was a love affair, then it became business. In the early days of our marriage, we discussed many times what way we should go—whether she should be a policeman's homemaker, or whether she should be a career person. So after many discussions, we agreed she had the greatest potential and I would resign from the police department."

Beyond just committing their resources to Simone's music, the couple decided that Stroud would assume the reins as her manager. She still had dreams of playing Carnegie Hall as a classical pianist. More pressingly, she needed a systematic, directed plan for what was becoming an erratic recording schedule.

"When [Andy] took over, for the first time I knew what it was not to be just floundering out there," said Simone. "Before then I played and sang, and that was my pleasure, but all of the agents and managers that I had known were just taking advantage right and left of me. When Andrew came into the picture, he straightened it all out."

Stroud formally began his new responsibilities in early 1962, initially working out of a home office. He started by evaluating the sorts of deals and contracts that Simone had been signing and then concluded that he would handle her concert bookings by himself—an unusual role for a manager.

The Newport Festival's George Wein, probably the most important promoter in the jazz world, asserted that he had seen female artists go down this road over and over again and that hiring a husband, family member, or friend as a manager was usually a mistake.

"Most of them were treated badly because they picked the wrong men to manage them," he said. "Singers wanted somebody close to them to manage them. They should have got people that were *not* close to them, business people. I knew [these guys], and they weren't professional managers. I always call them 'coat holders.' You need a professional manager, and professional managers are very rare people. It's not just a matter of taking phone calls and signing contracts. It's a manager directing your career, and a career is not just making a record. It's an overall structure of a person's life."

But Simone had total confidence in Stroud, partly because of his own history—including those famous, street-tested intimidation skills. "Andrew has a degree in business administration, and he simply applied what he had learned as a sergeant of police to my business," she said. "Which is very easy, because the business was so wide open. There are crooks in this business all over, so he applied what he had learned in the police department to show business and it worked."

"He didn't take no shit," said daughter Lisa. "There were times that he would grab people over the table when they didn't have the money. I guess being a cop helped, 'cause you could be your own security."

The middle of the year saw the release of two new Nina Simone albums. First came another live album, the set recorded at the Village Gate. That album included her version of "House of the Rising Sun," a song that Bob Dylan would record a few months later for his debut album and that would become a global hit for the Animals in 1964. She also sang Babatunde Olatunji's "Zungo" (the title track of the Nigerian drummer's follow-up album to his groundbreaking 1959 smash *Drums of Passion*) on *At the Village Gate,* her most African-inspired recording to date.

The progressive music community was widening its range to incorporate both folk and world music, and Simone was right on top of the pulse in multiple ways.

A few months later came *Nina Simone Sings Ellington,* on which she recorded eleven songs associated with the jazz giant, backed by strings and the Malcolm Dodds Singers. Material ranged from familiar Duke classics ("Satin Doll," a gospel-tinged "I Got It Bad") to more obscure selections like "Hey, Buddy Bolden" and "Merry Mending." Taken together, the two 1962 albums solidified the range and self-assurance of her work, but both failed to chart.

Privately, Simone continued to struggle with her feelings for Stroud, still reeling from the emotional fallout of the brutal attack the previous year. She felt that he hated sharing her—even with the public—and she always harbored fear for the anger she knew he could potentially release. In a letter to him, she wrote:

> *I've been scared to be happy. I think I figured the change or transition would be too much and kill me.*
>
> *Each day I grow more beautiful (for I feel beautiful) and it must be awful hard for you to watch your little "jewel" that you've polished and loved being admired all over the goddam place! I don't blame you—I'd want to put it in a box and hide it somewhere, too! Specially when you're the jealous type anyway!! I'm so glad I was able to see this more today, for unfortunately, my sweet, the words "I own and deserve you because I made you" coming from your lips automatically would antagonize me—and so I say them for you—and they actually are true—I want to lick you all over and keep saying "I love you, Andy" I love you—for you gave me my life back—and so, in turn, I give it back to you. I don't think I'll ever lose my fear of you (though I hope it won't be so extreme) and to a certain extent trust's good . . . for though I don't understand you when you're mean,*

it isn't as necessary for me to understand as it was. I just must respect and handle it (and hope I can) when it comes—not the beatings, Andy, not the beatings—those I can't take—for some reason, they destroy everything within me—my confidence, my warmth and my spirit! And when that happens I feel that I must kill or be killed—you know how I just about lost my mind the last time—well anyway, I do understand and I respect the message you so crudely got across (smile) that message was "I will be heard I will be seen I will love you And you will love me back, or I'll kill you!!!!"

By the time you get home today, I'll probably hate your guts but please keep this letter; especially for those times when you'd like to throw me against the wall—

Stroud maintained that Simone's use of "beatings" as a plural noun and the anxiety in this letter were exaggerations. "After that beating—and she did it the rest of the relationship—she's using that incident as if it was common," he said. "She told everybody that, told Lisa for years. One bad thing is recalled and remembered a thousand times and never forgotten. Like all the good things that followed didn't mean a thing; there's no healing."

Whatever her complex emotions about the marriage, Simone and Stroud ticked off the milestones of a young couple. Their next major step was buying a house on Nuber Avenue in Mount Vernon, a rolling, leafy, and largely black suburb in lower Westchester County just outside New York City limits.

As the civil rights battles were heating up in the southern states, new opportunities were arising in other black communities. Motown Records was fulfilling its motto as "the Sound of Young America," and Ray Charles (one of Simone's few rivals as an explorer of multiple genres) had one of 1962's biggest albums with *Modern Sounds in Country and Western Music*. Mount Vernon exemplified a new African American prosperity and was becoming a hub for black professional families; a generation later, a number of hip-hop stars (including Sean "Puffy" Combs, Heavy D, and Pete Rock & CL Smooth) would emerge from the town, rhyming the praises of "Money-Earnin' Mt. Vernon."

Finding the house seemed almost like kismet. It sat atop a hill on a one-acre corner lot, with entrances on three sides, the perfect home for a growing family. It sported a flagstone patio, a spacious glassed-in front porch, elaborate gardens bordered by twelve-foot lilac trees, a two-car garage with an apartment above (which Simone would dub her "treehouse"). The previous owners of the house were a black couple; the husband owned a fleet of taxicabs and a private, after-hours club in Stroud's Harlem precinct. The wife was a big Nina Simone fan, delighted to sell to the singer.

To raise the money for the down payment, Stroud approached Colpix Records with a proposal: Simone would record and hand over five albums in exchange for the advances for all of them at once. The sum would cover what they needed for the house, while also fulfilling her contractual obligations to the label (and giving Stroud the ability to negotiate a new deal with them, or the freedom to move to another company). Colpix apparently agreed to these terms, and Simone's team set up a home studio on Nuber Avenue, plugged in a four-track recorder, brought in her musicians, and quickly rehearsed and recorded enough material to fill the quota. Since Simone's albums were often assembled from different sessions scattered over multiple years, it's hard to track exactly how these recordings were ultimately used; regardless, Simone and Stroud got their payday and secured their new home.

Trading up happened at exactly the right time, too, because Simone was pregnant. It was not the first time; she had gotten pregnant while still living in Philadelphia, and then several times again in later years. Oddly, in different interviews, she had claimed that she had lost four, five, or six previous pregnancies, some through abortions and some in miscarriages, saying that she "sacrificed it all for my career."

She spoke in painful detail about her first abortion. "You weren't ever supposed to even fuck, let alone get pregnant," she said. "That was the end of the world, and my mother conducted funeral services over my body when I was sitting there with this tube in me, waiting for this thing to come down. I was in all this pain, didn't know what I was doing, had gone to some quack doctor in North Philadelphia. He had butchered me. I was in great pain. He put a tube up in me, and I had to stay that way for, oh, God, eighteen, twenty hours, but I was in so much pain I called my mother. She came down and did not help me at all, just told me how bad I was, how terrible I was, then left me there. That was cruel."

But if Simone was concerned that her body had been so badly mangled that it could not safely deliver a baby, she needn't have been. She was easily able to carry to term. In fact, she was three weeks past her due date when her sister Frances came to see her and instructed Nina to get herself to the hospital immediately.

Frances told Stroud that she didn't care what the doctor said, the baby was coming that day. He sped home in his Mercedes and shuttled his wife to the hospital, and the baby arrived forty-five minutes later. When Simone recovered from the delivery, she asked Stroud, "How's the baby?" He replied, "How's the mother?"

"I loved him for that," Simone said.

Lisa Celeste Stroud was born on September 12, 1962. And with her arrival, at least for a short time, Simone at last felt true bliss.

"The first three hours after Lisa was born were the most peaceful in my life," she said. "I was in love with the world. The dust that was in the air, I loved it, the air itself. There was nothing in me that had any tension at all. I'll never forget it. I had a feathery feeling of floating and loving, being completely at peace and loving everything, in tune with everyone."

But when she got home, she quickly began to feel overwhelmed by the responsibilities. Though they had hired staff to help with the housework, she claimed that she still took on most of the effort. "I had to show the servant girl how to clean the house, help her with the cooking, help her with the cleaning, help her take care of my daughter," she said. "I had to take care of Lisa, I had to supervise taking care of the house, supervise the gardener, I cooked, and I worked at night. So I worked at night and I worked during the daytime. And I thought I was supposed to do that." This micromanaging, of course, was probably better explained by Simone's need for absolute control than by the staff's incompetence.

To lessen these burdens, they hired a professional nanny, complete with white uniform, named Rose Stewart. "Nina hated her," said Stroud. "Rose Stewart was as crazy as she was when you get her upset. Rose Stewart would put her fist in her face and call her a bitch or whatever, and said, 'I'll kick your ass if you don't shut up and leave me alone.' Rose was one of the most beautiful people that you would ever want to meet—just don't cross her. Then the streak comes out and she could be very, very forceful, much more than Nina. And I loved her for it."

Stroud would later tell Lisa, "Let's face it, she didn't physically take care of you. When there's a nanny all the time, the mother doesn't have any responsibilities or things like that. She would handle you and play with you. You weren't a tit baby, so it was formulas for you." (Simone would say that Stroud had instructed her not to breast-feed Lisa because it made him jealous.)

With the addition of this staff to help take care of Lisa and the house, the Mount Vernon residence was rapidly filling up despite its spaciousness. Frances also came to live with her sister. She had a young child of her own but was having some issues with her husband and moved from Philadelphia to help Simone for several months. It also meant the chance to know her brother-in-law better.

"Andrew was funny, but also serious, a businessman," she said. "I don't know that he was domineering, but he was a strong character. This is an independent man, strong-willed. And self-motivating, self-starting, entrepreneur. Tough, but I think also gentle. I think he was very good for her.

"Andy had been married and had children before, so he had experience with newborn children. Nina never really had that experience. With an assistant, other people around to do the actual care, she never had the full or total responsibility of doing it herself. I told them, 'I wouldn't marry either one of you.' I used to tell them that all the time."

But Simone abruptly threw her sister out of the house, seemingly without provocation. Stroud came home from the office one day and she was gone. He asked Frances what happened, and she said that Simone had just exploded and sent her away. It was perhaps a sign of the stress she was feeling, and a harbinger of the instability and emotional outbursts that would escalate in the years to come.

After losing the room and board she had been given in exchange for helping with Lisa, Frances had no other income and was doing domestic work to pay her expenses. Stroud lent her some money, and she started attending business classes to begin a career in accounting. Simone lit into Stroud for giving Frances the loan, but he brushed her off.

"Subsequently, when Nina would visit her family, she never spoke to her sister," he said. "At somebody's funeral, Nina walked through the room where her sister was and it was if she did not exist."

That December, on "Andy's Birthday Our 1st Anniversary," Nina seemed highly self-aware, both loving and logical, when she wrote to him:

> *I am so proud of being a woman now—I gave your little girl back to you—that makes me happy!*
>
> *You know about my ambivalence toward work. But I think you should know that because I understand and know why I'm working, i not only don't mind it but at time find it enjoyable and exciting; which is definitely a contrast to the old me—anyway, you and I will be going through all kinds of stages during our marriage and I look at this one as simply being the work period—so try to get me another week in December (smiles)*
>
> *One day, I'll fix up the house—when we don't need money so badly—until then, don't you do anything around here that isn't—conserve your strength for the police work and getting me jobs and breathing down my neck when you hold me at night*

With the baby at home and the staff in place (though turnover was high), it was time to get back to work. The Mount Vernon house was now being set up as a full-service headquarters for the Nina Simone operation, a space to create, rehearse, strategize.

Nina and Andy had separate bedrooms. Her bedroom—about forty feet wide and twenty-five feet deep, with walk-in closets for her clothes and her shoes—took up the whole front of the house. That room was her real headquarters; it was where she met with designers and took lessons from her dance instructor, Pearl Reynolds. "Everything happened in that bedroom," said Stroud. "It was like a little studio where she worked."

Simone was concerned about the schedule and the pressure, but Stroud had broken things into more manageable pieces. He had her visualize her goals, looking at her career as a series of finite projects rather than something shapeless and indefinable.

"He used to tell me to put on the blackboard, 'I'll be a rich black bitch by such-and-such date' and then I could quit," she said. "And I always believed him, and I never could quit, and that's why I left him in the end, because he worked me too hard. And he was mean. I was always afraid of him."

Andrew said that we couldn't miss being successful - he used the example of a flour sifter - (if a couple of holes got clogged, it didn't mean anything because there were so many other holes for the flour to go through") As applicable to us: we have 1. Albums already made
2. Albums that have been pirated and we're collecting damages
3. Publishing company -
4. Approximately 30 songs in our own company - and no one gets that money but us
5. I've learned how to steal
7. 2 fanclubs
8. Been on TV on 9 ½ hrs shows ~~so far~~. in the last year
9. The 2nd time I ever saw Andrew cry was when he was telling me how tough things are now with him.

Nina believed in Andy's vision, and in his love. But she felt that both his professional and his romantic requirements were ultimately just too demanding. Her need for freedom, creatively and personally, was bringing her into increasing conflict with her formidable husband.

"Andrew loved me like a serpent," she said. "He wrapped himself around me and he ate and breathed me, and without me he would die. That's the way he treated me. And it was just too much."

CHAPTER 6

There were two things that people in the movement would fight over. One was if you took their books. The other was if you took their Nina Simone albums.

—ANDREW YOUNG

ndrew Stroud was making moves. He had resigned from the police force and was now in the music business full-time. In addition to his attempts to maximize Simone's career, he started a production company, with an office at Fifth Avenue and Forty-second Street. His staff included a publicist he hired from RCA, where she had worked with Elvis Presley. There was also a promotion person who had been at Atlantic Records, and someone specifically doing promotion to college radio stations—a full-service operation. "Every time a record came out, or concert appearances, we would do a mailing with a photo, a bio, and whatnot to the magazines, to get newspaper coverage and to bring out the critics," he said.

"He was the original Puff Daddy," said Lisa Simone. "He had pads where it says 'Andrew Stroud, exclusive manager of Nina Simone.' He had his office on Fifth Avenue, he had Stroud Productions and all these different artists and publishing companies. He really had a vision, and he was a very astute businessman who had a strategic plan in terms of how Mom's career was gonna go. And it was working very well until she got touched by civil rights and the plan went out the window."

The contract with RCA later gave Stroud the finances to sign and produce other talent, and he would work with such R&B artists as Sonny Til and Percy Mayfield. Stroud also did record promotion and joined the DJ Association so that he could attend their conventions.

Simone's career was benefiting from this increased focus. People started recognizing her, stopping her on the street. She seemed excited by the attention, if still a bit baffled by her whirlwind success. The couple decided that it was time to take a big gamble, to fulfill a deeply felt, lifelong dream. Stroud booked Nina Simone into Carnegie Hall.

Even if Nina seemed to have the devoted following to justify the appearance, Stroud was a complete unknown to the iconic theater's powers that be. Carnegie Hall wasn't about to rent the hall to some unknown manager, so just to be able to get in the door he had to partner with experienced classical promoter Felix Gerstman, who agreed to handle the actual booking in exchange for a commission on the ticket sales.

Despite the help from Gerstman, Andy was still heavily invested in promoting the event. Stroud paid for a thousand three-by-six-foot posters throughout the city, brochures that went into record stores and department stores, newspaper advertisements—"especially in the *New York Times,* because her fans were *New York Times* people."

The Carnegie Hall performance was on April 12, 1963. Backstage, Nina was swallowing her anxiety as best she could. "She was nervous," said Al Schackman, "and I said, 'Hey, it's your time now.' And she said, 'I know, but still, this is Carnegie Hall.' I said, 'Yeah, it's Carnegie Hall—this is where you were heading for and now you're here, on your own terms.' I said, 'Now, how about breathing?' And she went [exhale], 'Now can I have a ciga-rette?' I said, 'Come on—hold on,' and it was great."

She played eighteen songs in total, though only seven of them made it onto the resulting live album (another eight would make up the 1964 album *Folksy Nina,* while the remain-der would be located in a label vault in the 1990s and would fi-nally surface on a 2005 reissue). The complete set list reveals the extent to which she was still searching for any material she connected with, regardless of genre—two Israeli folk songs ("Eretz Zavat Chalav U'dvash" and "Vaynikehu," which may have been introduced to her by her Atlantic City friend Shlomo Carlebach), "Theme from *Samson and Delilah,*" Leadbelly's "Sil-ver City Bound," an original titled "If You Knew" that she had written for Stroud.

Her performance revealed none of her anxiety—on this night, she was in total command. As strong as the more theatri-cal (and more accessible) songs were that made up the bulk of the *Nina Simone at Carnegie Hall* LP, the more spare and personal folk-based repertoire that was collected on the follow-up album is, if anything, even more arresting. This magical night showed that her singing truly stood on its own, even separated from her stunning piano work.

The show also met its goals commercially; Stroud broke even and the couple was spared financial repercussions for his under-taking. More important than the money, the night was an artis-tic triumph. The live album became one of Simone's signature recordings and established her reputation as an artist who could draw in big crowds for big venues. It was impressive enough that she had been able to reach audiences from the folk scene down-town to the Apollo uptown, but conquering Carnegie Hall ele-vated her to the top tier of popular music performers, validating her as a musician to be taken seriously. And personally, it repre-sented something that couldn't be quantified: Simone's parents and even Mrs. Mazzanovich came to New York to witness her achievement.

"We had a party after and her father played a little thing on the piano," Schackman recalled. "Strange man, never really spoke. Tall, bony, sat down at the piano and only played the black keys." The guitarist felt that he could recognize some of Nina's eccentricities in her father's behavior. "I saw that and I said, 'Aha, that's some of it.'"

Simone had finally made it to Carnegie Hall, but as a pop singer instead of a classical pianist. If she felt any bitterness about this, though, she didn't let it show. "It felt glorious," she said many years later. "It was the same thing . . . didn't change what I felt in my heart and didn't change my classical training."

But the same night Nina was making her sensational, life-changing Carnegie Hall debut, Martin Luther King Jr. was arrested and jailed in Birmingham, Alabama. She had, of course, been following the developments in the fight for racial equality, but from a bit of a distance—she had listened to her intellectual friends debate the issues, had laughed at the hip Village comedians' topical jokes. But it wasn't until playwright Lorraine Hansberry took Simone under her wing that she really began to prioritize these issues—and after the concert, Hansberry pointedly pulled Simone aside and asked her what she was doing for the civil rights movement while its leaders were being put in prison.

Hansberry, the daughter of an activist family, was best known as the author of the classic *Raisin in the Sun,* the first play written by a black woman ever produced on Broadway. She was emerging as a mentor for Simone. "Nina idolized Lorraine Hansberry and had the utmost respect for her, never a bad word," said Schackman. "I think Nina really started to glean her ability to compose story lines and poetry and lyrics from Lorraine.

"New York was a hotbed of music, art, theater," he continued.

"Lorraine would come to the Gate. They hung out a lot together. There was so much going on in New York at that time. The art scene was incredible, and she gradually got used to being in the in crowd in the New York scene. We're talking about a country girl here from Tryon, North Carolina."

Simone was spending as much time as she could with Hansberry, who also lived in Westchester, and it was shifting her attitudes about social ills and racial barriers. "Lorraine was a very staunch activist," said Stroud, "and she was convinced that certain things must be done in order to push the revolution."

"When you reference political enlightenment, Nina Simone was really already there," said Attallah Shabazz, daughter of Malcolm X, whose speeches were also something Simone was absorbing. "What Lorraine Hansberry gave was permission to dare. I don't think there was a lot of teaching you give Nina Simone—I think she entered the world ready. Lorraine Hansberry was a free spirit, an open spirit, was not caged. So what someone like Lorraine Hansberry would be for Nina Simone is a wink of permission. It inspired her to just go head-on."

Like so many, Simone gave credit to Martin Luther King Jr. for first exposing her to activism. "I didn't get political until Martin Luther King came along," she said. "I wanted to be a classical pianist because there was no black classical pianist, but I wasn't focused on 'black,' if you understand the difference."

Though he helped open her eyes and her attitudes, however, Simone would often express her reservations about Dr. King's practice of nonviolent protest. "I never did agree too much with Martin Luther King," Simone said. "He was popular, but I never believed with him." The first time that Simone met Dr. King, she immediately said to him, "I'm not nonviolent." He considered that and replied, "Okay, I'm glad to meet you." She extended her hand and said, "I'm so glad to meet you, too."

Racial justice was simmering in Nina Simone's consciousness, but in 1963 a series of events would forever transform her life, her music, and her politics, radicalizing her into a figure identified with a particular brand of civil rights activism. First Medgar Evers, an activist and organizer, and the NAACP's first field secretary in Mississippi, was shot in his own driveway on June 12, 1963. He died in a hospital in Jackson after initially being denied entry because of his race.

In August, King delivered the "I Have a Dream" speech in front of 250,000 people gathered on the capital's Mall, the culmination of the March on Washington. That day, Simone was playing a concert in Detroit and saw the coverage of the march on television. According to Stroud, Nina went "ballistic" because she hadn't been invited to participate in the demonstration.

Then on September 15—just a month after Simone played a concert at Birmingham's Miles College, supporting the campaign for desegregation—four young girls were killed when a bomb exploded while they were attending Bible class at the Sixteenth Street Baptist Church in that very city. It was a profound and transformative moment for the civil rights movement, the murder of innocent children presenting in stark and absolute terms the stakes of the fight and the intolerable level of hatred and violence being directed at African Americans.

After the Birmingham bombing, Simone felt compelled to commit to the fight for racial equality in a deeper and more active way. Maybe it was because she had a daughter of her own now and the deaths of those little girls touched her as a mother, but on that day something in her caught fire.

"When they killed those children is when I said, 'I have to start using my talent to help black people,'" she said. "When they killed the little girls in Alabama, that's when I changed."

"It also put in perspective her childhood," Carrol Waymon said about the event's impact on Nina. "The town was segregated, but we never talked about it, it was just there. She began to reflect on the fact that had she not been black, she would have been in Juilliard, would have been in Curtis."

Her immediate impulse was to get violent, retreating to her garage and trying to build a zip gun, but within a few hours of hearing the news Simone had channeled her ravaged emotions into something else. She sat down and wrote a new song. Having previously dismissed the pop audience because "all they wanted to get was the words," she now embraced the emotional power that a lyric could carry. The melody was surprisingly upbeat, bouncy in a Broadway sort of way (in the recording, she said, "This is a show tune, but the show hasn't been written for it yet"). The cheerful style of the arrangement made the contrast with the lyrics all the more striking:

> *Alabama's gotten me so upset*
> *Tennessee made me lose my rest*
> *And everybody knows about Mississippi Goddam!*
> . . . .
>
> *Picket lines, school boycotts*
> *They try to say it's a communist plot*
> *All I want is equality*
> *For my sister, my brother, my people, and me*
> . . . .
>
> *Oh, but this whole country is full of lies*
> *You're all gonna die and die like flies*
> *I don't trust you any more*
> *You keep on saying, "Go slow! Go slow!"*
> . . . .
>
> *Do things gradually (Do it slow)*
> *But bring more tragedy (Do it slow)*
> *Why don't you see it? Why don't you feel it?*
> *I don't know, I don't know*

You don't have to live next to me
Just give me my equality
Alabama's gotten me so upset
Tennessee made me lose my rest
And everybody knows about Mississippi Goddam!

"Mississippi Goddam" marked a dividing line in Simone's career. When she premiered the song at Carnegie Hall in March 1964, she introduced a level of outrage and immediacy unlike anything else in the protest movement. This was not couched in biblical language, not a metaphorical yearning for freedom and progress: she was naming names and demanding answers. "You're all gonna die and die like flies," "You don't have to live next to me," "Mississippi *Goddam*."

This kind of directness was becoming familiar in the new wave of protest songs like Bob Dylan's "Masters of War," but it marked new territory for a black artist: Sam Cooke's majestic but still veiled commentary in "A Change Is Gonna Come" was considered a daring step when it came out nine months later. (The Birmingham bombing was also the inspiration for John Coltrane's moving, stately instrumental elegy "Alabama.")

"There is something about a woman," said comedian and activist Dick Gregory. "If you look at all the suffering that black folks went through, not one black man would dare sing 'Mississippi Goddam.' Not one black man would say what Billie Holiday did about being lynched [in "Strange Fruit"]—they weren't lynching women, they was lynching men, but it was women that talked about it, and nobody told them to talk about it. No manager going to tell you to talk about this, it's just something inside of them.

"'Mississippi Goddam'—that's using God's name in vain. She said it, talking about 'Mississippi, goddamn you.' We all *wanted* to say it, but she said it. That's the difference that set her aside from the rest of them."

The expletive in the title meant the song was banned by numerous radio stations (though it's unlikely that it would have gotten significant airplay anyway, given its unabashedly political rhetoric). When Simone appeared on *The Steve Allen Show,* the host—a sometime jazz pianist, who a few years earlier had humiliated Elvis Presley by making him sing "Hound Dog" to an actual basset—was impressively mature about the situation, expressing his frustration that they had to refer to the song as "Mississippi Blank-Blank" ("I think everybody up this late at night who can afford to pay for a television set is adult enough to recognize that one not only hears that expression, but probably most of you say it when you hit your thumb with a hammer"), and encouraging viewers at home to scream out the offending word when she reached that point in the chorus.

There was no going back from "Mississippi Goddam." Simone would say that it was the point of demarcation, not only in the content of her material, but also in her actual vocal sound. "Mom said that her voice broke," said Lisa, "and that if you listen to her songs, there was pre–getting mad and post–getting mad. She's singing love songs, and her voice and her approach is much lighter. And then from 'Mississippi Goddam' on, it was as if her voice just dropped, and it never returned to its former octave."

"There are people who see injustice and it becomes a part of them, and they can't run from it, and I think that Nina Simone was one of those people," said Ilyasah Shabazz, another one of Malcolm X's daughters. "When she was younger, she was fortunate. She didn't know about racism per se, she wasn't so conscious of injustice. And once she became completely aware of it, she couldn't turn around and continue to play classical music, she had to write about the things that she was feeling. I think that sometimes these things become so overwhelming, they challenge the core of who you are."

Spared from some of segregation's worst elements in Tryon,

Simone was shocked when she was kept away from her white friend and when her parents were sent to the back row at her recital. Protected by the hermetic insularity of classical training, she was stunned when she didn't make the cut at Curtis. Even after coming to New York, she moved in glamorous creative and intellectual circles, where the civil rights struggle was a project to support and tackle. But now, as children were being murdered and innocent men assassinated, she could no longer be surprised by the evils and injustices of American racism. It was time to get to work.

Those in Simone's music circles saw a shift in her ambition, though it was nascent. "I think she felt she could influence people, but I don't think she knew how to influence them," said George Wein. "She tried to influence by telling them directly, in a way they didn't want to hear. People like to be influenced artistically, not verbally, and she would talk to the audience in a very strong way during the middle of her performance. What really influenced them was the song that she was singing, and she wanted that when she wrote a song like 'Mississippi Goddam'—I mean, that was an influence, and I think she really felt she was carrying a message."

On the front lines of the civil rights movement, Simone's message was loud. Andrew Young—later a congressman, the mayor of Atlanta, and the US ambassador to the United Nations—was a ground-level organizer for the Southern Christian Leadership Conference during the 1960s, and he remembered the moment that he first heard a recording of Simone.

Young and Stokely Carmichael lived in the same dormitory at Howard University, and during their freshman year Carmichael played a Simone album over and over. Young went to the record store and bought an album for the first time—a copy of *Nina Simone at Town Hall*.

He noted that at all social gatherings at the time, whether

parties or demonstrations, the same music was a constant; Simone was providing the soundtrack for a movement in need of inspiration, solace, and relief. "Every home I went to had Nina Simone—I mean, every one," he said. "For all of the people in the civil rights movement, it was an identity, you know what I mean? Her music was just sort of what you heard."

In early 1964, as she was unleashing the force of "Mississippi Goddam" on the world, her own involvement in and relationship to the movement were still evolving. She performed at some benefit concerts but wasn't yet clear on the role she should play. "There was a concert in Chicago where there were some very high-power people there in the civil rights movement," said Schackman. "They had a big reception afterward, and Vernon Jordan from the Urban League goes up to her. She never really liked to demonstrate for civil rights, or 'Hey, there's gonna be a benefit, would you appear?' 'Yeah, how much? It's about the money, I want to get paid.'

"So Vernon comes up to her and says, 'Nina, how come you're not more active in civil rights?' And she says, 'Active in civil rights? Motherfucker, I *am* civil rights!'"

The second Nina Simone concert at Carnegie Hall took place on March 21, 1964. This time, tickets sold out. Spurred by her unapologetically controversial music, Simone was really a star. When she would return to Carnegie Hall in the years that followed, Stroud would no longer promote the shows himself—now the real players wanted a piece of the action.

The first week of April, she recorded overdubs and fixes for the album that would become *In Concert*. Though it opens with a languid "I Loves You, Porgy," the songs from the show that were chosen for the LP added to the sense that she was charging into an outspoken protest through song, though in a way that kept her distinct flavor. The album also included an original number called "Old Jim Crow," a commentary on the Jim Crow segregation laws, and a modified, satirical version of the folk song "Go Limp," about a mother begging her daughter not to join the NAACP because they would "rock you and roll you and shove you into bed."

In Concert also marked the first recording of a song that Simone did not perform often—she said it was too emotionally demanding—but that became one of her signatures: "Pirate Jenny," from Bertolt Brecht and Kurt Weill's *Threepenny Opera*. In Simone's hands, the tale of a lowly maid fantasizing about taking revenge against the contemptuous people in her town took on a very different, very clear subtext. The narrative—a "black freighter" sweeping into the harbor, destroying the town, and bringing the residents to Jenny, who orders the pirates to kill everyone and then sails off with them—could be understood only as a call for retaliation against racist America.

Langston Hughes singled out "Pirate Jenny" as a favorite, and Angela Davis wrote that as a young activist, at a time when virtually all of the dominant voices of protest were male, "here was a black woman musician redefining the content of this song to depict the collective rage of black women domestic workers. . . . She helped to introduce gender into our ways of imagining radical change."

"She was an actress," noted Stanley Crouch. "A real good one, a serious actress, because I remember a guy who taught theater and he used to play 'Pirate Jenny' all the time for his class. He says, 'Now this is the part here—it's not that good a part, but Nina Simone makes you *think* it's a great part.' That's what a performer can do, she can really make you believe all those words. And she was good at that."

The version of "Pirate Jenny" on *In Concert* was actually less extreme than the ways she would sometimes deliver the song.

Sometimes when she reached a part of the song when Jenny sings, "Kill them now or kill them later," families who had brought their children to the show would flee the theater.

Simone archivist Roger Nupie pointed out that her interpretation of "Pirate Jenny" was one of many times that she was able to convert material from another source into a protest song. The concept of killing everyone who stands in the way of your freedom was, he said, "a very Simone idea," but she was able to transform other songs, like Charles Aznavour's love song "Tomorrow Is My Turn," into something that was resonant for her mission and was also entirely her own.

In Concert was also Simone's first release for a new label, Philips Records. The company's Dutch owner, Wilhelm Langenberg, had heard "Mississippi Goddam" and become obsessed with Simone. He came to America to find her, showing up backstage at the Village Gate. "He was a gigantic man, he must have weighed three thousand pounds," said Simone. He informed her that he was there to take her back and sign her to his company.

The rapid-fire batch of recordings she had submitted to Colpix for the advance to buy her house had freed her up to sign with a new label, so she and Stroud worked out a deal with a man she called "my real daddy for about ten years." The towering, bombastic Langenberg was not intimidated by Stroud (who was part Dutch himself). "He used to tell Andy, 'Look at you, you have no color. You don't even know who you are,'" according to Simone. "He said, 'Nina has color and she has the weight of forty million people on her back. You must be gentle with her.'"

Though *In Concert* reached only number 102 on Billboard's rankings, it was the highest she had charted since the 1960 *Newport* album. When Simone hit the road again, though, something had changed.

She had started keeping a diary on tour, beginning in February 1964, and the early jottings were brief and trivial. She noted that Andrew had sent her six cards on her birthday, that she had been shocked when Cassius Clay knocked out Sonny Liston, that she had watched a TV show that demonstrated how to make masks out of papier-mâché. She expressed concern for her daughter while she was on the road, asking if Lisa was being bathed properly and was taking vitamins.

Even when she returned to New York, her thoughts were more superficial rather than dwelling on any personal or social issues. She bragged about going to a fashion show wearing a new Chanel suit ("I loved it"). But whereas these notes had been carefree and glib, after the Carnegie Hall show and the release of "Mississippi Goddam" the entries' tone shifted, becoming melancholy. In May 1964 she wrote:

> *Washington D.C. yesterday, Saturday ha[d] a severe attack of depression—the pain excruciating for 3 performances (did not change street clothes) Performances good Sunday—lost my desire to live realized that there was no reason to continue anything— washing my face, hair—No desire for sex, talk, nothing. lost desire to try anything . . .*

Though her words don't address it directly, tension was building between Simone and Stroud, as they engaged in a battle over the trajectory of her career. As she became closer to figures in the civil rights movement, she was being pulled in a more radical direction. Stroud had promised her that she would become a "rich black bitch," and things had been proceeding according to his plan until she became, in his words, "side-tracked with the revolution."

"She was becoming successful," he said. "She was getting airplay all over the country, magazines, doing college concerts. The fight and the hunger to get ahead in her career, to obtain success and money, was all happening at the same time as these other things were with the civil rights. I was busy trying to control her, keep her from ruining what I had built up."

In Syracuse, she began lecturing the audience, chastising them about their attitudes on civil rights, and they started booing. Stroud said that he told her that they had paid their money to hear her romantic songs, not to be scolded from the stage. "They don't want to be told not to hate niggers," he said. "This is not the place to preach."

Lisa Simone saw the seeds of her parents' eventual breakup in this conflict. "He wanted her to be able to win all the awards, and to become the huge star that he knew that she could be," she said. "Whereas she wanted something more—there was something missing, some meaning, and she realized that she could utilize the stage as a platform from which to speak out and feel like she was doing something meaningful for her people."

Stroud maintained that what was most difficult wasn't the clash with his ambitions for Simone but the fact that she still desired commercial acceptance and spent her money accordingly. "She wanted everything that money and success could buy," he said. "She'd see Nancy Wilson and Aretha and Gladys Knight and Diahann Carroll—Diahann was on Broadway and film and TV and doing the guest spots, and she's like, 'Why am I not there?' I'd go, 'Well, because of "Mississippi Goddam" and the other things that you refuse not to throw in the faces of the audience.'

"I said, 'Let's go out commercially, make the money, and then you can contribute to these causes like the other artists do.' And she thought that was a good idea—but the thing is, she would swear, she would promise, 'Okay, I'm going to be good,' then get onstage and go absolutely the other direction. She had no control over her emotions. When she got onstage, nothing else mattered. She had to do her thing."

But maybe Simone simply had a different vision for her work

and assumed that her fans would eventually catch up. Her re-fusal to compromise or adjust her music to comply with genres and expectations had been working so far. She had finally found a sense of purpose for her music, something she had lacked since leaving the classical world. It seemed as if—however realistic given her newly confrontational style—she expected to bend the audience to her will, or at least to be able to proceed precisely as she wished with her music and still maintain their acceptance.

The sense that she and Stroud were working at cross-purposes shows up in a letter, in which she indicated that even her feelings about Lisa were growing strained. In what would become a theme recurring throughout her life, she complained about exhaustion and proposed a temporary separation.

> *Dear Andy—I'm sorry you feel so bad—you must understand that I understand (at least with the part of me that's rational) that you couldn't help it—you had been pushed too far with worrying over me, trying to keep up with my ever-changing de-mands + moods, living 24 hrs a day in a constant vacuum of cry-ing, complaining, negativism and madness—And accept it for now—I must hurt someone—I can't help it—I'm also pushed too far. . . . Work most of the time is like a deadly poison seeping into my brain, undoing all the progress I've made, causing me not to see the sun in the daytime, not to smile, not to want to get dressed, not to care about anything except death—and death to my child-ish mind is simply escaping into the unconscious.*
>
> *Lisa is okay as long as she doesn't want too much from me and is just content with my presence and letting me watch her at play . . . And I'm too tired to even talk about it. Why working pains me to this extent I don't know—why I consider it my re-sponsibility to "give" something to those people show after show I don't know.*
>
> *so I'd rather it remained this way for a while . . . when I get*

*to the place where I must have human contact, I'll find you . . . I
don't wish to hurt you further so please try to do without me as
much as possible until this job is over—to make myself perfectly
clear: please do and go anyplace you like—However, when this
stage is over I shall want a verbal report of where you've been
and what you've done—Is that too much to ask?*

A note scrawled to herself on a record sleeve in September
indicates that the issues with Stroud had now extended into
their sex life:

*Do I want sex? yes, but why + how do I encourage it? do I tell
Andrew now I want it—let's go to bed?—So cold (so technical)
if not, what and who stimulates me—(nobody for years) . . .
     Andrew calls me a coward—why—because I've never hit
him back? Is that why?*

Despite this increasing strain, Simone continued to tour (she
returned again to Carnegie Hall on September 20, this time
opening for jazz trumpeter Harry James), but she was becoming
more volatile. Schackman said that she was becoming aggressive with people on the road, starting arguments with strangers,
and that he and the other musicians needed to start monitoring
her behavior. She was aware of this problematic irritability and
its potential consequences. She wrote in her diary,

*I can sleep when and if I choose I can stop picking on Rose—my
bad temper is due to all the times there was no one to take it out
on; plus I'm tired of teaching—but I must [not] justify it. I must
try always to remember how I would feel in the same boat and
forget the past—When I am working I must keep myself in a
trance. Must have many things going on in my head to relieve*

me—must be quiet and let it out on stage only—Andrew will
care for me more that way. If I keep this up, i will lose him—

As these emotions were being churned up, additional turmoil for Simone was introduced when 1965 started off with
profound loss. On January 12, thirty-four-year-old Lorraine
Hansberry—Simone's friend, inspiration, teacher, mentor—died
of pancreatic cancer. Referring to the horrors of living as a black
American, James Baldwin stated, "It is not at all farfetched to
suspect that what she saw contributed to the strain which killed
her, for the effort to which Lorraine was dedicated is more than
enough to kill a man." At her funeral in Harlem, the presiding
minister read a letter from Martin Luther King Jr. celebrating
Hansberry's life. "Her creative ability and her profound grasp of
the deep social issues confronting the world today will remain
an inspiration to generations yet unborn," he wrote.

Fueled by Hansberry's more radical political philosophy, Simone was increasingly becoming drawn to the black nationalist
teachings of Malcolm X. Although she heard him speak several
times, she said that she never met him. (Stroud, meanwhile, said
that he had known Malcolm during his police days, when he was
still a Harlem street hustler known as "Detroit Red.")

"I was always a Malcolm X fan," Simone said, many years
later. "I read *The Autobiography of Malcolm X* and certainly
agreed with him. I still think that separation of the races in
America is the best way to live. I think that now."

Then, on February 21, 1965—Nina Simone's thirty-second
birthday—Malcolm X was assassinated.

CHAPTER 7

Music can change your moods—Gospel music is as close to you as the nearest holiness church. It is most beneficial in helping you to cry or making you dance.

The murder of Malcolm X immediately affected Nina Simone and her family; it was both a foundation-shaking reckoning about being black in America and an event that changed the shape of their daily lives and introduced them to new neighbors. In the tragedy's aftermath, a group of friends and supporters banded together in search of a new home that could serve as a safe haven for Malcolm's widow, Betty Shabazz, and their children. Congresswoman Bella Abzug's family owned a house two blocks away from Simone and Stroud and offered it to the Shabazz family.

"Mount Vernon was perfect for our family, short of the fact that my father didn't make it there with us," said Attallah Shabazz, the eldest daughter. "I have to say that the community gathered quickly in that small-town way. The global community rallied around our family. 'Bring those babies in here, Betty,' is what Bella Abzug said to my mother. So thank God for those kinds of pioneers. It still is one of the things that affirms my idealism—believing in people, but also having to get the work done."

The Shabazz sisters were struck by the neighborhood's beauty, its sense of community, the chance to play in the street and explore the woods. They thought Andy Stroud was handsome and fun; when his sons Bucky and Renny would visit, they thought the boys were cute.

As for "Aunt Nina," the Shabazzes had no idea that she was a celebrity, just as they had no real sense that their father had been famous. But their memories of her are dominated by the music in the Stroud house.

"I think of her at home in front of the grand piano, playing music and singing," said Ilyasah. "We were so young, but when she sang these songs, you felt big. You felt like you had to make sure you were standing up straight. It made you feel happy and proud and there was something important, but you didn't know what that was."

Attallah recalled music being created on an everyday basis in the Stroud residence. "Music, impromptu music being sung as a kind of prayer through the house," she said. Nina might be at the piano playing an early version of "To Be Young, Gifted and Black," but it seemed like just a regular day in the family's home.

There was no getting around the fact that Simone was theatrical, and she stood out, even in a community full of creative and progressive people. Attallah remembered looking out the window and seeing Nina taking a walk, dressed in a cape, hood, and wrap—not exactly typical attire in "provincial" Mount Vernon.

When Nina toured, Lisa was quickly adopted as a member of the extended Shabazz family. "All I know is that we had a new sister," said Ilyasah Shabazz. "Lisa and I were the same age, and I think we called one another twins—because I really had twin sisters, who were the youngest, so Lisa and I became twins. She was number seven. I think that speaks a lot about my mother, to already have six girls and to not even think about bringing Lisa in our home."

"When you have a tribe, you have a tribe, what's one more?" asked Attallah. "She even kind of looked like one of the Shabazz girls. She was a very pure, soft, joyous little girl. The backdrop of life had not hit her directly so hard."

The same could not be said for Nina. Just days after Malcolm's assassination, Simone was again battling with her husband. Yet for as much as they fought, she battled even more with herself. Her diary entries spared neither of them.

Andrew says I've been giving him hell for the last 3 weeks (more than usual). He says that I'm more blase and less passionate than I've been—when we met I was hungry and starved for everything. . . . I don't like being around Andrew all the time— I've never liked that—some of my faults are: 1. I [slam?] and [shout?] all the time 2. I fuck when I don't feel it 3. Fight and argue 4. I blame him for my not having friends but I'm afraid to make new friends—afraid he'll take them apart. Now that I'm famous I distrust everyone much more than I need to—I wonder how badly my father and mother's failure at marriage has affected me?

. . . Since Andy has been with me the idea of separation from him hurts too much so that I tolerate certain falsities about our marriage in order to hold on to this little bit of security—what is the security? the feeling of belonging—I need people to like me in order to like myself—I can't seem to do alone—my ego and self confidence was shattered somewhere—

Nina's frequent arguments with Andy could be sparked quickly, even more so as a new divide began to open over her growing interest in the civil rights movement, which Andy viewed as an impediment to the smooth running of the Nina

Simone career machine. "The argument today started because I wanted to do a benefit for Malcolm X's wife instead of one Andrew had previously planned—" she wrote. "He told me I didn't respect him—I told him my energy was limited—(he keeps a calendar in his head about our relationship) the fight got worse included faggots, lesbians, friends, sex or lack of it . . ."

As nasty as these disputes might get, she continued working steadily on the club circuit. On March 16, she started another run of dates at the Village Gate, this time for a full three weeks. But in the middle of the engagement, on March 25, Martin Luther King led the historic Selma-to-Montgomery march in Alabama, and the Gate's owner, Art D'Lugoff, agreed with Nina that this event was too significant for her to miss. He allowed her, Andy, and Al Schackman to fly down and appear at the all-star concert that would greet the marchers at the event's conclusion in Montgomery.

As if the situation they were entering wasn't tense enough, they encountered further hazards during their trip south. They took a commercial flight to Montgomery, but as the plane was approaching the airport the pilot discovered that the runway was filled with trucks, blocking anyone headed to the march from landing. The plane was redirected to Jackson, Mississippi, where Stroud hired a tiny, four-seat private plane to get them to Montgomery.

Andy and Nina sat in the back, with Stroud holding Schackman's amp, while the guitarist sat, with his instrument in his lap, next to the pilot. As they took their seats, the weight in the rear was apparently more than the plane could take, and it tipped back, pointing its nose in the air. The pilot said, "Well, I don't think we can take off this way," so Andy and Schackman switched seats, moving the amp to the forward seat, and the aircraft's weight was balanced enough for takeoff.

The concert was held on a big athletic field, where rain had made everything muddy and messy. The stage was a huge platform with a scrim around the bottom. Schackman went to set up and asked Ralph MacDonald, Harry Belafonte's percussionist, where he could plug in his amp.

MacDonald told him to lift up the curtain, that the outlets were under the stage. Taking a step back, he kept an eye on Schackman. When the guitarist picked up the curtain, he felt a chill when he saw that the stage had been built on coffins, donated by the local black funeral parlors.

The duo performed alongside such other artists as Sammy Davis Jr. and Tony Bennett. But nobody brought the fire that Nina Simone did.

"She sang 'Mississippi Goddam,'" said Stroud. "And seated in front of the stage, facing the audience, was Martin Luther King, Ralph Bunche from the UN, and a lot of other worldwide dignitaries. And when she screamed out 'Mississippi Goddam!' the whole front row turned around and looked at her in amazement."

"A number of stars came down and performed," said Andrew Young, "but I think Nina Simone stole the show. And it was because her music so reflected the soul and the feeling of the people there."

Nina and Schackman stayed overnight in a hotel protected by federal marshals. The guitarist—in a suite with the likes of Langston Hughes, James Baldwin, Sidney Poitier, Bill Cosby, and Leonard Bernstein—remembers being told to stay away from the windows, and recalls the men staying up late telling stories, maintaining a mood that was a bit giddy with excitement and fear.

The next morning, they flew back to New York to complete their obligation at the Village Gate. "I wanted to stay down and help ferry people back from the march," said Schackman, "and

Nina said, 'Come on, you done enough, now let's go to work.' That was unusual for Nina, but I think she wanted to get out of there. It was great, but it was extremely dangerous, that whole thing.

"I think it was the first time that Nina could feel the vibe, the energy of a mass of people, the power of a movement. I think it affirmed her purpose."

While Nina was growing more confident in her activism, she became less certain of her marriage. Three years in, she strained to reconcile her complicated and contradictory feelings toward Andy—on the one hand, the love, the need for deeper intimacy; on the other hand, a lack of interest that sometimes bordered on disgust. This tortuous emotional whiplash played out in her writing. A diary entry describes a telling dream:

> *a wild Beast of a man (fat and hairy looking like Andy) who we thought was normal before—whom she had been in the room with before—and who upon seeing her desire for me turned naked and came to the door of the room and I knew instinctively he was going to attack her and I couldn't talk—I had knifed a little baby boy before who was trying to kill two of us in Bed (my sister, I guess) The woman coming toward me in the dream was white, golden haired and her eyes were hypnotic—I sensed that she didn't love me either, but just wanted me in her power—I just wanted Andy (my father) to get there quick*

In another entry, she writes: "Dear Andrew—I resented you so much tonight I couldn't even talk to you—but I want you to know I wish it were not that way—when the deal goes down, if I had control over my feelings, I would love you 24 hrs a day."

Although Nina's love for Andy could be intense, still another diary entry from the same time shows her frustration and ennui:

I live inside a cave of old fashioned rocks that refuse to budge when I try to get out. I'm trapped inside—I wish the work didn't take up as much of our time; I wished we valued something else as much as we do money and work. I don't "believe" in money any more than I do other things but I'm just going along because Andy says I should to show faith in him never mind if I'm tired, bored and frustrated—just go along with him to prove I trust him. I try—but i ain't got no faith but he's thee 2nd man in my life that made me feel like a woman so I'm grateful. Consequently, I whip myself into going along with him. I don't believe him. I don't believe anybody.

While her relationship with Andy had its ups and downs, Nina was also using her diary as a space to think about lifting herself out of those depressive moments. Around this time, she wrote ten "rules to remember in controlling [her] life" there. Some were simple maxims ("6. Plan your work—work your plan"; "8. you have always been where you ought to be"). Others revealed an insightful understanding of her own character and proposed strategies for counteracting her more negative impulses ("9. Keep in touch with Friends. They are valuable, As you are A loner by nature"). The tenth and last "rule" ("Do not anticipate Negativism in Any form—especially in something you want to do or something you say—remember you have the power to influence Andrew's reaction & attitude toward you by the way you Act & your Attitude At the time. But what you project comes first") revealed that she knew how her downbeat energy could affect her relationship.

Despite the ongoing tumult in her personal life, Nina's career continued to thrive. In June, she released *I Put a Spell on You,* one of her poppiest-sounding and best-known albums. With swinging arrangements featuring brass and strings, the record included not only the title track (her much-loved reading of

Screamin' Jay Hawkins's roof-raising plea) but also Jacques Brel's "Ne Me Quitte Pas," which would become a Simone concert staple, and her take on the Broadway number "Feeling Good." Though there were no original compositions on the album, there were two songs written by guitarist Rudy Stevenson and two credited to Andrew Stroud.

The album grazed the Top 100, but in England—where her theatricality may have fit more easily into the "music hall" tradition—it was a Top 20 hit, and "I Put a Spell on You" reached number 49 as a single. On top of this success, Simone was also entering the most prolific recording period of her career: over the next three years, she released eight albums, including much of her finest studio work.

At the end of June, Simone flew to London, where the Cumberland Hotel would serve as her base for her first tour of Europe. The trip lasted just over a month and took her to the Netherlands, Belgium, Spain, and France. In England, she built on her popularity there through the Animals' cover of "Don't Let Me Be Misunderstood," which she had recorded on 1964's *Broadway-Blues-Ballads* album (the song's lyrics, initially inspired by a fight that the album's arranger, Horace Ott, had with his girlfriend, seemed tailor-made for Simone's temperament—with lines like "Don't you know that no one alive can always be an angel" and "If I seem edgy, I want you to know/I never meant to take it out on you"). She even made several appearances on the BBC's new pop music TV show *Ready Steady Go!*

It was a time when many black American musicians, especially blues legends like Sonny Boy Williamson and Muddy Waters, were venturing across the pond, visiting the country that had embraced their recordings, and were greeted as heroes. Though Simone wasn't always quick to compliment other artists' versions of her repertoire—much less white acts performing material created by black musicians—she seemed to get a kick out of the London rockers who had popularized her work abroad, as she indicated in a letter home to her brother Sam.

> *The Animals (the rock & roll group that recorded my "Don't Let me be misunderstood") took us to a dance hall that was just like all the old singing negro halls where they dance the "Slow Drag," "Fish"—All the old dances that we used to do plus the new ones these kids do. . . . Sam, all these groups imitate us to a T and don't mind admitting it—they don't try to pretend that they started it. . . .*
>
> *They're more familiar with all negro blues singers more than all the colored kids in the States put together. Over here, I'm a big hit because (Listen to this) The Animals recorded "Don't Let me be misunderstood" and every time they sang it they said they got it from me. So that brought about an interest in me—so every where I play I have to sing that damn song!*

From the desk of . . .
ANDY STROUD

July 15 1965
London, England

Sam Dear -
This place is something - I've done lots of traveling in the states but London doesn't seem to have anything in common with the states except the Language and even that is used differently - for instance if they like something they say "Jolly Good" or "Splendid" or if you do something fast they say you're doing it "swiftly".

The clothes are so way out that it's easy to see why England is setting the fashion trend in the states. It's very stylish for all men to wear Brown suede shoes. and nobody, but nobody looks alike - Every one looks different And dresses differently. The young men (some of the "beatist" beatniks, rich and poor) wear their hair all the way down their backs, And mustaches (huge ones) And beards are prevalent.

All the music is negro - All the music, mind you. We're bringing back an album of some kids who sound-

From the desk of . . .
ANDY STROUD

very negro. And one night The Animals (The rock'd roll group that recorded my "Don't Let me be misunderstood") took us to a dance hall that was just like All the old swinging negro halls where they danced the "Slow Drag" "Fish" — — — All the old dances that we used to do plus the new ones these kids do . . but the Topper of the evening was a white boy who sounded absolutely colored. I asked him how he had learned - he told me he studied for years all the old time negro blues singers like Leadbelly, Muddy waters etc.

Sam, All these groups imitate us to a T And don't mind admitting it - They don't try to pretend that they started it. And of course, I make it a point to always ask them. The ironic part is some of the groups can't get on T.V. shows because they are discriminated against because they're white And sound colored.

Although she gave props to the Animals, her songs didn't have the same meaning when they were performed by the band. White Englishmen may have venerated her music, but they could not truly inhabit it the way she could. Nina also increasingly felt the need to emphasize the social mission and black pride that were now informing her work. In an interview with a French journalist, she said, "Because of the lack of respect that endures even after hundreds of years, each time I go to a new country I feel obligated, proudly, to assert my race. And don't fool yourself. No matter what I sing, whether it's a ballad or a lament, it's all the same thing—I want people to know who I am."

At one of Simone's *Ready Steady Go!* shoots, the Who were also filming a segment, and guitarist/songwriter Pete Townshend remembered the awe that he felt meeting her. "She was towering, formidable," he said. "She was wearing an African dress and holding a baby. I really wanted to talk to her—all of the girls at art college were huge fans of hers, because she was the first true music industry radical feminist. She was coming down the stairs and I was going up, and I said something like 'Really big fan' and she just kind of looked at me, didn't say anything. But that was important that she didn't bow to that, that she just was who she was."

Townshend remembered Nina as "really troublesome" at the tapings. Her own sexual questioning may have led to discomfort, even hostility. Vicki Wickham, a legendary figure in the UK music scene, was one of the show's producers, and she was a very open lesbian. "There was something that Nina didn't like about that," Townshend said.

"Nina Simone terrified me," Wickham later said. "She had a real presence. On the show they made me tell her she was only going to do one number, not two. She wasn't pleased." Still, her encounter wasn't as tough as the one suffered by Dusty Springfield, the white soul singer managed by Wickham. "It's not much fun having a glass of whisky thrown in your face by Nina Simone, who called me a honky and resented me being alive!" Springfield said. "She was having a few problems, which I thought I could solve by being nice. . . . I was warned not to approach her but—I knew better, didn't I?"

A story in London's *Evening Standard* by prominent journalist Maureen Cleave (who would, the following year, conduct the infamous interview in which John Lennon claimed that the Beatles were "bigger than Jesus") focused on Simone's personal story rather than her difficult reputation. "She is a tall, powerful woman of 32," wrote Cleave. "She has a great proud face, with a huge nose and a wide mouth. Her eyes fill readily with tears and her whisper is more compelling than most people's speech. On stage, as though she were not really arresting enough, she often wears sequins glued to her eyebrows. Her whole self . . . comes out and makes a grab for you and she is utterly irresistible."

Cleave described a pleasant domestic scene in Simone's hotel room, with Lisa asleep on her lap and Stroud seated quietly in the corner. The singer offered that her greatest triumph was finding a happy marriage and family life.

"Ms. Simone believes [Stroud] was the result of a bargain she made earlier. 'Don't hurt me by laughing at this,' she said, 'but somewhere in the back in my career, I said, "All right, God, if you want me to continue to play this music, you better give me a man. If you don't, I will drink and go to the dogs. You gave me this talent, but that doesn't mean I'm not also a human being. I'm a girl and I have desires like other girls. There's too much to enjoy out there."' So God sent her the man.

"'You see,' cried Ms. Simone triumphantly. 'I wanted it all. I wanted everything.'"

And in moments during this period, she seemed to have it. Judging from a lighthearted poem that Simone wrote about their time in Paris, Stroud struggled acclimating to the foreign city, but apparently not so much that his wife couldn't joke about it with a bit of tenderness.

"When Andrew Came to Paris"

When Andrew Came to Paris it was so very cold—the porters they were nasty the taxicabs were old—the fellows were bewildered the baby was asleep and Andrew was all alone because not a word of French could he speak—he was so very Angry at everyone around it would have been nice to take his walking stick and them all down—instead he kept his temper and took care of everything he felt as tired as a fighter who'd been knocked down in the ring But Alas! His spirits lifted and he went to get something to eat he remembered that he only had one night in Paris So he wouldn't admit defeat—he grabbed a taxicab and went to see the Eiffel tower the river Seine, and the Champs Ellyse and later grows the hour, he feels much better now, even though Paris greeted him cruelly—for next year when he returns he will conquer her most assuredly.

After Nina returned to the United States in early August, the *Pastel Blues* album was released. It was a more intimate, piano-based effort than her last few LPs, and it reached the Top 10 of Billboard's new "Black Music" album chart, the trade magazine's latest in an ongoing series of attempts at figuring out how to categorize shifting pop tastes. It included a new version of "Trouble in Mind," which had been a hit single for her in 1961, and her rendition of "Strange Fruit."

Most notable was the album's final track, the ten-minute "Sinnerman," based on lyrics that she had absorbed during her mother's revival meetings. It was another example of her ability to adapt a traditional lyric into an allegory about justice and civil rights, and, like "Mississippi Goddam," it was an upbeat (if menacing) treatment of a dark subject. It would be among Simone's most enduring recordings, turning up in numerous soundtracks and covered by artists including Bob Marley.

In the fall she returned to the studio, cutting songs that would appear on her next few albums, before heading back to Europe in December, where she would perform additional concerts and do a number of television tapings. It was a triumphant time for Simone professionally, but her husband felt that something permanently shifted for her then—perhaps prompted by these successes.

"The first five years was a love story," he said. "There was a lot of feeling and affection for one another. But after the European tour in '65, she realized she had achieved stardom—world recognition, so to speak—and she had attained her Carnegie Hall dream. Then came all the doubts after that—self-doubt, self-questioning. 'Who am I? Why I am here?' All that sort of stuff."

He felt that they worked for several years before breaking through in 1965 with the European tour and the hit with "Don't Let Me Be Misunderstood." From there, Stroud said, "it leveled off. . . . We had reached the summit, then it was maintenance, keeping her up there."

But having attained this success while accelerating her political engagement and onstage commentary, Nina presumably felt that she had won by sticking to her guns. So where Stroud saw that this was the time to strike, and try to really build a stable career, she wasn't willing to make that push. "That's when she started complaining about always being tired," he said, "and all of these other thoughts about having doubts about relationships, associations, the baby, and everything else."

Nina Simone was ambitious and driven when she was fighting to achieve something, but much less eager to work for its own sake. Unlike performers who find their reward in nightly applause and adoration, she maintained an ambivalent relationship with her audience, and even with her own talent. Whether restless, bored, or distracted, Simone would never fully come to terms with the idea of making music as a job.

```
CLASS OF SERVICE        WESTERN UNION
This is a fast message
unless its deferred char-   W. P. MARSHALL    TELEGRAM    R. W. McFALL
acter is indicated by the   CHAIRMAN OF THE BOARD              PRESIDENT
proper symbol.

The filing time shown in the date line on domestic telegrams is LOCAL TIME at point of origin. Time of receipt is LOCAL TIME at point of

FEA076 (28)(07)SYE277
SY MVA164 PD MOUNT VERNON NY 17 301P EST
ANDREW STROUD
  507 5 AVE NYK
EVERYTHING IS GOING TO BE FINE 1966 IS STILL OUR YEAR I LOVE
YOU
  NINA

1966.
```

After the second European tour, Simone spent most of 1966 in a steady routine of touring and recording. But although she proclaimed in a telegram to Andy that "everything is going to be fine 1966 is still our year I love you," her diaries indicate that during this time she was also grappling with fear, despair, and fatigue. For the first time, she articulated a desire to leave the United States. She was also beginning to experiment with drugs. Perhaps most significantly, she recognized the stirrings of her own emotional chaos—a self-awareness that would largely fade as her problems became more apparent. In January 1966 she wrote in her diary:

> *my frame of mind is the same as usual, these days, weary, tired, and alone. Last night on the plane, after 3 drinks I felt giddy and happy. Andrew & I had a nice fist fight on the plane (real fun) scared the other passengers—the time went fast and I felt totally "involved" for the moment—Maybe this death wish is just my protest against boredom. This T.V. show is all me—but it doesn't*

mean much to me. Perhaps I should live out of this country for a while—the same way we left the south knowing that in that atmosphere we'd never survive No matter how much we tried— maybe that is also true of the entire U.S. for me. I'm really scared

An entry from ten days later reads:

I'm looking at "The 3 faces of Eve"—think it's significant in a psychological study of myself. It is interesting how people sometimes think I'm going to strike them and "duck" (automatically when I'm in a certain mood). At a certain point in the movie, I burst out crying because the chick said that when Mrs White was going to kill herself another personality came out of her & saved her. Suppose someone had 6 or seven personalities? Is psychiatry prepared to help each person?

I like getting high now—I'm more relaxed I wish I could have some religious or spiritual or hypnotic experiences—maybe I'll have hypnosis again. I had LSD this summer

it's funny how I didn't record that before—I remember right this moment that I fought so hard the experience was "hell"— maybe I was scared (I don't know) but I'm anxious to try it again—I won't be as scared this time: when I'm tired, I'm not really tired, just bored I think—cause when something happens (a phone call etc) interests me I perk right up.

I am sure that sometime in the future I shall suffer a terrible punishment for the way I treated Lisa today—I do so want her not to be like me. I do so remember what Jerry said to me "Nina the best thing for you would be if you didn't care" (Just didn't care) Wouldn't it be marvelous. No guilt—no fear—Just irresponsible and having a ball—WOW!

Despite Nina's apprehension about how she was treating her daughter, Lisa's earliest memories of life in Mount Vernon are generally idyllic. "It was like a fairy tale," she said. "My mom was much less guarded when she was at home, the times that she could take time and be my mom, and didn't have to worry so much about every little thing, 'cause her and my dad were together, and they had the staff, and they had the whole machine."

Lisa remembers the glamorous details of the house—the flocked, paisley wallpaper; the sauna; the storage closet for her mother's fur coats and stage costumes. She dressed up her dolls in her old baby clothes and sang into a hairbrush in front of the three-way mirror to harmonize with her very own girl group.

Simone was clear about wanting Lisa to have a different childhood from her own, to experience things differently. "I don't want her to ever feel like she's alone the way I have felt it," she said. "I want her to just soak up life." She hoped to avoid not only the example of her own youth but also the way she was already feeling trapped by her career—singing about freedom while believing herself to be caged. "I want her to live as fully as she can and not become enslaved by music or by anything. I want her to always feel she has a choice in things, in where she lives and how she lives, what she wants to be. That's all I want for her, and I don't want her to ever have to feel the type of isolation that I have felt."

Perhaps seeking some respite from that solitude, on Valentine's Day she went to see her old friend Kevin Mathias. Though the diary offers no particulars, Simone writes that the visit was "a shocking revelation to myself about myself."

If this indicates some sexual activity, it would be consistent with her heightened focus on that topic throughout 1966. On June 10, she seems to allude to some kind of sex toy or stimulant in her diary. An entry titled "A List of Happy Times," dated June 13, is almost half-filled with allusions to sex with Andy ("3. My first real fuck with Andrew. 4. The time A. left home for two days, returned And we first fought on the grass And then fucked in the garage. 5. All the times he made up stories to soothe my mind—'Pimp Piggy'—'Abominable Snowgirl'—'The Indian Story' 'Pussybeater'—'Titty-tickler'").

The final "Happy Time" she mentions isn't sexual at all, however, but the joy of new motherhood: "The first moment of consciousness After Lisa was born And I held her in my Arms."

The sense of Simone from these entries is primarily someone still wrestling with her own identity—given that she'd always defined herself by her relationships ("God, if you want me to continue to play this music, you better give me a man"), was her role as a mother now her truest manifestation? If so, what impact did that have on her sexuality? Was her activism the driving force behind her or an obstacle to her purpose?

Despite Stroud's later claim that their relationship was never the same after the European tours, Simone's private writings generally depict these months as a relatively stable, even happy time in their marriage. Though she did note, on June 6, that "with Andrew it feels like we spend most of our time (At least for my Part) trying not to step on each others toes," most entries focus on her rekindled connection to her husband, such as this one in February 1966: "had a new feeling yesterday with Andy—a new old feeling of being totally alone with Andy—I got an inkling of the intimacy that can happen between two people when nothing is bugging 'one' (them) want to remember this feeling . . . it's important."

And the card Simone sent to Stroud on Father's Day certainly implies that their relationship was, at this moment, on solid ground: "Today is Father's Day & wouldn't you guess why It's because I've got the world's sweetest, funniest, most lovable guy Happy Father's Day! I love you, Nina 1966."

Nina and Andy had both fought hard for this sense of stability, and though it was temporary, it would be something she never stopped seeking.

CHAPTER 8

"Four Women" was a song about what enters the minds of most black women—their hair, their complexion, how they feel about each other, how they feel about themselves. That was a consuming theme all over America. Black women always had this problem.

In 1966, Simone made another dramatic, more public change, one that would prove pivotal in redefining her image and her role as a cultural leader.

"The first time I wore my hair African was after *Pastel Blues*," she said. "It reflected black pride, and that's when I changed it. I identified a lot with Africa, and learned what they did, and started wearing my hair in an Afro."

Her archivist and friend Roger Nupie tracked this revolutionary new look with a more regal bearing on- and offstage. Early on, he pointed out, she was wearing a wig in her photo shoots and on her album covers, as most black singers and actresses did in an effort to conform to white conventions. But Nina was the first celebrity to wear an Afro and dress in African styles. "The 'black beauty' thing started around those days," he said, "and it was very important that somebody like Nina Simone came onstage and was there in a very proud African way. And from that moment, her attitude changed completely, because when she comes on it's like 'Here I am. Who am I? I'm an

African queen'—or, as she sometimes said, the reincarnation of an Egyptian queen."

This decisive change represented a rejection of standards of white beauty—standards that Simone had been acutely aware of her whole life. In her diaries, she complains about the photographs chosen for her album covers, and Stroud noted that Simone had long struggled with her self-image. "She would get very depressed at times staring into the mirror," he said. "Even though she was so committed to the black cause and preached it and everything, most of her friends were white. So she's crying about her hair and her other features. Before she got her teeth capped, they weren't that nice. It came from deep inside—she was just unhappy to be black, and what she termed ugly."

In her private writings, Nina revealed this agony regarding her appearance. In one undated note, she wrote: "I can't be white and I'm the kind of colored girl who looks like everything white people despise or have been taught to despise—if I were a boy, it wouldn't matter so much, but I'm a girl and in front of the public all the time wide open for them to jeer and approve of or disapprove of." She went on to describe herself as "someone who has been brainwashed to think everything they do is wrong . . . someone who's been robbed of their self respect their self esteem some one's who's been convinced they have no right to be happy. But then why haven't I killed myself?"

The change in her outward appearance, then, was obviously about more than just style—to use a phrase becoming popular around this time, she was realizing that the personal is political. The new hair coincided with her increasing interest in black pride and a growing engagement in activism. In a diary entry written in February 1966 in South Bend, Indiana, there's a short but critical sentence scrawled at the end: "I decided today that I wanted to be more Active in civil rights."

Since "Mississippi Goddam," she had been closely associated

with the movement, performing at benefits and speaking out onstage. She later said, though, that she had initially been propelled into activism by raw emotion but had been slower to engage with its arguments and ideas. "The civil rights movement was something that I got into before I became fiercely political," she said. "I was just doing it because—well, I loved it. I approved of what they were doing, but I didn't talk about it a lot. I was just composing songs to spur them on."

To Nina, "politics" was rooted more in her work and her example than in organizing and legislating; what resonated was an idea, the model of independence and pride she practiced—as she told Vernon Jordan, "I *am* civil rights!"— rather than strategic action. "I didn't educate myself very well," she said. "I was so busy working that there wasn't time to reflect on what I was doing."

Later, she would even claim that she was moving at such great speed that she had no real recollection of such historic events as the trip to Selma. "My mind during this time was on automatic," she said. "I don't remember most of this job because all I did was work, work, work. At times people's faces are not even clear in my mind. I'm sure that stacked somewhere in the back of me when I'm not so tired is all this memory. I don't remember doing all this."

In some ways, it was as if she was providing a soundtrack for a community that she wasn't entirely able to connect with. "One of the things she said to me was that she really felt bad that she was not more active in marching and protesting and things like that," said Andrew Young. "And I thought how very strange and odd for her to say that. One of my friends who was there commented to me later, 'God, she was so present—she was everywhere, in all our projects, in all our work.' What she was doing, going around the country spreading the word of the movement—nothing was as cogent of the frailty and the humiliation and the sadness and the joy of what we did than her music.

"More than any other artist, I think that her music depicted and reflected the time. It just seemed to be so very current, so very fluid, and expressed so completely the aspirations, the anxiety, the fear, the love, the rejection, the hurt, the horror, the anger of what we were feeling at the time. Her music always seemed to be so on top of our situation."

As Simone's involvement increased—in the language of the time, as she became more "militant"—some of the greatest leaders and spokespeople of the movement became first her fans and then her friends. She was getting more engaged with the thinkers who were leading the historic action.

"Langston Hughes was befriending me, and he invited me to his house to have coon, like a possum, to eat," she proudly recalled. "I started to want to become part of these people. I met Stokely Carmichael at church in Philadelphia. He told the whole audience that he knew who I was, and that I was their cultural heroine and I was their singer of the black movement and how proud he was of me."

Even Andy, who was skeptical of the intellectual predilections of new friends like Amiri Baraka and James Baldwin, saw how eager Nina was to contribute to the conversation. "She thought herself the equal of anyone for intellectual discussions," he said. "She was as bright as you can get, I was amazed listening to her sometimes.

"This was like going to church. She loved being with these people; being around them was the air under her wings. It elevated her, it energized her. She got uplifted in these kinds of surroundings."

The new company she kept and the ideas they exchanged would shape not just her work but her understanding of the power that music could have in the world. "During the '60s, my people started having riots and saying, 'We want this and we want that.' I said, 'Well, okay, now I can change my direction from love songs and things that are not related to what's happening, to something that is happening for my people. I can use my music as an instrument, a voice to be heard all over the world for what my people need and what we really are about.'" Contributing to the cause was no longer just an option; it had become an obligation, and she was becoming increasingly fearless, even reckless, onstage. "I think it's my duty to express in music what they're feeling, and I'm privileged I can do that."

Stroud, already wary of Nina's distraction from her career goals, claimed that her sense of activism could be irrational, even destructive. He said that she would talk about poisoning the local reservoir or grabbing one of his guns and shooting people. "She went absolutely crazy," he said. "It got really heavy and bad. She wanted to just go in and devastate the community, one way or the other."

Nina's songs, statements, and onstage demeanor were starting to affect bookings. The movement had already pivoted from King-style nonviolence toward a more aggressive push for Black Power, complicating its relationship to the white liberals who made up much of Simone's audience, and her fierce words and unpredictable behavior made promoters increasingly nervous. "The protest stuff . . . created a negative atmosphere, people were turned off," said Stroud, who as her manager was acutely aware of the impact of her priorities on the bottom line of her touring.

"She became embittered by what was going on in this country," said promoter Ron Delsener, who had booked Nina at Lincoln Center and Carnegie Hall, in 1991, looking back at a time when urban violence and radical politics were dividing the audiences of many black artists. "It came out in her performance and she started to turn off the white audiences who were now afraid to go to her shows . . . afraid of hearing some message they were sick and tired of hearing."

The public and industry response to her amplified political commitment was instilling in Nina a bunker mentality. The more her ideas were challenged, the angrier she became and the more she railed against the status quo. Simone was also feeling a greater sense of mission in her work, and with that came, even at this early stage in her career, the conviction that she was underappreciated. "I have no faith that the greatest talent in this country will get any recognition while they're alive," she said in a 1966 interview. "Perhaps Bob Dylan, but me, and Billie before me, and Coltrane—in the jazz circles, yes, but not the general public. I don't believe that the talent that would be considered artistic in this country is going to get any recognition, and that includes me."

Simone's greatest contribution in 1966 (and among her most important works ever) wasn't focused on integration. It was a song that only her black audience could truly understand, a penetrating and scathing examination of America's complicated attitudes toward skin tone. The song, called "Four Women," had to do more with her decision to grow out her natural hair than with her participation in protests.

In 1984, she gave a lengthy description of the song to Mary Anne Evans, one of the several collaborators who attempted to write a memoir with Simone.

> "Four Women" is four distinctive descriptions of four women. And it capsules completely the problem of the blacks in America among the women.
>
> The first woman is called Aunt Sarah. She is 104, she's dark-skinned, woolly hair like me, her back is down to here from carrying all them damn shit all her life. And she lives in Harlem, she talks with a southern dialect, and she's old and feeble now,

she can barely make it. She knows who she is, and we have seen her all over America. All black people have seen her.

The first words are "My skin is black, my arms are long, my hair is woolly, my back is strong. Strong enough to take the pain that's been inflicted again and again, what do they call me? My name is Aunt Sarah"—and "Aunt" is important, it comes from "Auntie," like the whites used to call the mammies to suckle their babies. Everybody black heard it and they knew what I didn't say and what I did say. Whites heard it too, but the blacks really got mad behind it.

Second woman, "My skin is yellow, and my hair is long. Between two worlds I do belong, my father was rich and white, he raped my mother late one night. What do they call me? My name is Saffronia." I don't know where I got that name, it's just a common name down South. That gets all them yellow bitches who think that they're better because they have long hair and their skin is yellow. What I'm doing is getting rid of the load 'cause I have been just burdened down with all these problems. It's bad enough to be born black in America, but to be burdened down with the problems within it is too much.

The third woman, "My skin is tan, and my hair is all right, it's fine"—so she imply she don't give a damn, it's fine. "My hips invite you, daddy, and my mouth is like wine. Whose little girl am I? Well, yours, if you got enough money to buy. What do they call me? My name is of course Sweet Thang."

The last woman—and it's all done with music and there is a big rumble, and a very big pause and very fierce. And she reminds me of the Israelis and Stokely Carmichael. "My skin is brown, my manner is tough, I'll kill the first mother I see because my life has been too rough. I'm awfully bitter these days because my parents were slaves, what do they call me?" And then, you expect her to say "King Kong," then she goes "My name is"—and she says it fiercely—"Peaches."

All my songs, the important ones, have razor cuts, I call them, at the end. I cut you, I make you think and it's immediate. So the whole thing was that she's gone to Africa, she's got her ass together. Her name is Thandewye, look that's my name, so they expected that. "My name is Peaches," and you say, "My God, she probably was the sweetest of all." She turned. I sing it angrily and that also is a cut because it just doesn't make no sense.

That's it. When any black woman hears that song, she either starts crying or she wants to go out and kill somebody. 'Cause all I did was I just took them and said, all right, there is the problem. Every black in the world who heard that fucking song knew what it meant. It's personal to thirty-two million blacks out there.

Simone said that images of the four women came to her on an airplane, and that she wrote the song but kept it to herself for a full year before performing it. She waited even longer to record it and featured it as a track on the 1966 album *Wild Is the Wind*.

According to Lisa Simone, Andy told her that he assisted in the composition of this landmark song. "Dad claims, and I'm inclined to believe this, that he helped her write that song," she said. "Sweet Thing is a prostitute, so she was asking him questions about different females. I'm sure she came up with the music all by herself, but in terms of the characters and the breakdown of those different characters, Dad and her did it together, according to him."

Al Schackman knew exactly which woman represented Simone herself. "Nina was Peaches," he said. "'You don't mess with me,' 'I'll kill every motherfucker I see,' and that's the last woman that you hear. Peaches is the part of the persona that Nina became. You did not want to mess with her—she pulled out a knife in a second, she didn't take any of the shit that the other three did or play the white folks' games that the others did."

Percussionist Leopoldo Fleming, who played with Simone for many years, noted that part of the power of "Four Women" was the dramatic, stately music moving with the different characters, reflecting the shifting moods. "I could feel the emotions of the four women," he said. "You use different dynamics in the number. It doesn't stay on one level. There is the harshness of some, and then there is the tenderness of the other. It's like drama, and you have to use different colors in it."

To Attallah Shabazz, the song was a tough but empathetic critique for a population rarely given the chance to engage in accurate self-reflection. "'Four Women' was an opportunity for black women to do an internal look at how we coexist," she said. "She had the ability to tell a story, herself, and be all women while writing it—she didn't change, she was the same person, but became all of them. And we all know one or two of those women, and so you feel represented. It's introducing you to yourselves."

But that hard-hitting look in the mirror wasn't welcomed by everyone. Though *Wild Is the Wind* hit number 12 on the black charts, many black radio stations would not play "Four Women." Simone said, "I thought it was stupid for black radio stations to ban the song. I should think they would have been the ones who would have supported it."

The song was also sometimes met with confusion or dismissed by the audience when she performed it live. In a diary entry from February 20, 1966, she wrote that at an appearance in front of a black and Puerto Rican crowd at New York's Hilton Hotel she was "very hurt when they giggled" at her performance of "Four Women."

"Black people thought it was insulting," said Roger Nupie.

"Her message was 'I just depict the four different types, and you have to think about it.' And that was probably too difficult for the audience. Now it's different—now it's regarded as one of the most important songs in the civil rights movement."

Despite the fact that this brave, radical song went over many people's heads, Nina was still on the rise. That same year, she was presented with the Jazz at Home Club's annual Jazz Culture Award. Accepting the prize in Philadelphia, she said, "I have always admired the late Dinah Washington and Billie Holiday and I know they never in their lifetimes were so honored as I am tonight."

It's interesting that Simone herself brought up Holiday in such a public forum, the singer to whom she was most often compared and about whom she expressed wildly varying opinions at different times. That same year, she praised Holiday again, saying the jazz legend was "the kind of woman who had so much integrity as an artist, and even at the expense of dying as she did and with dope and all, she just never let go of her integrity and what she had to say. We don't find them like that anymore, this day and age everybody is going for the dollar. And if it means giving up what they have felt was good music for years, they do it. But Billie didn't, so I look to her for inspiration."

Later, however, she claimed that she was insulted by the association. "I think they do it because I recorded 'Porgy,' and because I'm black and because I'm southern. And they needed somebody to fill Billie Holiday's shoes when she died. . . . If they're going to compare me to somebody, they should compare me to Maria Callas. She was a diva, I'm a diva. I'm not a blues singer."

Simone's feelings about Holiday were so conflicted, in fact, that she would even praise her and condemn her within the same conversation. In 1989, she told Stephen Cleary, "I was never influenced by Billie Holiday—I hated her songs. I didn't

Nina was highly style conscious and had her own distinctive fashion sense—a perfect blend of elegant sophistication and black pride.
Courtesy of the Estate of Alfred Wertheimer

Nina's home in Mount Vernon, New York, where she and husband
Andrew Stroud entertained luminaries like Ossie Davis and Ruby Dee,
Harry Belafonte, and Sidney Poitier. *Courtesy of the Estate of Alfred Wertheimer*

Lisa Simone, age two, at the piano. Nina always had music playing in
her home growing up and continued the tradition with her own family.
Courtesy of the Estate of Alfred Wertheimer

Nina in a contemplative moment on the road. *Bernard Gotfryd/Courtesy of Lisa Simone Kelly*

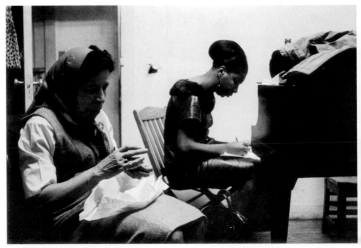

Trained as a classical pianist, Nina taught herself to incorporate multiple, independent music lines into one improvisation that blended everything from Bach to pop. *Courtesy of the Estate of Alfred Wertheimer*

Nina with her dear friend James Baldwin. *Bernard Gotfryd/Courtesy of Lisa Simone Kelly*

Nina's new Afro coincided with her increasing interest in black pride and a commitment to using her talent in the fight for racial equality.
Jack Robinson/Getty

Nina loved to look theatrical when she went on stage; she often had sequins glued to her eyebrows and eyelids for her performances. *Courtesy of the Estate of Alfred Wertheimer*

Nina pointing to her name on the marquee at the Luxor Theatre in Arnhem, the Netherlands. *Gerrit De Bruin*

With Andrew in their hotel room on the road. He became her manager in 1962 and helped her realize her dream of playing Carnegie Hall the following year. *Courtesy of the Estate of Alfred Wertheimer*

Nina greeting fans after a show; she often complained that Andrew worked her too hard. *Bernard Gotfryd/Courtesy of Lisa Simone Kelly*

Nina reviewing her set list before her Carnegie Hall appearance. She was the first black female soloist to appear at the legendary theater.
Courtesy of the Estate of Alfred Wertheimer

She played eighteen pieces, an eclectic set list ranging from an Israeli folk tune to a Leadbelly song.
Courtesy of the Estate of Alfred Wertheimer

Nina was aware of her power as a performer—she described it as "mass hypnosis . . . a spell that you cast." *Bernard Gotfryd/Courtesy of Lisa Simone Kelly*

Released in 1963, *Nina Simone at Carnegie Hall* was an artistic triumph and became one of her signature albums. *Courtesy of the Estate of Alfred Wertheimer*

After a trip to Africa, Nina developed a deep love for the continent's people and culture; this affection inspired the many African gowns she commissioned upon her return. *David Redfern/Getty*

A disciplined perfectionist who was finely attuned to her audiences, Nina often paced the theater before performances to get a sense of its sound. *Guy Le Querrec/Magnum Photos*

Nina posing for a photograph in 1978. *John Minihan/Getty*

Nina on a European
tour in 1978. Facing tax
evasion charges in the
States and bitter about
the rampant racism
there, she moved to
France that same year.
Gerrit De Bruin

Nina sometimes found the constant touring physically draining and
mentally punishing, but she continued to perform until the very end of
her life. *Courtesy of the Estate of Alfred Wertheimer*

Tel Aviv, 1978. Nina spent many of her later years abroad; while she traveled extensively through Europe and the Middle East, she felt most at home in Africa. Upon her death, she asked that her ashes be scattered across several countries there. *AP Photo/Max Nash*

London, 1997, enjoying her final act as an international icon. *Bernard Gotfryd/ Courtesy of Lisa Simone Kelly*

Nina in 1990 with a triumphant fist raised on stage. "An artist's duty, as far as I'm concerned, is to reflect the times," she said. *David Redfern/Getty*

admire Billie Holiday." Within that very interview session, she went on, "As for Billie Holiday, every time I listen to her, I hear more in her music than I heard before. I can't pay her a greater tribute than that."

Holiday was only the most obvious scapegoat for Simone's mixed feelings about jazz in general. To her, being identified as a jazz singer was a reductive insult, ignoring her classical foundation and categorizing her only on the basis of her race. Still, Nina offered her greatest admiration to the giants of the form— what she responded to most of all was a sense of true artistry and ambition, regardless of genre.

"I would travel five hundred miles to see Miles and Dizzy Gillespie, Coltrane, Art Tatum, Duke Ellington—those were the great masters," she said. "But other than that, I didn't like jazz. I didn't like blues because it made me blue. I could play them, and I would play them sometimes, but they made me blue. And that's what I didn't like. Depressing."

The year she recorded "Four Women" wasn't all political fire and frustration. At home in Mount Vernon, the mood was generally positive, the atmosphere alive. Black cultural leaders like Ossie Davis and Ruby Dee, Harry Belafonte, Sidney Poitier, and Miriam Makeba would gather at the house on Nuber Avenue, and Lisa and the Shabazz girls would put on shows for their esteemed guests. Simone and Betty Shabazz would chat on the phone and visit; the kids would play in the yard, frolicking on a tree swing.

Attallah Shabazz recalled the camaraderie among the civil rights women during this happy time. "These were brilliant, well-read, well-traveled, experienced women," she said. "Charming, alluring, charismatic women, in a time that said, 'Not you.' So to sit and listen to this relationship between a Lorraine

Hansberry and a Nina Simone and a Ruby Dee—some things I'll never tell. They were rich in their humor and how they were able to zero in on every iota of social existence, how they could assess a thing. They were raw of laughter, and free."

There were increasing signs, though, that not everything was well within the Simone-Stroud family. Ilyasah Shabazz remembered Nina yelling at Lisa when the girls made a mess with Silly String, and another occasion when they were so afraid of the singer that they hid from her at the top of a tall spiral staircase. "I loved her, and she was like an aunt, but she was strict, she was a disciplinarian," said Ilyasah. "I was a little intimidated—I didn't know the word, but I was intimidated by her."

When Nina would get upset, she would disappear to her "treehouse"—the apartment over the garage that was fully equipped with a bathroom, kitchen, telephone—and stay there, sometimes for several days. Other times, she would just get in her car and vanish.

Lisa claimed that she was stunned when she read the accounts of her father's abuse in Nina's diaries, but in retrospect she could summon up certain troubling moments from her youth. "I remember sitting in the car with them one day," she said. "At that time, the cars had one long seat—you had the driver, and the middle, and then the other passenger, and you didn't have to wear your seat belts and the whole nine. I was sitting in between them and they were arguing about something, and I remember my father reaching across me and backhanding her."

The frequency of physical violence is difficult to assess, since neither party was entirely forthright, but tensions were definitely rising on all sides. A note from Simone to Stroud, written on a record sleeve and dated December 1966, indicates a growing strain between her husband and Lisa, which she attributed to his unresolved feelings about his late daughter from a previous relationship.

Andrew—Again I say, "you have Lisa, now" Celeste is dead"!
I'm fully aware that you put on quite a show of loving Lisa
by fighting with her all the time under the disguise that she'll
know how to defend herself but it's a lie. You don't love her at
all (though she's prettier, smarter than your original Celeste) she
tries to reach you, but all you do is fight. (you don't fool a fucking
soul Baby—) I let you believe that you fool me cause I'd do any-
thing to please you, but honey, I'm just what you always thought
I was—I don't miss nothing (and don't forget it) I love you—but

you make me sick cause you're dead: and you have the nerve to be egotistic about it. you don't even love me—(you worship me but that's a far cry from love motherfucker. Lisa loves you, but just like I can't get over Edney, you can't get over Celeste well, you better it's december 1966—this is it. your daughter knows everything. you better start loving her to you'll get your ass read like you never imagined one day (not from me but from her and your Boys, baby!

The harshness of that message may have also reflected her mounting professional pressures. A story in *Sepia* magazine asserted that "Nina Simone has exploded into national prominence with all the force of a super musical bomb." Next up was a major national tour opening for Bill Cosby—once a comrade in the Greenwich Village club circuit, he was now one of the country's most popular comedians.

Simone was feeling exhausted and disoriented before the shows even started. Still, she was able to pull it together enough to get things rolling on the road, and the tour seemed to be going well. Simone's sets were being warmly received, and she and Cosby were getting along.

The final stop was Baltimore, in February of 1967. Before each show, Nina would typically get dressed at the hotel and then go directly onstage when she arrived at the venue. On the night of one of her last performances, Andy came to the hotel to get her and found her behaving erratically.

Most alarming, Nina was putting shoe polish in her hair. When he asked her what was going on, she replied in gibberish. Further efforts to get her to explain her actions led nowhere, so he decided to let it slide and see what happened. "I wasn't going to interfere," he said. "If that's what she wanted in her hair, that's her thing."

"My husband discovered me putting makeup in my hair, and I kept saying that I wanted to be the same color all over," said Nina. "I said, 'I'm very tired and you're not my husband, and we're going to fly away, we're going to go home to heaven and you had better do what I tell you to do.' I could see through his skin. I actually could see it. I was too tired, so I kind of left here. He said, 'Do you want to finish the tour?' I said, 'Yeah, don't tell Bill that I'm this way.'

"I went a little crazy. I had visions of me walking on the edge of a laser beam, and I thought that Andrew was my nephew."

Taking her word that she wanted to go ahead with the concert, Stroud took Nina to the theater, holding her by the arm. She was, he said, still "partly incoherent," but she insisted that the show go on. When she was up, he walked her onto the stage and took a position directly in front of her in the wings. He signaled from backstage for her to start playing; she made it through her set.

He thought she was having a nervous breakdown. The Stroud family was supposed to go to Hawaii for a two-week vacation after the Cosby tour, but Stroud called and canceled all the reservations, insisting that Nina stay home and rest. When she got back to Mount Vernon, she slept for three straight days.

Despite the harrowing experience of watching his wife unravel, at the time Stroud chalked it up as an isolated incident brought on by the vigorous performing schedule and, presumably, exacerbated by the passion and intensity she delivered onstage. "After a few days' rest, she was okay," he said. "She was normal. There was no further thought given to the matter." In retrospect, he realized that it was a defining moment in her emotional condition.

While nothing else may have happened immediately, this frightening episode would prove to be the beginning, rather than the end, of Simone's more public battles with stress. The incident was a turning point in her history—the most obvious manifestation yet of problems that were very serious. A retreat to her bed was a sufficient solution for now, but keeping Simone in condition to perform would gradually come to dominate her life and the lives of those around her.

CHAPTER 9

I've had a couple of times onstage when I really felt free, and that's something else. I'll tell you what freedom is to me—no fear. I mean really, no fear.

After releasing eight albums in just over three years with Philips, Simone signed with a bigger label, RCA Victor. The title for her final record with Philips was inspired by the regal nickname that had been bestowed upon her, *High Priestess of Soul*. It wasn't quite as successful as her last few releases—it peaked at number 29 on the black albums chart—but her reputation was still growing.

Whether her sound was already changing when she switched labels or whether working with new people shifted her music's direction isn't entirely clear, but the timing of the RCA deal aligned closely with a new phase in Nina's music. "If you compare the Philips records and the RCA records, they're completely different," said close friend Gerrit De Bruin. "The Philips Nina is a wonderful, mellow girl, and beautiful arrangements in the music. RCA, that's a woman, a bit angry. Philips was very sophisticated, and RCA was more raw, more bluesy. . . . Nina's problems became more apparent, and that also changed her music. In the Philips time, she said, 'Hopefully, time will change things.' In the RCA time, she said, 'Wrong. I should kill to stop this.' She got hard and harsh, a fighting woman."

Given her ambivalence about the genre, it's notable that her first album for RCA was titled *Nina Simone Sings the Blues*. Less surprising, though, is that the record took a more expansive view of the sound and scope of the style; the musicians were not standard blues players but jazz- and soul-based session musicians like guitarist Eric Gale and master drummer Bernard Purdie. The moments when they took a conventional approach were the least satisfying. But the more stripped-down arrangements resulted in some of her greatest recordings.

The set encompassed blues history: a sensual, unforgettable version of Bessie Smith's "I Want a Little Sugar in My Bowl," a spare and languid reading of "My Man's Gone Now" (from *Porgy and Bess*), a barrelhouse-style rerecording of "House of the Rising Sun," even a new song called "Backlash Blues," which bore the remarkable writing credit "Langston Hughes / Nina Simone."

"They are songs of the soil, of the people and their troubles," wrote DJ Sid McCoy in the album's liner notes. "What we have here is an acceptable artist really giving it to us about the most unacceptable pangs of life." White rock-and-rollers had brought the blues to a new generation, but for black listeners the form was often a reminder of a past they wanted to escape. Simone's approach personalized the blues, retaining the fundamental human truths of the songs while transforming them beyond old-fashioned period pieces.

Despite the breakdown in Baltimore, after a brief pause the touring rolled on. In April, Simone returned to Europe for shows in England, France, and the Netherlands, including some dates opening for comedian Dick Gregory. The size of the crowd varied wildly. In Bristol the bill sold only thirty tickets, but in London they were a sensation.

"I remember Royal Albert Hall, they was in the street lined up," said Gregory. "Sold that house every night. But I never heard her 'cause she was opening. I knew that she was the buzz in my neighborhood, with the people I hung out with. They'd memorize her songs. The white folks that was coming, they understood what she was talking about. And I know them jazz musicians couldn't wait to get offstage so they could put their horn down and come and listen to her—this woman with no sugar in it, just, here it is."

In Europe, Simone had also met someone who would prove to be critically important to her several decades down the line. Prior to her performance at the Concertgebouw in Amsterdam, Al Schackman was greeted at the stage door by a young man who offered to help carry his guitar and amp. Assuming he was part of the crew, Schackman handed over his gear. Backstage security, in turn, thought he was with Simone's entourage and waved them through, but as soon as they got inside and heard Simone warming up on the piano onstage, the stranger handed Schackman his equipment back and ran inside the theater. Gerrit De Bruin had devised a clever way to sneak into the sold-out concert.

"I climbed up the stage, and I said, 'Miss Simone, my name is Herr De Bruin and I'm your biggest fan in Holland,'" he said. "And she looked at me and said, 'Well, since you're my biggest fan in this country, I might as well get you a chair.' She yelled for somebody to bring a chair, and she asked me, 'What can I play for you?' And I said, I like the song 'Just in Time,' but she said, 'No, that I'm gonna do in the concert.' So she played for about ten minutes, and then we had to go offstage because people were coming in."

Andy Stroud passed along an invitation from Nina to join the after-show party at the Hilton Hotel. After she returned to the States, she and De Bruin began corresponding and soon became fast friends.

Simone spent much of the summer in America playing the newly thriving circuit of jazz festivals (in Austin, Cincinnati,

Detroit, and of course returning to Newport). She went back to a familiar base in October for a two-week stand at the Village Gate, though this time she clashed with the club's audience. In Atlanta, she was named "Female Jazz Singer of the Year" at the annual convention of NATRA (the National Association of Television and Radio Announcers). Despite the new record deal and steady work, though, she continued to express dissatisfaction with her own celebrity, looking for more respect—and more cash.

"My music, I feel, is the same as it's always been," she told Sid Mark, her old friend who had initially broken the "I Loves You, Porgy" single, in 1967. "I work on emotion. Each tune, no matter how many times I do it, it's different, and I trust that instinct that lets me go where I go with the tune. But I have not gotten the kind of recognition that I think I deserve, and I certainly have not gotten the money. I'm waiting for a feeling that I have been recognized and accepted. And when that happens, I feel that I can do the kind of music that ordinarily people don't listen to."

Her next album—her third of the year, called *Silk & Soul*—mostly stayed away from pushing things too far forward musically or politically. As the title indicated, it was a smoother ride, with more focus on love songs and sweeping string arrangements. The material ranged from songs by Andrew Stroud and her brother Sam Waymon to Burt Bacharach and Hal David's "The Look of Love."

The songs that did advance her agenda, like Martha Holmes's ambitious "Turning Point," which addressed the origins of racism through the story of the burgeoning friendship of two young girls, felt out of place, awkwardly earnest in the album's lush musical settings. And, despite the softer rhetoric, *Silk & Soul* wasn't quite the commercial success RCA had hoped for; it reached number 24 on the black charts, a few ticks higher than Simone's last few albums, but not a significant climb.

But there was at least one song on the album that would become part of Nina Simone's legacy—her version of jazz pianist and educator Dr. Billy Taylor's "I Wish I Knew How It Would Feel to Be Free." Once again, the contrast between the emotion of the lyrics ("I wish I could share all the love that's in my heart / Remove all the bars that keep us apart") and the song's swinging melody and arrangement added depth and power to the performance. She understood the impact of this tension: the upbeat, finger-popping, gospel-based sound rang out as a hopeful but realistic vision of emancipation, offsetting the more somber tone of the piece's words. The song quickly became a civil rights anthem, a standard that would be recorded dozens of times by other artists in the years to come.

In October, Nina fulfilled another ambition—though it was more Andy's vision than her own. "She will play Las Vegas yet," Stroud had told jazz journalist Leonard Feather. "When she does, it will be just the way it has been everywhere else she's worked: wild cheering crowd, standing-room-only replays and then, of course, they let her sing anything she likes."

She was booked into Caesars Palace, but in the lounge known as Nero's Nook rather than the main stage; she shared the bill with Xavier Cugat and Charo. The market still represented a pinnacle for "mainstream" entertainment, but the results were predictably disastrous.

If she was still having issues with the audience in New York, the Vegas crowd and their short attention span infuriated her. Nina's attitude antagonized the technical crew, who paid her back with a microphone that frequently cut in and out.

"I gave up in two weeks," she said. "I was supposed to play four weeks. It was very hard. We had to play five shows a day. And you had to play when nobody was there—at five o'clock in the morning, when there was nobody there, I had to play anyway, and it was too hard. So I cut short my job there after two weeks." (Even a two-week stay might have been an exaggeration on Simone's part. In her memoir, she said that she bailed after four days.)

The experience at Nero's Nook may have fueled her desire to go more aggressively against the grain, to start pushing her live performances further. "I've always thought that I was shaking people up," she said, "but now I want to go at it more, and I want to go at it more deliberately, and I want to go at it coldly. I want to shake people up so bad that when they leave a nightclub where I've performed, I want them to be in pieces. I want to go in that den of those elegant people with their old ideas, smugness, and just drive them insane."

Though she had no further meltdowns for a while, Simone was still walking an emotional tightrope. As a December 1967 diary entry illustrates, her professional life and her personal—even her sexual—life were so enmeshed that she wasn't sure where to direct her exasperation.

> *I don't sleep with [Andrew] too often—I am not needed— Everything I've had in terms of security (most especially my music) seems to be slipping right between my fingers. And Andy (he'll get out of it without any feelings of guilt) he like an analyst just sits back + says "She wants no part of me; there's nothing I can do"!*
>
> *I haven't been needed in a while. No where in the press am I mentioned, voluntarily. Am I evolving again??? What is left for me now? I get no preferential treatment from Andrew.*

At this moment, Stroud didn't seem overly concerned with his wife's mental state. Keeping her on track was a matter of continuity rather than an urgent crisis. "I didn't picture it as a problem," he said. "I pictured it as a situation that could be managed like I did everything else. I figured with enough success that would alleviate a lot of these phobias that she had, and ghosts. She never frightened me—she frustrated me."

One achievement capped the up-and-down year of 1967: she received word that her recording of "Go to Hell" from the *Silk & Soul* album had been nominated for a Grammy Award in the category of Best Female Rhythm & Blues Vocal Performance. Ultimately, she lost the award to Aretha Franklin.

Simone ended the year spending the holidays with her family, seemingly in fine (and apparently sometimes marijuana-assisted) spirits, still fragile but on good terms with her husband and her parents. On Christmas night, she wrote to Stroud to express how much she had missed him—not just during this trip but for months. She wanted to close the distance between them, writing that "unless I get to you soon, I feel as though I'll dissolve and never be heard of any more and people won't even remember that there was a me."

A few days later, she described an idyllic scene with her parents, helping her mother with the wash at the laundromat and watching her father play guitar ("I don't think I'd ever realized what a great musician he is"). She sounded thrilled to be at such ease around her family, jokingly suggesting that Stroud start managing her father. "This vacation is wonderful," she wrote, "I'm really enjoying myself."

After an active, productive year, Simone was becoming very aware that she was employing a lot of bodies between her band, her business, and her home staff, which meant increasing pressure to continue generating income for everyone.

"There are nineteen people who depend on me for their livelihood—that's a hell of a lot of people," she said. "Because

I know that if I say, 'Look, I'm too tired to work tonight,' I'm gonna get it from both ends. Nobody is gonna understand or care that I'm too tired. I'm very aware of that. Now, I would like some freedom somewhere, where I didn't feel those pressures, and I think that some songs would flow out of me then, because they wouldn't have to come."

The rigor of her schedule was increasingly heightened by the emotional demands of being a public figure and overseeing a growing business. "As the fame grew, and the loss of privacy, her life was not her own, but it was that of the public," said her sister Frances. "She got to a place where she felt all the burden of supporting thirteen or fourteen people. She would talk about her musicians and their families, and all of her other staff and their families, because their livelihood was dependent on her livelihood. So then she felt responsible for all of those different sectors. That took away the pleasure of doing the songs and the music and rehearsals and so forth. If she didn't work, other folks' lives were affected by it."

She was telling those around her that she wasn't making money from her albums, only from the concerts. This not only put pressure on her to keep touring but also added to her rising suspicions about record companies. Occupying the top spot on the Nina Simone organization pyramid inevitably meant juggling elements other than music, which was always difficult for her.

Of course, the other way to look at this was that Simone refused to make the effort that would keep her career growing. She still insisted on treatment that severely restricted her moneymaking potential. "If a band does a European tour, you book as many gigs as possible—let's go out there and make the bread," said Al Schackman. "You could do five or six concerts a week, and we would do two. Nina demanded a travel day, a rest day, concert day, rest day, travel day. Six days, and maybe we've done one or two concerts. She resented working—that was her slogan, 'You work me like a dog.'

"If you want to get ahead, you've got to take care of your business, if it's going to grow and survive. These are the rules. If you don't want them, back off. And she's never been able to accept that."

But Eunice Waymon hadn't grown up dreaming of being a pop star. She wanted to be a classical musician, an artist, playing in a world where pianos were perfectly tuned and audiences were quiet and attentive. Where the compensation for all that discipline and practice was respect, not radio play. She believed that excellence would be acknowledged for its own sake, not because you hustled for your reward. So the notion that she wanted a swimming pool for the house but didn't want to take on extra dates to pay for it presumably didn't seem like a problem to her; Stroud said that her favorite thing was selling her songs for commercials and getting paid without doing any work at all.

"[Stroud] didn't understand Nina," said Sam Waymon. "He did not understand the complexity and the madness of being an artist—the confusion, the joy, the happiness, how one day you love what you do and the next day you may hate the very same thing that you loved the day before."

The first few months of 1968 saw her returning to Carnegie Hall, traveling to Cannes for the MIDEM (Marché International du Disque et de l'Édition Musicale) trade conference, playing in Detroit and Vancouver and for two weeks at the Troubadour club in Los Angeles. In February, a massive birthday celebration was held for Huey P. Newton, the imprisoned cofounder of the Black Panther Party, at the L.A. Sports Arena. During the event, a (short-lived, ultimately) merger was announced between the Panthers and the Student Non-violent Coordinating Committee. Speakers included H. Rap Brown, Stokely Carmichael, and Bobby Seale, but not a single woman.

"It was Nina Simone's voice that bestowed on that gathering an aura of historical transcendence," wrote activist Angela Davis, one of the event's organizers. "In representing all of the women who had been silenced, in sharing her incomparable artistic genius, she was the embodiment of the revolutionary democracy we had not yet learned how to imagine. At that moment we were no longer powerless individuals but rather a formidable collective force that was moving irreversibly in the direction of radical change."

While Simone continued to complain about being tired, there was a sense of new momentum and mission informing her work—a need to draw attention to the condition of her people, to point toward some kind of transformation in society. "It's very frustrating to find that you're not moving as fast as you'd like," she told filmmaker Joel Gold for the 1968 documentary short *Nina*, "and sometimes I get afraid that I won't be able to do all I'm supposed to do before I die. But I know where I'm supposed to go and I'm on my way, slowly but going. . . . I don't know what's gonna happen, but all I know is that force that's inside of me is pushing me toward something."

And then, on April 4, 1968, Martin Luther King Jr. was assassinated in Memphis, and the world would never be the same—not for Nina Simone, not for anyone.

"How did you feel when Martin Luther King died?" the host of the British TV program *Hard Talk* asked her decades later. "Oh, God, man, I was devastated," Nina answered. ". . . I think I must have cried for two weeks, and it killed my inspiration for the civil rights movement, and the United States."

Following Dr. King's murder, there was mourning, and there was chaos. Riots broke out in 125 American cities, resulting in 46 deaths and more than 2,600 injuries. The nonviolence he had preached was in danger of turning into something close to civil war. Music was one of the only outlets for black sorrow and rage—in Boston, Mayor Kevin White appealed to James Brown not to cancel his concert but to televise it on the local PBS affiliate; the city, known as a hotbed of racial tension, was one of the few urban centers that remained peaceful.

On April 7, three days after Dr. King's death, Simone performed on Long Island at the Westbury Music Fair. "We're glad to see you, and happily surprised with so many of you," she greeted the audience, in a tone of sorrow and chilling calm. "We didn't really expect anybody tonight, and you know why . . . but we're glad that you've come to see us and hope that we can provide . . . some kind of something for you, this evening, this particular evening, this Sunday, at this particular time in 1968. We hope that we can give you some—some of whatever it is that you need tonight."

That night, she delivered a version of "Backlash Blues" that far surpassed the studio recording, and a brief, wrenching rendition of the gospel classic "Take My Hand, Precious Lord." She was calling out for guidance, for help, trying to look ahead while straining to make sense of a senseless world. Most notably, she introduced a new song, written for the occasion by her bass player, Gene Taylor. It was titled "Why? (The King of Love Is Dead)," and it went on for thirteen minutes, ending with the sobering question "What will happen, now that the King of Love is dead?"

"We learned that song that day," said Sam Waymon, who was playing organ in her band at the time. "We didn't have a chance to really, like, have two or three days of rehearsal. But when you're feeling compassion and outrage and wanting to express what you know the world is feeling—we did it because that's what we felt."

A five-and-a-half-minute edit of the song would be included on her next album, *'Nuff Said!*, but the full live recording wouldn't be officially released until it was included decades later on a collection of her protest songs titled *Forever Young, Gifted and Black: Songs of Freedom and Spirit*. The sprawling, pleading performance is almost too much to take. "They're shooting us down, one by one," she spoke through tears. In a lengthy, anguished monologue toward the end of the song she reeled off the names of other black luminaries who had died in recent years. "Lorraine Hansberry left us, Langston Hughes left us, Coltrane left us, Otis Redding left us—I could go on . . . Do you realize how many we've lost?"

The assassination of Dr. King was pivotal for Simone, and for black America. Coming on the heels of so many other early, needless deaths, it produced in many a swirl of rage and grief that led to alternating feelings of urgency and paralysis. Nina found herself torn between moving toward an even more radical, outspoken activism and giving up hope in the civil rights movement's ability to change anything. King's death was also, of course, a reminder of how high the stakes really were—losing concert bookings because of her politics was one thing, but the true costs of being outspoken about racial equality could be impossibly high.

"Participation in activism during the sixties rendered chaos in any individual's life," said Attallah Shabazz. "We had already experienced the risks—we know about Kennedy, we know about Medgar Evers, we know about my father, we know about King. The risk meant that if you crossed a line there could be an ultimate price. So what does that do to a household, and a family, not because of income, but because of your soul not being able to do what you need to do?"

But Simone believed that she had no choice, that her purpose was clear. "I choose to reflect the times and the situations in which I find myself," she said. "That, to me, is my duty. And at this crucial time in our lives, when everything is so desperate, when every day is a matter of survival, I don't think you can help but be involved. Young people black and white know this. That's why they are so involved in politics. We will shape and mold this country, or it will not be shaped and molded at all anymore. So I don't think you have a choice. How can you be an artist and not reflect the times?"

And so, Nina went back to work. She returned to what was becoming a regular circuit—back to Europe in June, jazz festivals through the summer—sometimes focusing more on spiritual themes than on activist ones. Introducing a song called "You'll Go to Hell If You Don't Pray" at a television taping at the Greenwich Village club the Bitter End, she said, "If you just think about what everybody is looking for—and I really think that even though they use the words 'I love you,' and they talk about their boyfriend or girlfriend—what they're really saying is they want something terribly deeper than that, and I think it's religion that we're looking for."

By this time, more outspoken protest music was growing in popularity. Simone's own song selection was also incorporating more compositions by current pop songwriters, and, perhaps because of these shifts, in the fall of 1968 there was a sudden burst of interest in Simone's records. The edited version of "Why? (The King of Love Is Dead)" was released as a single and reached the Top 20 on both the US and UK R&B charts.

Right on its heels, her version of "Ain't Got No / I Got Life," a medley from the musical *Hair,* was issued as a single (in a slightly different edit from the way it appeared on the *'Nuff Said!* album). Merging one song about lacking material goods and comforts with another that's a joyous celebration of the human body and its vitality, in Nina's hands the medley became a call for freedom and respect of all people. It grazed the US pop charts—her first appearance in the Top 100 in seven years—but the song exploded in Europe, reaching number 2 in England and even hitting number 1 on the Dutch pop chart. The follow-up,

Jimmy Webb's "Do What You Gotta Do," outperformed "Ain't Got No" in the United States and also got to number 2 in the United Kingdom.

But during this unexpected commercial boom, Simone was having a harder time offstage. It's impossible to know the exact combination of influences that made it increasingly challenging for Nina to keep herself together. Over a year had passed since her breakdown on the Cosby tour, and life on the road had not grown easier. One can only guess at the effect of the added stress that Dr. King's assassination and its impact on the civil rights community had on her state of mind. But whatever the causes, it was clear that Nina's suffering was becoming worse and that she was growing more and more difficult to be around.

"Andy told me that in 1968 something changed in Nina," recalled her friend Gerrit De Bruin. "From that moment on, it was difficult for him to have influence on her anymore. She felt like she needed to be more aggressive. She got less mellow, she got harsh, and the people around her saw it, too."

Andy said that Nina was aware of her transformation, that she struggled to keep her ungovernable emotions under control. "In her sane moments, she was very concerned about her inability to handle these fits of depression and anger that came over her," he said. "She was very concerned about it when she was feeling good."

They went to various doctors, even a hypnotist, but eventually signed her into Columbia Presbyterian Hospital for a battery of tests that took several days. "She was looking for answers," said Stroud. "They conducted every known type of examination to try to get to the source of her problems, but they couldn't find anything showing any probable cause."

Returning to the studio, Simone followed 'Nuff Said! with an album that was one of her more experimental efforts, Nina Simone and Piano! Other than reprising an exclamation point in the title, the record's tone was very different from the live-band feel of the previous release; the sound was stripped down to just two instruments—Nina's piano and her voice.

"If you listen to some of those great recordings from the '60s, it's so easy to forget that the same woman that's singing is playing the piano," said Paul Robinson, who would later play drums with Simone, describing the multiple musical lines that had transfixed Miles Davis. "The independence of thought, of doing a vocal line one way and still playing the piano and supporting that way, she was great at that."

With a curious mix of material—from Blind Willie Johnson's "Nobody's Fault but Mine" to Leonard Bernstein's "Who Am I?"—the album was a project that Simone was proud of, but it failed to find its audience. Even though she was coming off of her biggest hit single since "I Loves You, Porgy," *And Piano!* was her first album not to chart in almost four years.

Perhaps disappointed by her latest venture's lack of commercial success, Simone was clearly unsettled when she made a remarkable appearance on the radio show *Night Call* in May 1969. Hosted by Del Shields, the program was a rare broadcast forum for black social issues. Simone responded at length to the callers, voicing her confusion about whether her own community was hearing her messages.

> *I think that the artists who don't get involved in preaching messages probably are happier, and use less energy. But since the stage is my life 90 percent of the time, I must use it to say the things that I feel. And, let's face it, being colored is not easy, and so I have taken upon myself to do these songs. . . . If [people] happen to be entertained, I'm glad, and I guess it's fair that they should get a fair amount of entertainment. But it's more or less a stage for saying what I feel about the situations that are happening around me.*

*I don't know how much I really reach people, especially with
the protest songs. I get the feeling at times that it's much smaller
than I imagine.*

Simone also used the airtime to muse on the responsibility of
an artist to push boundaries—and how far one could take things
before those opinions became dangerous.

*To me, an artist doesn't necessarily have to take a political stand
or a stand like I have taken with the protest songs. To me, that's
not necessarily his duty, but some type of reality that he lives in,
he must reflect that, that's what makes him an artist.*
    *I have no clear idea of what's going to happen. I am scared
most of the time. Nobody knows what's going to happen. All I
can do is expose the sickness, that's my job. I am as scared as you
are. . . . To me, American society is nothing but a cancer, and
it must be exposed before it can be cured. I am not the doctor to
cure it however, sugar.*

Simone's behavior remained inconsistent. If she wasn't acting
out onstage, she was doing so at home. "We go to bed happy and
holding one another," said Stroud, "and I wake up and she'd be
sitting up in bed with her arms folded, looking at me and thinking about killing me."

In August of 1969, she decided that she needed a break—
from her husband and from her work—more significant than
just a retreat to her treehouse or a temporary disappearance in
her car, and she impulsively booked a trip by herself to Barbados. She left her wedding ring on her bedroom nightstand and
took off without telling Stroud that she was leaving or where she
was going. "I walked out on Andy," she wrote in *I Put a Spell on
You*. "It was the only thing I could do."

But she didn't necessarily see this break as a definitive end to her marriage. "I wanted a rest from him, I knew that," she said. "I was hoping that maybe when I got back, he would have come to his senses, but I didn't want him to jump on a plane and come down there. I wouldn't have cared if he did, however."

The diary she kept in Barbados and the letters she wrote while she was there reveal just how tangled her feelings were at this confusing time. At first she mainly expresses relief that she's no longer working, perhaps feeling she was able to breathe at last. In a Barbados diary entry labeled "Vacation!" she writes, "Had no idea how tired I was—it is extremely hard to stop forcing myself to do things—it is incredible to believe that I have nothing to do—That's the hardest—Am sleeping & unwinding slowly."

In letters to Stroud, she both misses him and lashes out at him:

> It's nice to to [sic] feel like a queen down here, be the most beautiful, and envied by all the women. Money made these feelings possible—So Andrew, I thank you for teaching me this—though I'll probably forget it the moment I get back to Hell. I turn into a monster there—& the atmosphere is part of the reason. I'm happy here and slowly unwinding more.
>
> I still love you, Andrew and I'm trying—Thank you for making it easy to vacation without you. P.S. This place is a sort of paradise—like Morrocco—the United States is really Hell (when you compare)

And a few days later:

> Let's face it—you + I are partners (our marriage has just about been swallowed by the business) so please don't make me suffer any more pain because of your "still learning stage" of making a

*star—and always your silly notion that you can do everything
yourself.*

Most significant, though, are her diary entries about her
sometime dance teacher, Pearl Reynolds, who was also on the
island:

September 1
*I think this was the night Pearl arrived, around 3 A.M. I had
been swimming in the moonlight—there she was—sandals &
dirt reddish dress & hair up.*

September 2
*Argument with Pearl & very decisive one—went on motorcycle
ride (very fast—around 45 miles)*

September 4
*Pearl attended a classical concert (chamber music) at Harrison
College—I planned it, but at the last minute I went to the mov-
ies to see a western & a comedy—the audience was a gas. She
wore the black polka dotted velvet dress—my African earrings
& gold sandals.*

Sat. September 6
*Had loads of Fun with Pearl—she bought me a straw hat that
I'd been looking for—There was a dance at Saint George's
park—I didn't go—understand Diary?*

Sunday September 7
*Pearl leaves today at 3—Taking Lisa's birthday present with
her. it'll be her 7th—Congo drums, a small story book, and a
wire basket—all made here took Pearl to airport. I gave her
swimming lessons for three days—it was a pleasure.*

Happy Birthday to Kenny.

Sam Lord's Castle
Barbados, W.I.

Telephone : 97351

September 2, 1969

Cable Address : Samlords

P.S.S. Send me an acetate (if you can) of the recent record session.

Hi —

I'm two days late with this horoscope but here it is.

reading — it's Sundays —

What is happening with the Vogue-BAZAAR project? I have been advised that the best way to get it done (or rather one of the ways) is to have a series of pictures made first — I don't know — but Andy, there is a certain way this can be done but whoever is in charge must be an expert at this sort of thing — so it is not botched up by some inexperienced fool who will in his or her awkwardness ▮▮▮ cause me shame. (As I now have over many of my record covers and the recent pictures in Ebony) Let's face it — you + I are partners (our marraige has just about been swallowed up by the business) so please don't make me suffer any

After Pearl leaves, the entries go from joy to loneliness and anxiety, returning to residual anger toward her husband and memories of responsibilities back home, doubts about her attractiveness, and even uncertainty about her own sexual preference.

Tuesday September 9
Today was my happiest so far.

Wed. September 10
It's Amazing to me how I can feel the tension & sickness leaving—Last nite I cried—I knew the "Black bird" is clean inside—not sick like the ones in the states—that's all I kept feeling & saying to myself "He's not sick"—Andrew, Sam, everyone at home who depends on me flashed through my mind & how heavy the weight is—N.Y. seems far away—more so every day yet I'm beginning to get a little scared Love is a serious business I'm a little lonely today—spent 6 hrs on the beach

Fri (Lisa's Birthday) September 12
I had called home for Lisa's birthday—Got Andy—he upset me quite a bit—later, I got drunk, threw up all over the place—lost my blue crocheted vest to my swimming suit. Found it later.

Sunday September 14
Everyone here is white—at times it really makes me sick. Have decided to leave a week from today—I must master the meditative exercises & self-hypnosis—for I get upset so easily. I read from Revelations (the Bible) today.

Tuesday September 16
I don't feel pretty anymore. Had argument with girl in drugstore. She said "you may look queer, but you're no different from the rest of us." I got mad—took me a while to realize I could take that as a compliment. She didn't mean "queer" the way they mean it at home.

Wednesday September 17
Today is next to my last day here—very very depressing today—things are so still here. I am glad I am going—I think I've been here too long—However, some things have come quite clear to me—for instance that I am stuck between desire for both sexes

*but even though Andy & I have known this, I've never really
imagined other people knowing it. Now it is obvious to me that
they must know. Makes for quite a problem for me those who
aren't on the borderline.*

When Simone returned to Mount Vernon, she was stunned
to see that Stroud had moved out. The house was empty, her
husband and daughter were gone. She had never thought that
he would take her sudden departure so seriously. It might have
been an extreme, unpredictable response to her emotional problems, but it wasn't news to anyone that she was going through a
difficult period.

"Half of it was in jest," she said. "I took my ring off and put
it on the table, and I went to Barbados. I thought we'd be separated, but I didn't think that we would be divorced. I was surprised that he was gone when I got back. I was upset."

Stroud, though, can't exactly be blamed for taking his wife's
sudden departure—without her wedding ring—as something
more than a joke. He said that the doubt he had about their
future was confirmed after Simone came home and contacted
him. "The first day she arrived [in Barbados], she fucked the
bellboy after going for a ride on his motorcycle," he said, referring to the man named Paul with whom she had begun an affair.
"That's what type of person you're dealing with. She comes to a
strange country, goes to a hotel, rides a bicycle or a motorbike
with a bellboy, and goes to bed with him all within a few hours.
Plus all the time writing about how she's waiting for her female
lover, Pearl Reynolds, to come."

Though Simone hoped the Barbados trip would give her an
opportunity to rest and gain perspective, Stroud claimed that
nothing improved in her after she got back. In fact, her behavior was even more unstable. He said, "Now that she had been
by herself with no one to tell her what to do, where to go, or

any pressure on her, she began to think that this is the way she wanted to be."

For the sake of the business, Simone and Stroud decided to try to continue their working relationship while putting their marriage on pause. They sat apart on flights, stayed in separate hotel rooms—even separate hotels—while Simone did another round of shows in Europe.

When the tour stopped in Rome in November, Stroud met an exotic-looking woman who claimed to be an Ethiopian princess. He bought her lunch and listened to her story, then told Simone about the encounter on their flight to Oslo, where she was taping a performance for television. Sensing his attraction to this mysterious woman, she proposed that he get them all together for a threesome.

Was this a fulfillment of her own fantasy, some kind of dare to Stroud's masculinity, a peace offering? Was she still eager to hold on to some part of his attention and affection? Whatever Nina's motivation, Andy arranged for the self-proclaimed princess to fly to Norway and meet them at the hotel, where they all retired to his room and had sex.

Nina apparently felt regret immediately. A few hours later, after the women had left, two house detectives came to Stroud's suite, accusing him of having assaulted Simone. "Did she have any marks on her? Did you see any bruises or scars?" he replied. "She's hallucinating. She's a nut. I haven't touched her."

The next day, the touring party flew back to New York. On the flight, Simone asked for cash. As soon as the plane landed, she jumped in a cab while Stroud handled final arrangements with the musicians. By the time he got to Mount Vernon, Nina and Lisa were gone. Once again at a breaking point, he put most of his things in storage and moved what he needed into the Mansfield Hotel on Forty-fourth Street.

The episode marked the beginning of a more permanent

end to their turbulent relationship. Stroud believed that Simone couldn't handle the fact that he had seen her having sex with a woman. "The fact that I knew and I saw, I was an eyewitness to the sexual preference and how it worked," he said. "I knew all along that she was having these relationships with both men and women, and I should've walked out before.

"Anyway, that was the turning point. After that incident, we never got back together. She had nothing to do with me."

CHAPTER 10

People seem to think that when she went out onstage, that was when she became Nina Simone. My mother was Nina Simone 24/7. . . . She couldn't be herself, and she wasn't loved for who she was when she was not at the piano and not singing.

—LISA SIMONE KELLY

T he summer of 1969 saw perhaps the most rigorous tour schedule Nina Simone ever faced. With plans put in place by Andy and spurred by her recent chart success, she played a full slate of shows in the United States (including the Harlem Cultural Festival appearance) and also made a quick trip that took her to France for a festival in Antibes and then to Algeria for the first Pan-African Festival.

As the "folk-rock" boom had given way to psychedelia and then the first stirrings of the singer-songwriter movement, pop songs had an increasing sense of gravity and ambition that seemed to appeal to Simone. She followed her hit from *Hair* with another single from a current pop source, covering the Bee Gees' "To Love Somebody" and reaching number 5 on the UK charts. The song also became the title track for Simone's next album, which had the most contemporary song selection she ever attempted: three songs written by Bob Dylan (she was one of the few truly great Dylan interpreters), Leonard Cohen's "Suzanne," the folk song "Turn! Turn! Turn!" (with lyrics taken from the Bible and credited to Pete Seeger, the song had of course been a huge hit for the Byrds a few years earlier).

She also cut two more Bee Gees compositions and a modified version of the Beatles' "Revolution," later praised by John Lennon himself. Such a track list broadened her audience and inevitably interested young, white rock fans, which led to her first booking into Bill Graham's famous venue, the Fillmore East.

A review in the *Village Voice* indicates that Simone was at the peak of her power in the East Village rock mecca. "She now possesses an absolute mastery of her material," wrote Don Heckman. "Like all great singers, she has passed the point of sheer technique and takes for granted nuances of performance that other singers would have to make strenuous and conscious efforts to achieve."

In August, she also recorded the song that would be her final contribution to the protest repertoire—though it was one of inspiration and uplift rather than fury. Lorraine Hansberry's ex-husband and estate executor, Robert Nemiroff, had adapted some of her writings into a new off-Broadway play titled *To Be Young, Gifted and Black*. One Sunday morning, Simone opened the *New York Times* and saw a story about the production, with a photo of her old friend Hansberry.

"This picture caught hold of me," she said. "In her eyes, she kept trying to tell me something, and the memory of being with her many times kept flooding back. I sat down at the piano at that moment and made up a tune. I knew what I wanted it to say, but I couldn't get the words together. So I called up my musical director, Weldon Irving, Junior, and I said, 'Hey, Weldon, I got a song, and I want you to finish writing it.' I hummed it over the phone, told him what was on my mind, explained to him a little bit about Lorraine Hansberry. And he captured the mood, and it was finished on Tuesday, forty-eight hours later."

Like all great anthems, the lyrics to "To Be Young, Gifted and Black" are simple and clear, the melody forceful and memorable but not cloying.

> To be young, gifted and black,
> Oh, what a lovely precious dream
> To be young, gifted and black,
> Open your heart to what I mean
>
> In the whole world you know
> There are a billion boys and girls
> Who are young, gifted and black,
> And that's a fact!
>
> Young, gifted and black
> We must begin to tell our young
> There's a world waiting for you
> This is a quest that's just begun
>
> When you feel really low
> Yeah, there's a great truth you should know
> When you're young, gifted and black
> Your soul's intact!
>
> Young, gifted and black
> How I long to know the truth
> There are times when I look back
> And I am haunted by my youth
>
> Oh, but my joy of today
> Is that we can all be proud to say
> To be young, gifted and black
> Is where it's at!

Speaking about the song at the time of its release, Simone revealed a true sense of purpose, a look beyond the historical outrage of "Mississippi Goddam" and "Four Women" to a mission for the future. "To me, we are the most beautiful creatures in the whole world, black people," she said. "I mean that in every sense, outside and inside. We have a culture that's surpassed by no other civilization, but don't know anything about it. So my job is to somehow make them curious enough, or persuade them by hook or crook, to get more aware of themselves, and where they came from, and to bring it out. This is what compels me to compel them, and I will do it by whatever means necessary.

"As far as I'm concerned, my music is addressed to my people, especially to make them more curious about where they came from and their own identity and pride in that identity. We don't know anything about ourselves. We don't even have the pride and the dignity of African people. We can't even talk about where we came from, we don't know. It's like a lost race, and my songs are deliberately to provoke this feeling of 'Who am I? Where did I come from? Do I really like me, and why do I like me? And if I am black and beautiful, I really am and I know it, and I don't care who says what.' That's what my songs are about, and it is addressed to black people. Though I hope that in their musical concept, and in their musical form and power, that they will also live on after I die, as much as they are universal songs, too."

"To Be Young, Gifted and Black" was a Top 10 R&B hit and, peaking at number 76 on the pop charts, also Simone's biggest crossover success since "I Loves You, Porgy." The song would be covered by Aretha Franklin (who made it the title of a 1972 album) and the masterful soul singer Donny Hathaway; a few years later, Simone even performed the song sitting on a stoop on *Sesame Street*. The Congress of Racial Equality named it the "Black National Anthem," and the themes articulated by the song would be explored by such artists as Stevie Wonder and the Staple Singers.

"I'm born of the young, gifted, and black affirmation," said Attallah Shabazz. "It wasn't that we didn't know it. It was daring to proclaim it, and then share it joyously. It's stated in a way that you know your African-ness without apology, without explanation, and it's put into a contemporary, hip song, which means you get to hum it in public. And you didn't have to be black to sing it, because it was just a truth."

The studio version of "To Be Young, Gifted and Black" was released only as a single; Simone's next album would be another live set, titled *Black Gold* and recorded at an October show at New York's Philharmonic Hall. The closing number was a nine-and-a-half-minute version of the new hit, which she introduced by saying, "It is not addressed to white people primarily. Though it doesn't put you down in any way . . . it simply ignores you. For my people need all the inspiration and love that they can get."

As the focus of her work increasingly shifted to singing about and for her black audience, Simone's political thrust had moved from the drive for civil rights and racial equality to the priorities of independence and self-sufficiency that defined the Black Power agenda. "She made the transition from movements demanding the acknowledgment of our rights as citizens to insurgent movements calling for the economic and political restructuring of our society," wrote Angela Davis. "With her, I moved from an assimilationist project to a revolutionary project."

Black Gold would be Simone's only gold-selling album with RCA Victor. It was nominated for a Grammy for Best Female R&B Vocal Performance (although she would once again lose to Aretha Franklin). A separate LP containing an interview with Simone was mailed to radio DJs for promotion; in this conversation, she expressed her satisfaction with the record.

"There is a great deal of electricity in this album," she said. "There is a great deal of rapport between the audience and myself, which has been missing in so many of the previous albums."

Simone was finely attuned to her audiences, and to which nights she was truly on her game. If this meant that her performances could be uneven, it also resulted in her ability to maximize her powers when she felt in command. "If I'm in a good mood, in very high spirits, I can tell how I'm going to move them," she said. "But, on the other hand, if they are in a very different mood, they may be able to sway me their way. Usually I know as time goes on how it's going. Sometimes I may know the minute I get onstage."

Following the run of "Ain't Got No / I Got Life," "To Love Somebody," and especially "To Be Young, Gifted and Black," the mainstream media began paying attention to Nina Simone in a way they hadn't since the days of "I Loves You, Porgy." In the fall of 1970 alone, there were features about the singer in *LIFE* magazine, the brand-new black women's publication *Essence,* and *Redbook,* who had Maya Angelou—a cultural icon with the publication of *I Know Why the Caged Bird Sings* the previous year—pen an extensive, ambitious profile that was presented in an introduction as "the impressions of a poet."

"Nina Simone is able to stand upon a shadowed stage, take in all light and then return that luminescence to her audience in opulent, pulsating rays," Angelou wrote. "At other times and with no seeming reluctance she rejects the audience, rejects their physical fact, rejects their loyalty, rejects their devotion."

But despite her sudden turn as a media darling, she was still plagued by the same issues. George Wein said that he booked her for a successful show at the historically black Hampton Institute but that when he put her on the bill at the Playboy Jazz Festival she was acting strangely. "You really could not grab ahold of this woman. You could not do it, much as you tried," he said.

Trouble seemed to follow her. Wein had a house in France near James Baldwin's house, and the two men had become friendly. Simone came to visit Baldwin and got into some altercation. Whatever transpired, it was ugly enough that Simone was asked to leave. "I don't know the details, but Jimmy could put up with anything," said Wein. "Jimmy Baldwin was one of the most generous, sweetest, nicest people, but he couldn't make it with Nina, and that was very bad."

But Baldwin's friendship ran deeper than one bad night, and he would return to save Nina during a dark moment at the Village Gate in New York. Tickets for the show were ten dollars (expensive for a nightclub), and the set started about ninety minutes late. "She had a certain kind of regality, mixed up with a kind of pretentious arrogance," said Stanley Crouch, who was covering the show. "She was really a very frightened person; she wasn't as arrogant as she seemed. She was definitely afraid of being rejected, but she was ready to go out and tell the audience, 'I am here, I am Nina Simone, I don't care.'"

Al Schackman remembered this particular set. "At the Village Gate, she wouldn't have anybody play with her, just the two of us. We're on, and somehow she gets this thing going about Jews, 'That Jew, he owns this club, all these Jews,' and I'm going to myself, 'Oh, shit, Nina, most of your audience is Jewish.'"

Song after song collapsed midway through, with Simone complaining about the microphones and the lights, until eventually Baldwin came out and sat with her onstage. He said, "Nina, I think you should sing," and she replied, "James, yes, of course—I like you, I know you like me, so if you think I should sing, I will sing." Schackman recalled, "Jimmy was an angel come to earth, he really truly was."

"He was a little drunk, and you couldn't tell if she was

drunk," said Crouch, of Baldwin and Simone that night. "She stopped and said, 'I bet you all think I'm drunk—well, I am not, and you better remember that, because if you act as though you think I'm drunk and you abuse me, I will just stop and leave and you still have to pay and I am still going to get paid.'

"She had that kind of thing in her, that if you actually outdid her in a form of obnoxiousness, she could be more obnoxious than you could. And at a certain point, you would just surrender, because you would realize that you were not going to win, because she was going to be more obnoxious than you could be."

Still, when she turned it on, she could transport crowds to incomparable heights. If she and an audience could feed each other's energy, the results were something beyond a concert experience. A breathless review in the *San Francisco Chronicle* by John L. Wasserman offers an example of her still-incandescent potency.

"She is Priestess and she is Leader, mystic and political scientist, dancer, actress, playwright and chemist," he wrote. "I have never, ever seen a singer exercise the kind of control, the kind of benign manipulation that Miss Simone did on Saturday night." Wasserman described the show as "one hour 35 minutes of spiritual sex . . . if one talks about sex in singing, Tina Turner is a stripper, Nina is a woman." She is, he concluded, "a person making the final merger of life and art."

"If you're striking at the heart of five thousand people, there's more being plugged into you," said Simone. "There's more electricity coming from you, because you're getting it from them and they're getting it from you. It's like when lightning strikes a town, or a hurricane or a tornado, it builds. If it's getting ready to capture or to hurt thousands of people, it comes stronger as it goes through the oceans and the waves get bigger—it gets stronger all the time, because it's been building wave by wave by wave all that time. That's the way I think of myself."

If Simone saw herself as a force of nature, her young daughter was just becoming aware that hers was not a typical upbringing. "I didn't know that my mother was famous, or that she sang for a living, until I was maybe ten," said Lisa Simone. "I just knew that Mom was always traveling, and I never knew half the time that she was leaving or when she was coming back. I looked at her passport, and I saw the name 'Eunice K. Stroud, aka Nina Simone.' And I asked, 'What's aka?' And she's like, 'It means "also known as,"' and then I started to really consciously realize that my mother had two different lives."

But this awareness wouldn't be something that Lisa would have much chance to work through with her mother. "By the time I started to put things together, and get a wider sense of our family and the roles taking place in our home, [my parents] divorced."

She doesn't remember Simone and Stroud ever telling her that they were splitting up. At this point, her parents didn't seem to know what to do with her. She had already spent third grade in Rutherfordton, North Carolina, where she lived with her aunt Lucille for a year. But then one day her father was gone, and her mother was still touring. Lisa went to stay with the Shabazzes. Betty Shabazz couldn't reach Simone, so eventually she enrolled Lisa in school with her own daughters.

It was confusing and painful for a nine-year-old girl to be abandoned by her parents, but Lisa still found something to be positive about. "They stayed together ten years," she said. "That's a long time, so there had to be something fantastic to balance out all the other stuff. Maybe that was me."

Her love for her daughter may have been strong, but left to her own devices, Nina Simone wasn't always able to meet even the basic requirements of responsible parenting. "I went to the camp where we all went and I saw the director," said Ilyasah Shabazz, recalling research she had done for her own book. The camp director reminded her that one year, at the end of the camp season, all the kids were gone, but Lisa was left there alone—her mother hadn't come to pick her up.

"When he mentioned it, I started to understand why she was with us," said Shabazz. "And it was never anything that my mother ever talked about, we never even addressed it. She was with us for about six years, from when we were six to twelve or thirteen, on and off. I had no idea that her parents had split up. I had no idea."

"The breakup was really sad," said Al Schackman. "There was so much that they offered each other in the relationship, and Nina was always fighting it. Nina was just against Andy promoting her and making her work. He would say, 'Nina, you're making money. We've got a career here, and that's not gonna continue if you don't nurture it.' And she couldn't care less, and she could get violent, she could get really physical. She came to resent Andy, and he represented a part of her giving of herself that she only wanted to give when she wanted to give it."

For the rest of her life, Simone would blame Stroud's role as her manager for their breakup. She resented how hard he pushed her and hated what she perceived as the grueling pace of work he insisted upon. "He treated me like a horse, a nonstop workaholic horse," she said in 1999.

Stroud maintained that even if he had wanted to drive her harder, there was only so much he had control over. "All contracts were with her approval," he said. "She had to approve everything. I could never push her or make her do anything.

"But I took her out of the big booking agencies, because they were taking 15 percent of the expense money. I took her out of the clubs and put her in concerts where she made twice the amount in one night that she made in the clubs for one week, two shows a night. I made her have hit records. That's all that I did."

The people who surrounded Nina later in life would take a more nuanced view of Andrew Stroud and his ultimate impact on her career and her attitude. According to Gerrit De Bruin, Stroud was "the best husband for Nina that she could have had. Andy was a good guy, and I know he loved Nina very much."

Others agreed that Stroud was one of the rare people who could motivate Nina. "He was a strong guy who could control her, who could take care of her and her career," said Roger Nupie. "And up to the very last years, she kept on calling him, and deep inside I think she still loved him."

The most immediate need upon Andy's departure was to decide on a new manager. Simone again opted to keep things close to home, asking her brother and sometime band member Sam Waymon to take over the job. Having toured and recorded with her in the last few years, he was in the unique position of being close at hand and being someone Nina trusted. And Sam, not surprisingly, had a less generous opinion of Stroud.

"Andy was a son of a bitch," said Sam. "I think he realized he had a good thing, a workhorse. I think he realized that she was not as knowledgeable about contracts, about the business end of the music industry."

When Simone first offered the job to Sam, he talked it over with their mother and indicated that he was aware of how severe her issues were becoming. "Mom, she's my blood," he told her, "and nobody is going to hurt her as long as I'm around. If I can be of some good to her, if I can keep those bastards away from her, if I can show her that things are not like she's been used to, if I can show her that 'if you keep hanging in there, Sis, day after day, you'll see some improvement, things will get better'—the paranoia, the voices that she hears."

Al Schackman was not convinced. "I always had a problem

with Sam. . . . It was like a push-pull relationship, and I really didn't want any part of it. When Sam was around, I was not."

In addition to the change in her business structure, the divorce also meant a new chapter in Nina's romantic life. In fact, she told Stephen Cleary that after splitting from Stroud she had the one real same-sex affair of her life. "I've had sexual relationships with one woman that I loved very much," she said. "And it's just one. I'm not bisexual. I prefer men. I'm essentially a heterosexual person, and when I left Andy is when I had this relationship with this girl. But I loved that girl."

Simone said that she was "stupid" to break off the relationship. "I wouldn't dance with her in public," she said. "I was more hung up about music than I was about her."

As she navigated this uncertainty in her love life, Simone had moved, along with Lisa, to a Manhattan apartment near Lincoln Center. It was a different existence than they had in quiet Mount Vernon, but, at least for the time being, mother and daughter were together—even during Nina's frequent travels.

Perhaps not surprisingly given all the upheaval in her life, she released only one album in 1971, the mostly indifferent *Here Comes the Sun,* which again focused on recent rock songs (more Beatles, more Dylan) and was most notable for a radical up-tempo reworking of "My Way." In *Rolling Stone,* Timothy Crouse wrote that "unfortunately, neither Nina's *grande dame* intensity nor her old musical bravado find their way onto her new album." He felt that her signature eclecticism had become a distraction, noting that "except on her very first LPs, Nina has seldom found more than two or three really good songs to put on each album."

Her biggest priority at this time seemed to be spending time in Barbados, where she continued her affair with Paul, the hotel porter with the motorcycle, and where the actor Geoffrey Holder was showing her the sights of the island. Though she was blissfully happy there—"All I saw was its beauty"—she felt that Paul, who refused to come visit her in New York, didn't fully appreciate her celebrity and was taking their relationship for granted.

"One day I got mad," she said, "put my clothes on, took my daughter, and said, 'Okay, I'm gonna show you who I am, Paul, you dirty rat.' I said, 'Take me to the prime minister.' Went, walked in, said, 'My name is Nina Simone, this is my daughter,' and before I said scat—a southern term there—there were reporters all around us. We were on the TV news that night."

The prime minister—the first in the island's history, in fact—was named Errol Barrow. A member of the Royal Air Force during World War II, he had helped lead his country to independence from Great Britain as a founder of the Democratic Labour Party and would later be named one of ten official National Heroes of Barbados by the country's parliament. When he met Simone, he was approximately fifty years old and had held the top position in Barbados since 1966.

Barrow was immediately taken with the island's larger-than-life new celebrity, and he invited Nina and Lisa to live in one of the cottages on his beach estate. A servant named Mrs. Drake was delegated to take care of them. He would come to the cottage every night about one o'clock, when he finished the day's work. In light of this luxury and the attention from the island nation's most powerful man, Paul the hotel porter was soon left in the dust; Simone and Barrow began an affair.

Simone returned to the island every few months, breezing past customs and being picked up in a waiting Mercedes. She begged Barrow to divorce his wife, which he refused to do, but when he came to visit her in New York—showing the respect that Paul refused to grant—she decided that she would officially move to Barbados and live there full-time.

"I moved everything down to Barbados—my piano, the rugs,

the furniture, everything—and didn't tell him I was moving," she said. "I took the stuff to [luxury resort] Sam Lord's Castle, and I didn't see hide nor hair of him. Someone came to the Castle and said I had to post a bond to live there, that the Queen didn't want any foreigners there. I somehow got the bond, but I was surprised that Errol Barrow didn't come to my aid at that time. To my surprise, he wasn't particularly happy that I had moved down to Barbados. So I rented a cottage on the estate of Sam Lord's Castle and moved into that."

Barrow moved her into another house, but she became frustrated with the limits of their relationship. Though he treated her with genuine affection and tenderness, she hated that he wouldn't say that he loved her. She sought his constant attention in dramatic ways. One day, she stripped naked in a meadow, just to get him to run after her. "He was chasing me all over," she said, "the prime minister chasing this naked woman, and he cooked for me that night and made Chinese food, and sang a song called 'The Folks Who Live on the Hill.'"

"Out of all her boyfriends, Prime Minister Errol Barrow was the only one I liked," said Lisa. "He was very sweet, very kind, and he was different from my dad. His energy was different. I remember when he would come around, I always felt good, he was very nice to me, and that wasn't something that happened a lot with people at that time."

"I think [the Errol affair] was all theater," said Schackman. "I think he was infatuated with a star. And she was very magnetic, but it wasn't this wild love affair. She was having fun with it, she was having a good time. We went dancing at night, swimming in the sea, and it was good, it was good for her."

Whether the relationship was ultimately impossible to sustain, as much fantasy as reality, Al Schackman captures the good humor of this era in a story from his first visit to Barbados, which he arranged as a time to rehearse with Simone. Upon his arrival, she had asked him, with little explanation, if he could change the locks on her doors because someone had been coming around the house and scaring her, so he went into town and got a new tumbler and new keys. When he got back, Simone was gone and he set to work alone.

As he was fiddling with the lock, a Town Car drove up to the house and a black man got out. He walked over to Schackman and asked, in a British accent, if Miss Simone was home. Schackman replied that she was out, prompting the man to ask who Schackman was. "I'm her guitarist. I'm a friend of hers," he said, adding with some suspicion, "Who are you?" The stranger said casually to tell her that Errol came by; then the stranger returned to his car, and left.

A few nights later, Simone and Schackman were invited to a dinner reception at the prime minister's mansion. They arrived and went through the reception line, mingling with well-dressed guests.

"I meet this ambassador, I meet this minister and stuff like that," recalled Schackman. "I meet the prime minister's wife, a lovely woman, and then the prime minister. I go up to shake hands and look at him. He looks at me and grins. And I said, 'Oh, no.' And he says, 'That's all right, my friend.' I said, 'I'm so sorry. I had no . . . how could I know?'

"He said, 'That's right. What can any of us know with Nina Simone?'"

CHAPTER 11

My dad was God to me until the time I turned on him. He was my dad. When I pray now, and say, "Our Father, who art in heaven," to me I ain't praying to God. I'm praying to my daddy.

Simone's time in Barbados was notable as a period of some respite and stability. Lisa was doing some work for a moving company on the island, and she fondly remembered a time when her mother did something unexpected. "Mom decided to make me lunch one day," she said. "She made me a peanut butter and flying fish sandwich, and I dutifully bit into it and was amazed that the flavors actually kind of went together. She was just so proud of herself. When she wasn't playing piano and she wasn't performing, she was like a fish out of water when it came to those kinds of little things. So for her to even do that was really a big deal to us both."

Elsewhere, though, her actions continued to spiral in disturbing ways. As her daughter was coming of age, Simone wanted to avoid replaying the distance that she felt from her own mother as a young woman. But her relationship with Lisa was so irregular and her judgment so skewed that the intimacy she attempted to cultivate with her child by educating her about puberty sometimes manifested in wildly inappropriate ways.

"She made a vow that when she had children she would make sure that we knew more than she [had] about [sex]," said Lisa. "I think that things started to get a bit twisted for her, the sense of right and wrong. I think a lot of times she forgot that I was her little girl, and what I needed was someone to make me feel safe, as opposed to treating me like I was your girlfriend."

But Nina's instinct to teach her daughter about her changing body could also play out in maternal ways, like when she helped Lisa with her first period (something that Simone had specifically recalled her own mother avoiding). "The best conversation I ever had with my mother," said Lisa, "that helped me come into my womanhood, was that she showed me what tampons were and what Kotex was, so that when that time came for me I wouldn't be afraid. She was very meticulous, and very loving, and it was a very special time for me to just have her take time with me." If Simone's actions with her daughter weren't always fully thought out, her intentions were at least loving.

But, of course, Nina wasn't always so tender, nor were her decisions always clearheaded. Her anger at Andy Stroud continued to flare up and make her want to lash out. During this time, Lisa overheard her making plans to have two men show up at Stroud's brownstone and shoot him when he answered the door. When they arrived, he wasn't home. After this hasty, botched attempt on her ex-husband's life, Simone lost interest and abandoned the plot.

Though Barbados had offered some temporary peace, those around her continued to worry about her deteriorating condition. "Early on, I thought there was something eating at her, and gradually that got stronger," said Schackman. "I realized that she was fighting demons that could appear at any moment. The change in her would be dramatic, like a switch, and after a while I realized that I wasn't with my sister, I was with *that* one, and that one was menacing. I felt a multiple personality thing going on."

The guitarist recalls an argument with Simone when she was

so upset that she spoke in an entirely different voice, low and guttural and involuntary. "We finally realized this was a lifetime project of really trying to get Nina through those times," he said. "To keep her creative spirit alive, and keep her emotional space calm, where she wasn't being so destructive to herself."

Still, she kept working. In 1971, Jane Fonda and Donald Sutherland asked Simone to sing for the black American soldiers who had just come home from Vietnam to Fort Dix. The show was part of their FTA tour, an acronym that officially stood for Free Theater Associates but was usually referred to as either "Free the Army" or "Fuck the Army."

She met the actors in Greenwich Village and told them that she would perform, but only if they promised to use her music in their next two films. Fonda burst into tears, asking why she wanted to make this a commercial exchange.

"I said, 'I don't want to sing for your people, I want to sing for my own people, and so I want something for my services,'" Simone recalled. "She couldn't understand my attitude, that I wanted something in return for my services. So they wrote on a napkin, 'The next two films that we do, Nina Simone will do the soundtrack.' And of course they didn't, then I never saw them anymore."

With this uneasy settlement reached, she went through with the Fort Dix show, where she was struck by how docile the GIs were. "It was very strange, because they weren't full of joy," she said. "They were very depressed. They had just come back. They were just quiet. It was about five hundred of them maybe, and they didn't say anything, they didn't do anything. They responded to the choir, and they clapped appropriately. But they didn't jump up and down."

The show was recorded, and some of it—though it isn't entirely clear how much, since material was rerecorded in the studio and the label copy doesn't specify what comes from where—was used for Simone's next album, *Emergency Ward!* Though the album cover was made up of newspaper clippings about the Vietnam War, the material (just three songs over two sides) feels more spiritual than overtly political. The entire first side is an eighteen-minute medley of George Harrison's "My Sweet Lord" with interludes from a poem by David Nelson titled "Today Is a Killer." It's a fascinating, odd record, the lengthy, meandering tracks journeying through sections hypnotic, dull, and stirring.

But this focus on the war, even though it wasn't very specific, earned her points from the rock-and-roll crowd. Calling the album "undoubtedly her greatest record," Stephen Holden's review in *Rolling Stone* said that *Emergency Ward!* was "the most direct, desperate musical outcry against the war and the system supporting it that I've ever heard."

Holden attributed almost supernatural power to Simone's music. "Today, more than ever, Nina Simone's art comes directly from the cutting edge of reality, where love, rage, and despair are inseparable, and there is no other choice but action," he wrote. Still, the album—which obviously couldn't spin off any singles, given the length of the tracks—was demanding and a bit perplexing and didn't connect with a larger audience. It was her first LP in several years not to chart.

Simone's mind-set didn't make for an easy fit with the antiwar activist community, but she remained in close contact with the leaders of the Black Power movement. In 1971, she went to visit jailed activist Angela Davis in her California prison cell. When she didn't appear at the scheduled time, Davis was afraid that the appointment had been canceled.

The delay was actually caused by the jail's refusal to allow Nina to bring the gift she wanted to present to Davis into the secured area—a red helium-filled balloon. Even in a high-security environment, she was ready to argue with the authorities about the rules, and to win. "As it gradually lost its buoyancy, this balloon remained one of the few permanent fixtures in my cell," wrote Davis. "Even when it was entirely deflated, I preserved it as a treasured artifact of my time with the amazing Nina Simone."

While she was visiting Davis, further disaster struck in Mount Vernon. The house, which had been abandoned and was now in disrepair, overgrown, and unsafe, was further compromised by a fire, which also destroyed all of Simone's professional records. The Internal Revenue Service had started inquiring about unpaid back taxes. Simone's financial situation was headed for trouble.

Based once again in New York while still shuttling to Barbados, Simone continued to visit her family but remained frustrated by her relationship with them. She felt a distinct lack of gratitude and sympathy, that they didn't understand or care to understand her life. "I lived apart from them," she said. "I worked and gave them money, but they didn't come to share my life. They didn't know what was going on with me. My personal insecurity goes unnoticed. Even when I go home now, we don't talk about what I do."

Her anger toward her mother was most acute, still the same resentments building up year after year. "My mother acts like I've never even left the house. She never asks me what I've been doing and how I feel and where have I been, and how do I feel and who I've met, no. My mother was never close to me—I just played for revivals for her, and she never took any interest in me."

But in 1972, she caught a conversation between her father and her brother Sam that abruptly upended her feelings about John Divine Waymon and changed everything about their relationship. She claimed that she heard him tell Sam that he had been the provider, the one to bring in the money and take care of the family. Knowing that he had struggled to maintain steady work for much of her childhood, and that her mother had carried the financial burden of supporting the large Waymon family, Simone was horrified and felt betrayed by the father she adored—so much so that she dramatically, unbelievably disowned him on the spot.

"We were brought up to think that lying, killing, stealing were simple things," she said. "And my father lied, and it was the first time I had heard him lie in all the years I had known him. That doesn't begin to tell you how much it bothered me—if you take in consideration twenty, twenty-five years of no lying, and the affection I had for my father, and his for me, his lying to my youngest brother . . . It just crushed me."

The pressure that she put on her father to be perfect, and her extreme reaction when she felt he had disappointed her, are echoed in the idealized relationships she had with her lovers— her expectation that they could fix all her problems inevitably followed by confusion and anger when faced by more complex realities.

Later, her anger would dull, tempered by some compassion. She would say that she understood what her father was doing, that he was telling Sam something he needed to hear, that it was a case of "an old man being tactful to his son." But at the time, that rage was uncontainable, and she obstinately insisted that she had no father.

Soon after this rift, her sisters told Nina that their father was sick, that he was in the hospital with cancer and probably wouldn't survive. Though she was staying close by, with her eternal confidante Mrs. Mazzanovich, she refused to visit him.

"I was determined not to see him," she said. "As far as I was concerned, I didn't have a father, whether he was sick or not."

Her sisters couldn't believe this stubbornness and told her day after day that he was asking for her and was getting weaker and frailer.

Though she often made choices impulsively, inconsistently, this time she dug in her heels. "I wanted to see him, but I had said I wouldn't see him, and I had to go by what I said," she reiterated. "And my daddy died without my seeing him at all in the last six months of his life. After he died was when the full shock of it came to me.

"I didn't realize that death means that you never see them again. I didn't realize it was so final. I was unaware of what I was doing. I guess I didn't know anything about death."

John Divine Waymon died on October 23, 1972. Five days later, Simone flew to Washington, D.C., for a concert at the Kennedy Center. Skipping the funeral, she went onstage at the same time he was being buried in North Carolina.

She performed a song that she had been writing for her father during the last few weeks of his life, a very loose interpretation of Gilbert O'Sullivan's recent hit "Alone Again (Naturally)," with nine lengthy verses grappling with the story of his death.

> *I remember this afternoon*
> *When my sister came into the room*
> *She refused to say how my father was*
> *But I knew he'd be dying soon*
>
> *And I was oh so glad, and it was oh so sad*
> *That I realized that I despised this man I once called*
> *   father*
> *In his hanging on, with fingers clutching*
> *His body now just eighty-eight pounds*
> *Blinded eyes still searching*

For some distant dream that had faded away at the seams
Dying alone, naturally
. . . .

And after he died, after he died
Every night I went out, every night I had a flight
It didn't matter who it was with
'Cos I knew what it was about
And if you could read between lines, my dad and I close
   as flies
I loved him then and I loved him still, that's why my
   heart's so broken

Leaving me to doubt God in His Mercy
And if He really does exist, then why does He desert me?
When he passed away I smoked and drank all day
Alone. Again. Naturally.

"Nina's relationship with her father was very complex, very confusing to her," said Schackman. "I think there were some memories, some aspects of her relationship with her father that she really never talked about."

This unbreakable connection continued after her father's death, taking on a supernatural quality. During one concert, she noticed that a fly had landed on her piano, and she said to the audience, "My father is here tonight." For some reason, she had adopted the fly as the symbol of her father, and wherever she was, if the insect appeared, she would tell the people around her that her dad was visiting.

Further evidence of the mysticism that anchored Simone to her father can be found in her recollection of how she finally forgave him several years later (and, perhaps, forgave herself for her treatment of him on his deathbed), in an elaborate three-day ritual performed while she was living in Africa. Feeling especially unsettled, she arranged for a witch doctor to come to her home, where he threw some bones and asked, "Who is this person on the other side who likes Carnation milk?" She recalled feeding her father the sweet milk when she was a young girl tending to him after his stomach surgery and knew immediately who the witch doctor was talking about.

He went on to describe John Waymon's appearance and said that Waymon could help her from the other side if she let go of her anger toward him. As instructed, she slept with Carnation milk under her pillow for three nights to complete the rite. The witch doctor claimed that her father's spirit would be with her from then on.

In 1973, Simone embarked on a longer tour, spending two weeks in Japan and then heading on to Australia. She pulled her daughter out of school to keep her company on the trip, but their relationship became so strained in Japan that Lisa refused to go on with her to Australia.

At a restaurant one night, on the Japanese leg of the tour, Nina started screaming at Lisa; Al Schackman said that Lisa was stoic, "like stone," taking this abuse from her mother. "I remember Mom saying that I was a robot, and that was my only protection, that I didn't show any emotion," Lisa said. "Because when Mom would see you cry, she knew she could push your buttons, and that's what she wanted. And I would not give her that satisfaction. When she would hit me, I would look her dead in her face. And she's like, 'You better cry, you better cry.' I wouldn't do it."

"Nina was berating her, it was just horrible," said Schackman. "I had enough of that, and I told Nina that this wasn't gonna work. And she said, 'Just get her out of here.'"

Her anger directed at Lisa may have been driven by a need to exert control, which could also manifest on her daughter's be-half. At other moments, Nina would want to protect her child with a primal ferocity. "We were in that same dining hall on a different day," said Schackman, "and there was a man standing near Lisa and he reached up and patted her head. She had an Afro at that time, and Nina flew in a rage and tried to attack the man. He said, 'I didn't mean anything, I liked it,' and he was South African. We had to restrain her—'How dare you touch my daughter?' So there was that there, too."

After these incidents in Japan, Simone gave Lisa the choice of going to see her grandmother in North Carolina or continu-ing on to Australia with her. Lisa opted to go back to the United States. Bouncing from residence to residence, after this tour ended, she went to stay at Schackman's farm in Massachusetts rather than return home to Nina. "Those are the two places that wound up being my salvation," she said, referring to the farm and her grandmother's house. "Al said that at one point I was walking on the porch and I fell through the floor and I started crying, and he had never seen me cry. He was my blanket of comfort, he was always a ray of sunshine, and he was always available for me to talk to or just be in his presence."

The tension between mother and daughter, along with Nina's deteriorating condition, pushed Lisa back toward Andy. "When my parents divorced, she changed, and so my father became my knight in shining armor," said Lisa. "It didn't matter to me what she said, I knew that if she was acting a certain way I could call my dad and she would back off. I didn't believe her—had I be-lieved her, I don't know if I would have made the same choices, but she was the person that was beating me when they divorced, so I would call my father, and he would protect me."

Lighter-skinned than Simone, Lisa looked more like her fa-ther than her mother. That resemblance alone could be enough to set Nina off. (Schackman remembered the writer of "Four

Women," so acutely aware of the power of skin tone, telling her daughter, "You're just like your father, you're like a half-breed.") "Whenever she looked at me, she saw my father, so I couldn't win for losing once they separated," Lisa said. "I think she was jealous of the fact that I was light-skinned with smaller features, and oftentimes I was persecuted for that when she was having a bad day. And I'd say, 'Well, I didn't pick Dad, you did.'"

But Nina's complicated feelings toward her daughter went beyond the reminders of her ex-husband. Schackman believed that she also resented the economic privileges that Lisa had growing up—a luxury that Simone never enjoyed as a child. He guessed that she felt competitive with her daughter. "Nina had an awful lot of anger and destructiveness toward Lisa," he said. "As far as Nina was concerned, she saw something in Lisa that she didn't like—her character, personality, whatever—and Lisa was lovely, just a beautiful young girl."

Lisa maintained that she wasn't miserable, in spite of her unstable home life—she liked school, had her favorite music and cartoons. But during this tumultuous time she did her best to stay clear of Nina as much as she could.

"I think she was very resentful, very angry, and very afraid," she said. "And a lot of times when people are afraid, it doesn't necessarily come out as wild-eyed and screaming, it comes out in anger, because oftentimes they don't know that that's what they are. And children and animals are usually the first ones to be on the receiving end of that."

Ironically, this same year Simone was honored for "Human Kindness Day." The all-day tribute took place in Washington, D.C., on May 11, 1974. It was one of the bright spots of this period—made more special by her own mother's attendance.

Cosponsored by the National Parks Service and put on with the support of government agencies and major corporations, the event was packed with festivities celebrating the singer. Things kicked off with a breakfast reception at the Kennedy Center, followed by a luncheon for her at the Museum of African Art. Next up was one of the main elements: a free seven-hour concert held on the Washington Monument grounds, with big acts like the Pointer Sisters, New Birth, and Herbie Hancock performing.

Additionally, there was a special musical and theatrical program titled "Tones of the Lady of Ebony—A Tribute to Nina Simone," directed by Harry Poe and staged at the Smithsonian Institution. The day also included art and writing awards for students, and a collection to raise money for a dam in the drought-stricken area of the Sahel in Africa.

Simone was in high spirits during the day, as demonstrated during her own evening performance. "Nina was ill and she had seen a doctor," said drummer Leopoldo Fleming. "She says to me, 'Leopoldo, I'm not feeling too well, so please don't make me dance.' I said, 'Okay, Nina.' So we do the concert, and during the concert she starts dancing. After she comes to me and says, 'Leopoldo, I thought I told you not to make me dance.' I said, 'Nina, I didn't make you dance—it was the drums that made you dance!' She loved dancing, you can see that when you see clips of her in concert."

During the tribute, Simone carefully monitored her mother's reaction. It was a rare opportunity for Mary Kate Waymon, usually so uninterested in Nina's career, to see what her music meant to people. "She didn't know what they were going to do to me, to her child that day," she said. "Because that was an all-compassing day—I mean, they crowned me, and my mom was watching to see what they were going to do to her child. It was beyond her imagination, what happened that day."

Photographs of Mary Kate on the day betrayed her uneasiness with the attention; more tellingly, Nina's own thoughts about what her mother may have been feeling reveal the combination of arrogance and fear that had haunted her since childhood.

"[The pictures] captured this anxiety," she said. "Can you imagine your child being so exceptional that people come in, they want to look at it and they want to feel it and they want to touch it and they want to take it here and they want to take it there? And you, as a mother hen would do, you watch and say, 'Okay, all right—only so far now, only so far. Bring her back.' That was all in my mom's face that day. It was in the pictures. She never said anything."

Though Mary Kate supported Simone by attending Human Kindness Day, she still never acknowledged Simone's involvement in the civil rights movement, or any of the other reasons that her daughter would be receiving such an honor. Simone continued to feel no acceptance or approval from her mother for her music or her activism. "She acts as though it doesn't exist," she said. "It was all just unreal to my mother."

Whether her mother was still uneasy with Nina's career making nonsacred, nonclassical music or whether she simply couldn't comprehend this level of celebrity, she never engaged with her daughter's work. With her father now gone, his final months and his death stirring up a morass of emotions for Nina, this sense of Mary Kate's indifference was more painful than ever.

Meanwhile, Simone had continued her attempts to maintain the relationship she was most excited about, returning to Barbados every few months to keep up her affair with Prime Minister Barrow. Eventually, though, he grew tired of her unreliability. One incident in particular pushed him away. She had been begging Barrow to take her to Martinique for lunch on his private jet. Finally, he relented and arranged for a day trip, telling her to be ready at seven o'clock the next morning. But Simone went out dancing that night and stayed out until 5:00 a.m. When Barrow's men came to pick her up for the flight to Martinique, she went to the door, bleary-eyed, and said she couldn't go.

"Well, this hurt the prime minister so much, he didn't say anything," she said. "He just quietly closed down the villa on me. And the next thing I knew, I was asked to get out, and I had to go back to America."

She would consider Barrow one of her great lost loves, and throughout her life she would try to win him back. After he broke up with her, though, she had to contend with reality and was faced with a life in serious disarray.

Simone returned to the States with Lisa, and the two lived in the unfurnished apartment in New York. The communications from the IRS became increasingly urgent—until ultimately a warrant for her arrest was issued. The county court had taken control of the Mount Vernon property. Simone and Stroud were arguing bitterly about who was responsible for the unpaid taxes, blaming each other for the failed payment.

Lisa indicated that Simone was remorseful about their transient lifestyle and regretted how chaotic everything had become. "After she divorced my dad and the house we had in Mount Vernon was taken by the IRS, she called us nomads," she said. "Her biggest lament was that she never was able to provide me with a home. She didn't know that as long as I was with her and she was not having a bad day, that wherever we were together, that was home."

Things looked bad for Nina Simone in the mid-'70s. But around this time an unlikely ally appeared, offering her a small morale boost. In July 1974, she took Lisa to a David Bowie concert at Madison Square Garden. About a week later, she went out, on a whim, to a private club called the Hippopotamus, and shortly after she arrived Bowie himself walked in with a small entourage and sat in a corner of the club. When Simone got up to leave and walked past his table, he invited her to sit down.

Though they had exchanged only a few words, Bowie asked for her phone number and then called her that night at exactly 3:00 a.m. "He said, 'The first thing I want you to know is that you're not crazy—don't let anybody tell you you're crazy, because where you're coming from, there are very few of us out there.'"

For a month, he called her every night and they would talk for hours. Finally, he paid a visit. "He looked just like Charlie Chaplin, a clown suit, a big black hat," said Simone. "He told me that he was not a gifted singer and he knew it. He said, 'What's wrong with you is you were gifted—you *have* to play. Your genius overshadows the money, and you don't know what to do to get your money, whereas I wasn't a genius, but I planned, I wanted to be a rock-and-roll singer and I just got the right formula.'"

What Bowie was affirming for Nina was her true calling as an artist, a sensibility that he could recognize as something different from that of a pop star. At a period of such turbulence, it was a lift that she needed. "He's got more sense than anybody I've ever known," she said. "It's not human—David ain't from here."

Bowie later would record "Wild Is the Wind," the title song from the 1966 Simone album, as the final track on his stellar *Station to Station*. And soon, as Bowie had done before her, Simone would leave her home country in search of a more sympathetic environment. She had no permanent address, a dwindling connection to her family, persistent frustration with how her music was accepted (or not), and doubts that she was being compensated fairly for her record sales, plus she was being pursued for tax evasion. Other than the Human Kindness Day appearance, she had performed only a handful of concerts in 1974. With everything going wrong in the States, she decided to pack up and leave.

"The most prevalent view was that she was being tremendously harassed by the government," said Andrew Young. "And we were very sad, but we understood the nature of government harassment—at this point, the government was burning our mail."

In a constant search for acceptance, for her true calling on earth, Simone was now fighting without a community left to bolster her work. Young felt that she was paying a higher price for her activism than the political organizers were. "At least with us, there were people whom we could cling to and lean on and draw strength and support from. But she was probably very isolated. In her community of artists, there's not a great circle of support."

Lisa remembered feeling that something dramatic had shifted in the activist community and in American culture. "It's almost like it just ended one day—it was going on and the next day it wasn't," she said. "So many people were leaving, whether they were assassinated or they just decided that they were tired—once we were allowed to vote, it was almost like, 'Okay, yay, we got the prize, everything is fine now.' And she's like, 'No, no, it's not.'

"I know she felt like she was alone, and she was still fighting while everybody else was happy that they had gotten their certificate. She never stopped speaking out against injustice. I think that Mom's anger is what sustained her, really what kept her going. It just became who she was."

Simone maintained that she was "chased out of this country," but she had also grown disillusioned with the possibilities for true social change. "I was angry, I felt naive," she said. "I felt that there was no more movement anymore and that I wasn't part of anything."

"Through her involvement in civil rights, she used the music for some purpose," said Roger Nupie. "And with the civil rights movement ending, she was a little bit lost because she didn't have this purpose anymore. She only had this music, her Nina Simone music—which wasn't the kind of music she wanted to play in the first place, because it was not classical music."

Before Simone left it all behind, she released one final album, ending her contract with RCA Victor. It was another live recording, with largely African instrumentation. The LP had two songs that were written by Bahamian musician Exuma, but also her versions of Jerry Jeff Walker's "Mr. Bojangles" and a song that had been recorded by Ike and Tina Turner called "Funkier Than a Mosquito's Tweeter."

The record, which would be the last new music she would release for four years, shared its name with a phrase that was one of Jesus's seven "Last Words on the Cross."

The title of the album was *It Is Finished*.

CHAPTER 12

They treated me like I was gold, like a human being, which is not the way they treat me over here. My heart is in Africa. . . . The Western world needs Africa, just to try to rape it all the time. The Western world needs me. That's why they can't let me go.

The chance for Nina to make her home outside the United States came from one of the few singers she viewed as a peer. Miriam Makeba, nicknamed "Mama Africa," was a South African–born singer and activist credited as the artist who first introduced African music to a worldwide audience. Because of Makeba's campaign against apartheid, South Africa revoked her passport in 1960. She met Simone soon after, when she sought asylum in the United States.

"She said that she had listened to me in South Africa and that when she came to America she wanted to meet me," said Simone. "I went to see her at the Blue Angel in New York City, and we became friends then." The pair occasionally performed together, first sharing a bill at a 1961 Carnegie Hall show.

Of course, the two forces of nature collided at times. At one point, Simone told Andrew Young that she and Makeba were not speaking (though he replied that it was very difficult for anybody to get along with Makeba). And drummer Leopoldo Fleming recalled the first time he met Simone, at a party at Makeba's New Jersey house. Simone had borrowed a fur coat from Makeba, and when she returned it that night the coat had been altered into a shorter, Eisenhower-jacket shape. "Miriam said, 'This is not the coat I gave you!'" he said. "She said, 'No, I had it restyled—I thought you would like that.'"

Despite their clashes, the two women were close and understood each other. In 1974, Makeba invited Simone and Lisa to her home in Monrovia, Liberia, for some political events celebrating the country's new government. The Simones made the move in September; Nina had not been back to the continent since the 1961 AMSAC trip to Nigeria.

"I've always wanted to go to Africa, I always knew that I would belong," said Simone. "It took [Makeba] twelve years to take me, and she was a star and she knew everything that I knew about show business. But most of all, she knew about my homeland, where my ancestors came from. We shared the same goals. We had the same color. We had the same hair. We shared the same interest in men. She loved to dance and drink champagne, and make love, and so did I. And we loved African men. And she used to come and see me and bring two men for me and three for herself."

Simone found the people of Liberia—a country first formed as a place to relocate freed slaves from America and the first democratic republic in Africa's history—to be generous and warm. When she first arrived, she was greeted with nonstop parties. Makeba arranged for her to go out on six dates in six nights, all with men who had made their fortunes in palm oil.

A few nights after arriving, she was taken to a private club called the Maze by drummer Fleming (who was playing with both Simone and Makeba at the time) and some friends. She was having fun, feeling loose and dancing. Fleming had to leave because one of his party had to go to work in the morning. When he woke up the next day, he discovered that everyone was talking about Nina, who had stripped naked on the dance floor.

"I was so happy to be at a place where I could do this," Nina recalled. "I was so happy to be home. I was in Africa. This was maybe the third day that I was in Liberia. The next day the president heard about it, and I got scared—he said, 'Who is this woman who came from America and stripped at the Maze?' I thought surely I was gonna get arrested. But the next night the president was at the place."

Simone later incorporated the striptease and the abandon she felt that night into a song called "Liberian Calypso," a re-working of "Run Joe," a tall-tale song that had previously been recorded by Louis Jordan, Chuck Berry, and even Maya Angelou during her days as a calypso singer:

> *Bodies started moving all around*
> *I was so happy to be in town*
> *And as I slowly began to strip*
> *Everyone thought I was so hip*
>
> *I danced all over the place, you know*
> *All over the ceiling, all over the floor*
> *Up in the balcony, all around*
> *I felt so good just being in town*

(Elsewhere in the song, recorded in 1982, she thanked God, saying, "He brought me to Liberia / Everywhere else is inferior.")

Back in America, Andrew Young was relieved that Simone had made such a decisive break from the system that was causing her such pain. "I was delighted that she was at a point in life where she could withdraw from all of this and lessen the intensity of it. I mean, you'd go absolutely mad if you didn't have some place of refuge. And many people in and outside of the movement just lost all sense of sanity. It was a particularly troubling and very difficult period for us."

As Simone was at last experiencing a sense of freedom she could never find in America, Lisa, who was starting seventh grade, was also beginning to settle into life in Monrovia. The first year, she stayed with a couple—a Liberian husband and American wife—who had a sixteen-year-old daughter. Eventually Simone bought a house of her own on the beach and had the space for her daughter, though Lisa was slow to move in.

About six weeks after arriving in Liberia, Simone had another chance at romance. She was at home alone, after turning down tickets for the Muhammad Ali–George Foreman fight in Zaire, when the telephone rang. It was Doris Dennis, a Liberian woman she had recently met, inviting her to come and meet her father-in-law. When she got to the Dennis family's house, there was a card left for her that read "Don't move. I'll be back in an hour. And we will be married in six weeks, signed C.C. Dennis."

Intrigued, she waited, and after about an hour a tall, handsome man swept in, seventy years old and wearing a stylish gray suit. He grabbed Simone, kissed her squarely on the mouth, and told his daughter-in-law to fetch the silver set. The cups were filled with wine, and he surprised Nina by toasting their upcoming wedding. He explained, "You've been sent here to me— my wife put me out her door after my second son, and I have to marry a younger woman." She had arrived in Liberia on his birthday, he explained, a clear sign that she was to be his bride. Simone may have been enjoying life away from performing while in Liberia, but her ego was still flattered when he indicated that he had been studying up on her and knew, for instance, that her piano was still in Barbados.

They drank and talked for hours before Dennis announced that she must be tired and eager to get home. He instructed that she would be picked up at seven o'clock the next morning and they would drive to his house in Bomi Hills, two hours outside the city. After watching her down many glasses of wine, he told

Simone that he was concerned about her alcohol consumption and would reward her if she didn't drink for the first three days they were in Bomi Hills, and that, after the sixth day, promised she would get to teach him about sex. Simone was smitten with how confident he was in his desires. "I never met a man like that in my life," she said. "I don't know where I am."

After returning to her house on the beach, Simone went to speak with an elderly neighbor named Martha Prout, who had become a surrogate mother figure for the singer. When she recapped the evening's events, she was surprised by the older woman's response. "I know where you're going," Prout said. "Are you going to live in the city or in the country?" Simone was taken aback, and replied that Martha must be confused, and that she had no idea what the older woman was talking about. Martha said, "Yes, you do, child—everybody in Liberia knows you're going to marry Mr. Dennis."

At promptly seven the next morning, Simone was whisked away to Bomi Hills in a car with Mr. Dennis. When they arrived at the mansion, an old man hoisted the flag, calling the staff together to greet their guest with a forty-five-minute prayer. Simone was fed Spam on crackers, and she changed into a white satin negligee in a style worn by Marilyn Monroe, an outfit Dennis asked her to keep wearing in order to impress his staff.

The elaborate, confusing story of her week at Dennis's estate dominates a disproportionate number of pages in *I Put a Spell on You;* to Nina, it seems to have represented her final chance at true love, and thus assumed greater significance as she lived out her days still single. The rituals and the old-fashioned romancing made her feel wanted, important. But there were still many steps to take before the plans for a future with Dennis could proceed.

Four days passed at the Bomi Hills estate, and despite the instructions she had been given to wait until the sixth day, Simone could wait no longer; she went to Dennis's room and tried, unsuccessfully, to seduce him. Distraught, Simone went back to her beach house and sought the wisdom of Martha Prout, unaware that Prout had been pursuing C.C. Dennis herself for thirty years.

"She took the opportunity to fill me full of wine," said Simone. "She says, 'Tell me all, child.' So I told her everything. She planted a rumor in the neighborhood that I had hit her, and she got his sister to come over, and they divided up the community against me."

A few days after her run-in with Prout, Simone left Lisa in Liberia and, looking for guidance, flew home to see her mother, without informing Dennis that she was leaving or where she was going—much as she had fled Andy for her trip to Barbados. "It was the stupidest move I ever made," she said. "My mom hadn't the faintest idea what to tell me." Nina returned to Monrovia after about a month with no more information about Dennis than when she left. Maybe he had run out of patience for Nina or felt insulted that she disobeyed him, maybe his romantic vision of her and their relationship had simply been shattered, but she saw the man only one more time. Eventually, she found out that, indeed, he had married Martha Prout.

Simone never forgave herself for losing Dennis, but she remained in Liberia for two more years. She was serious about taking a break from work of any kind; there were no performances or recording sessions in all of 1975, and just two concerts—one at the Montreux Jazz Festival and one in Paris—in 1976.

"She always said Africa was the happiest time in her life," said Roger Nupie. "She could just be there, enjoy herself, and do nothing. She was invited by kings and they gave her a beautiful house, and they just asked her to sing a few songs. She lived the life of a queen."

Simone later said that the high she got performing was

replicated in even the most ordinary moments in Africa. "Every-day life was fulfilling as my stage appearances are now," she said. "It took two hours to get from your house to town, because you had the rainy season and the dry season, and you fought the weather as much as we fight to get onstage here. I wore nothing but bikinis and boots, all day long. That's all I wore."

According to some of her musicians, though, things weren't always pure bliss for Simone, and she was still finding it hard to let go of her ex-husband. "I found Nina to be very, very lonely," said Leopoldo Fleming. "I had met some Moroccans, and my Moroccan friends took Nina out on the town. We took her swimming, we took her dancing, we took her to hang out in the coffee shops. She had such a wonderful time. And while I was dancing with her, she was telling me about how much she loved Andy."

For his part, Al Schackman claimed that, although Nina may have enjoyed herself, other people didn't. "They couldn't stand her in Africa," he said, chuckling. "Her maids—oh, she was just awful. If she were a queen, the streets would rumble."

True to form, Nina eventually grew bored in Liberia. Before she made her next move, though, and fresh off her rejection by Dennis, she took one more shot at winning over Errol Barrow. They met in Florida, but no romance blossomed, though he was courteous and inquired after Lisa's well-being.

When Simone replied that Lisa was happily living with her in Africa but that she was concerned about her daughter's education, he advised that she should send her daughter to boarding school to establish some consistency and stability. "I resented the fact that he said it," Simone said, "but I respected the fact that he was a prime minister and he seemed to know what he was talking about."

The people around Nina clearly felt some obligation to help her take care of Lisa; sometimes it seems as if she was crowd-sourcing her child-rearing. Claude Nobs, the founder of the Montreux Jazz Festival, recommended a school in Lausanne, Switzerland, for Lisa, who enrolled and moved there shortly afterward. Though Barrow had suggested to Nina that it would be best to establish some genuine separation from her daughter for a few years, about seven months later she rented a house in Switzerland, much to Lisa's dismay.

Lisa had been having a great time at school, at least until her mother appeared—"It's always that," Lisa said, "it's like the sun is shining and the birds are singing, and then the rain comes." Simone wanted her daughter to visit her every day, even to move into her house. Different people suddenly started asking Lisa why she refused to live with Simone.

Lisa could tell that her mother was instructing her contacts to report back on anything they could glean about Lisa's real feelings. She met with Nina's banker, and he began probing Lisa about why she didn't want to live with her mother. Tired of the game, she gave him an honest answer, unloading her anger and exasperation. After she left, he called Nina and told her what Lisa had said. Nina, in turn, called Lisa and asked her to come home so that she could take her to a party—but Lisa knew what was really coming.

"When I got to the house, the door was ajar," she said. "The house had a hallway, and I saw a branch go by—it wasn't a switch, it was the branch of a tree. And she proceeded to beat my ass for telling the truth. I got a black eye, and then she took me to the party."

"She had grown up too fast," said Simone. "She was making a fuss all over the neighborhood, and people were coming to my house complaining about my daughter. And it was because I had visited her and [Barrow] had told me not to."

Back in the orbit of Nina's harsh and sometimes violent behavior, Lisa turned to her father in an attempt to escape. She flew to New York for a three-day weekend to visit Stroud. "For many years, [my mother] told me that he didn't love me," she said. "I told her, 'I'm going to go see Daddy, and I'm going to prove to myself that he doesn't love me, like you've been telling me all these years, or I'm going to prove to you that he does.'" She called her father and told him she was coming—but didn't inform him that she hadn't purchased a return ticket.

When Lisa arrived and it was revealed, after a weekend had passed, that she didn't have a way back to Europe, Andy, living in a one-bedroom apartment with his girlfriend, called Simone and said she needed to pay for a flight back to Switzerland. She said that she would do so only if Lisa agreed to live with her.

"I said, 'Well, then, I'm not going,'" said Lisa. "I put him in a very awkward position, because what do you say to your child? 'I don't want you to be here?' So he took responsibility for me." In yet another in an endless series of abrupt life changes, Lisa went from attending boarding school in Switzerland one week to enrolling at a public school in New York City the next.

Nina remembered it a little differently, blaming Andy for Lisa's move back to New York. "I let her come back during midterm to see her father, and he never returned her to Switzerland."

Eventually, Lisa moved in with Stroud's sister-in-law in upstate New York. Simone stayed in Switzerland and would not see her daughter again for many years. "So what the prime minister predicted actually happened," she said in 1989. "It happened. I'm not close to my daughter now because of that time."

One thing the move from Africa to Europe signaled was that Nina was ready to get back into music. "Switzerland was the complete opposite of Africa," said Roger Nupie. "She needed the quietness to be able to get into show business again, and the fact that everything is very, very well organized in Switzerland. In Africa that's a totally different situation, of course, so I think it was her choice to find a basis to put her life back on track and be able to reenter show business."

Back in the game, Nina was plagued by the same sorts of trouble and ran into yet another fraught, murky situation with management. Apparently during the inactive years in Africa Sam Waymon had drifted out of his role as manager, and a lesbian couple named Susan Baumann and Josephine Jones wanted to take over her operations, an arrangement she vaguely accepted while refusing to sign any formal contract.

Jones and Baumann had made their initial inquiries about Simone through Raymond Gonzalez, who had booked some of her European dates. They had already promoted a Ray Charles show via Gonzalez and then asked for an introduction to Simone.

"I explained that she was very difficult, especially that particular time," he said. "I'd see what I could do and we left off like that. She wanted to live with them and I guess it went well for a couple of weeks and after that it just went completely wild."

In January 1977, Simone returned to the MIDEM international music trade show in Cannes. She used her set as an opportunity to blast the gathering of record executives from the stage, including them on her long list of tormentors.

"I am a genius," she said. "I am not your clown. Most of you people out there are crooks. I am an artist, not an entertainer, and five record companies owe me money." She was booed and walked off the stage in silence.

"I cursed out the entire music industry and didn't remember it," she said later, indicating perhaps that returning to the stage was a catalyst in her stress. "I called them snakes, thieves, spineless worms. They asked me to do two concerts, and I resented them asking me to do it for free, but since I had no money, and since it was a chance to tell them, I said, 'I'm going.' I did the first concert and it went smoothly, but the second concert, I was too tired. I remember saying to myself, 'I don't feel like doing this, and I shouldn't be doing it, anyway,' and something changed in me. I went on the stage and I remember playing the first number, and that's all I remember."

Getting back into performance mode with Nina Simone came with all the expected obstacles. Leopoldo Fleming recalled that she was essentially operating without management after things with Jones and Baumann went awry and thus had to pay the musicians herself. After long delays, Simone eventually gave them cash, but couldn't work out the correct exchange rate—giving them a tenth of what they had earned.

"Sometimes she just got fed up with you and she let you go, and then after a while she calls you back," he said. "I think sometimes it was because the money wasn't enough, and she also liked to experiment with different sounds. She was always changing up. She had fired me several times, but she called me back."

After Fleming had not heard from Simone for a long time, she called him one day and said that she wanted him to come back on the road but that he needed to bring a gun with him. "For what?" he wondered. "There was no reason for a gun. She had a little bit of paranoia and she was on the warpath, but there was really no war."

Simone returned to America for a few landmark moments. On May 29, Amherst College awarded her an honorary doctorate; it was a tremendous source of pride, and for the rest of her life she would insist on being called "Dr. Simone." In June, she returned to New York, with a concert scheduled at Carnegie Hall as part of the Newport Jazz Festival, which George Wein was now holding on various Manhattan stages.

"I talked to her," said Wein, "and I said, 'We want to do a

great concert.' We put an orchestra together, and we had the rehearsal at Carnegie Hall, and everything was okay, we thought."

Apparently, though, everything was not okay. Simone finished her sound check, went to the airport, and booked a flight back to Switzerland. Wein's wife and a friend went to the airport hotel where Simone was staying until the plane left the next morning in an effort to locate her; the house detectives thought they were prostitutes wandering the halls. But Nina never appeared, and Wein was forced to announce that the concert was canceled and then make a statement to the press.

"I said that she was a woman that could not adapt to being an African American in the American scene," he said. "We lost a lot of money, but I never held that against her. Nina was somebody that you accepted with all the craziness because she was such an artist. Promoters and producers learn to live with that problem. It's difficult, you try to get to trust in people—sometimes you do, sometimes you never gain their trust. I could do that with Miles Davis, I could do that with Monk, Mingus. I never could get that with Nina completely."

Simone rallied for a few more concerts in Europe over the next few months—in the Netherlands for the North Sea Jazz Festival, in Paris, in London for her first appearance in that city in eight years. On New Year's Eve, she played in Jerusalem— where, for once, she felt she was given the treatment she was due. "Israel is the first place I felt like a star, the first time in my life I ever felt like a star," she said.

In London, Simone met Creed Taylor, whose CTI label was becoming a leading force in jazz in the 1970s. With polished arrangements and a stable of top session players, CTI was helping to establish the "smooth jazz" format with popular albums by artists like George Benson, Bob James, and Freddie Hubbard. Taylor persuaded Simone to return to the studio for what would be her first new recording in four years.

They started the sessions at a studio outside of Brussels, but Taylor was annoying everyone and soon Simone insisted that he leave—not just the studio, but the entire country. He exited and the recording proceeded, though he had already established what much of the material and sound would be. The album was a wildly mixed bag, with moments of transcendence matched by overwrought orchestrations, and repertoire ranging from traditional gospel numbers to the recent Hall and Oates hit "Rich Girl." Simone would often express her distaste for the album, mainly because she had no input in the arrangements, song selection, or cover photo—and, of course, because she said that Taylor never paid her, though the album would reach number 12 on the jazz charts.

She did allow that she liked the title track, Randy Newman's spare, bleak "Baltimore," which perhaps mirrored some of her own views on urban America and on which she delivered an emotional vocal. "There's a song I sing called 'Baltimore,'" she said, "and it directly refers to 'See the little seagull, trying to find the ocean, looking everywhere.' And it refers to, I'm going to buy a fleet of Cadillacs and take my little sister, Frances, and my brother, and take them to the mountain and never come back here, until the day I die. When I went to Africa, I thought that I would be taking them with me."

At the very least, *Baltimore* established, for the moment, that it was possible for Nina Simone to make it through the sessions for an album at this unsteady stage in her career. Al Schackman recalled, though, that she remained as unpredictable as ever, and it was impossible to anticipate when she would fly off the handle.

After the band sessions, she wanted to record a few things with Schackman alone, even letting him play piano on one track. They got back to the hotel late after this additional tracking, and ace studio guitarist Eric Gale joined them in Simone's presidential suite. The musicians sat together on a sofa, under a huge mural, while Nina sat facing them, in front of windows overlooking the city. They were making idle chatter when she suddenly picked up a silver bowl of peanuts from the coffee table and hurled it across the room. "Man, I'm telling you, a quarterback couldn't have thrown a better pass," Schackman said.

The bowl flew over their heads, hitting the mural and tearing it. As Nina sat shaking in her chair, Gale jumped up and said he needed to go get some sleep. Schackman followed his fellow guitarist into the hall, where Gale gave him a hug and said, "God bless you that you're with her, bro."

CHAPTER 13

> I don't want anything to do with her. That's it. . . . We would wait
> for the call in the middle of the night. She might be dead or in
> jail or whatever.
>
> — CARROL WAYMON

In 1978, the IRS contacted Carrol Waymon, asking if he knew where his sister was. He hadn't seen her for years, but they spoke often. "She was losing it emotionally by that time, because she was convinced that she could not come back to this country," he said. He became the liaison between Nina and the agency.

Carrol had more questions after looking over her records. He discovered that she signed her payments over to Stroud, who kept their holdings under several corporations. "He was very smart," said Waymon. "He would sign a contract today for this company, but it would go into this other company. All kinds of shenanigans."

(Around this same time, Simone actually approached Stroud about taking over her management again. He handled her through a brief American tour, but she felt that he was no longer up to the task and dismissed him.)

While she was in the United States, she appeared before a federal court in New York to face the tax evasion charges. Her lawyers had worked out a deal in which she would plead guilty to not filing her 1972 return (perhaps tellingly, this was one of the last years Andy served as her manager), in exchange for other charges being dropped. According to a story in *Jet* magazine, she was "visibly shaken by her ordeal," potentially looking at a year in prison. She was ultimately put on probation and given a ninety-day suspended sentence.

Simone's trouble during this time didn't begin and end with the IRS. She had found a wealthy patron named Winfred Gibson, who offered to cover her living expenses while she got her career back on track. He put her up in a London hotel, but after a few weeks she determined that he had not been paying his bills and was avoiding the staff. She confronted Gibson, and the two got into a fight in her hotel room, she said. He knocked her unconscious and ran out. "I had to crawl to the telephone with my neck twisted, and I had to call the police," she claimed. "The police come and will not do anything. They threaten to arrest me." She took thirty-five Valium, and a nurse came to pump her stomach.

Simone was taken to St. Stephen's Hospital in Chelsea. "I had to have my neck straightened out because of the karate blow," she said. "I was pleased that I was still alive, but I was by myself. That was the lowest point."

Given her estrangement from her family, it was a complete surprise when Simone showed up in 1979 at Lisa's high school graduation in Hudson, New York, accompanied by her lawyer. Far from being invited, the singer had found out about the ceremony only because Mary Kate Waymon had mentioned it to her.

"Everybody was all just full of joy and happiness," said Lisa, "and by the time I walked down the aisle and glanced down the row of seats, all of [their] faces looked like something sad had happened. Then when I got down to the bottom of the aisle, I heard my name—and of course we all know our mother's voices. I turned, and I saw her face, and I think I held up the procession line briefly. The entire time that I was up on the dais I had a smile on my face, trying to appear involved, but I was praying that I could get through the ceremony."

Andy didn't notice Simone until after the graduation and didn't stick around to say hello. He just got in his car and drove back to New York City. "I avoided her as much as I could," he said. "The few times I was nice, she'd be asking for information. Then I would hear from an attorney a week or two later, looking to use the information against me, to sue me for something. When they called, I would always ask, 'Did you get any money or retainers yet?' And they would go silent. I said, 'Because you're about the fifth attorney that has called—and they've all called back later wanting to know where the money was.' Because she hadn't paid them, looking to get money from me and put a lien on any money coming in for her."

Lisa, in turn, surprised her family by announcing her post-graduation plans; she had enlisted in the air force. Clearly she was searching for some of the consistency and discipline that she had never been able to count on during her life. Her inseparable childhood friend Ilyasah Shabazz reconnected with Lisa during her time in the military and found that time had changed the girl she called her "twin" when they were growing up.

The two former neighbors met up when Lisa was passing through New York. "We went out to eat," Shabazz said. "I reached to get something on her plate, and she yelled at me, and I was shocked. I didn't know where that came from, because I never knew any of the challenges she had experienced. I would never take a fork and dig in someone's plate today—I might do it to one of my sisters, and Lisa was one of my sisters. So it was the nerve, the audacity that I would do that, but I was surprised that she snapped at me. But then I started to learn more about some of the things that she was experiencing."

The anecdote is telling; the first time Nina met Andy Stroud, she had taken French fries from his plate, and recognizing and respecting boundaries was clearly an issue that manifested in various ways for her. If Lisa's sense of guardedness remained heightened, perhaps her opening up to Ilyasah related to things unraveling further with her mother. On the heels of her encounter in the hotel with Gibson, Simone told the lengthy story of another bizarre, life-threatening scenario, this time during a stay in California and indicating even more paranoiac tendencies. She claimed that while she was in Hollywood she was tricked into entering a psychiatric institute. There the staff allegedly tried to silence her with medication until an Ethiopian priest mysteriously appeared to discharge her.

Simone invented wild theories for why she had been committed, indicating just how far her fears about the US government had gone. She concluded that a social worker had her put away in order to steal an unreleased concert video and prevent her from receiving royalties.

"They figured if I got my money, I'd have too much power in the United States," she said. "So I'd never get my money, and the black community would never know what happened to me until it was all over. That was the only real time I knew they were trying to kill me."

Carrol Waymon, living in San Diego, was the family member who was both geographically and emotionally closest to Simone; he was a witness to her declining state. "By that time she was under medication, but we couldn't get her to take the medication on a regular basis," he said. "She would say nothing's wrong with her. Yet at the same time she was having all these episodes of getting into scraps here and there.

"She couldn't get any work. She lived off of friends. Began to be more paranoid than ever. She'd call everybody, all our friends, any time of night, any time of day. My phone bill was four hundred and some dollars. She became so upset here that she got mad at me and I took her down to one of the hotels. Two days later, the hotel called me up and said they were going to arrest her."

But when their mother had a stroke, Simone was contacted by the hospital and decided to go home. She stayed in North Carolina for a week while her mother recovered, and things were calm; they stayed that way, at least with her family, for a while. "Part of it is that Nina has chemically multiple personalities," said Carrol. "I tried to deal with her around that, but she rejects it. Part of the memory is that one part doesn't really remember the other. There are different compartments. She's not in contact with all the realities around. She doesn't remember some things—literally, she doesn't. And she's aware of that, but she won't go through all the therapy."

The intensity of Simone's emotional swings can be heard in the interviews she was recording at this time, in one of several abandoned efforts to write a memoir. This time she was working with southern-born, Philadelphia-based arts journalist Mary Martin Niepold—at least, until she abruptly decided that she wasn't.

"If we're through with all this shit, let's put it in the waste-paper basket," Simone erupted suddenly one day. "You're draining my energy. I bring you in here in good faith thinking you need it and you take it back. If we don't need this shit, let's throw it away. Are you finished with that? Then throw it the fuck away. I don't like to keep this shit around. I only kept it around because of you.

"I'm not answering. You're not going to play me no more for

this fuckin' book. You don't care nothing about my music. All you care about is your book."

In April of 1980, Simone received bad news. There had been a coup in Liberia; the standing government had been overthrown and numerous officials had been killed, including C.C. Dennis's son and the country's president. C.C. Dennis had burned down his own house rather than have the new government seize it; he was paraded naked through the streets with Martha Prout, and shortly thereafter died of a heart attack before he could be assassinated.

"I didn't realize until he was dead that I made the biggest mistake of my life," said Simone, perhaps overeager to romanticize another in a series of powerful, ultimately unattainable men. "It was another world that I lived in when I was with him. He was rich, he was tall, he was handsome, he was older than me, he would have taken care of me, given me money. He told me I was beautiful and wonderful and that he loved me, he told me he loved me from the first minute I met him. He was the most honest man I've ever known."

As her condition deteriorates, it becomes almost impossible to track the chronology of Simone's different residences. In the early '80s, she stayed in Montreal for a while, in an effort to be close to the United States without paying its taxes. She briefly seemed to settle in, playing occasionally in a local café called the Rising Sun, but then she left the city without so much as returning to her apartment; eventually, her furniture and belongings were cleared out.

It was becoming increasingly difficult just to get her to show up for a performance, even dates that were only a short drive away. Longer trips had become epic challenges. She refused to get on flights, and when she did board she behaved so badly that the pilots would threaten to make an emergency landing just to get her off the plane.

At least once, in Paris, she simply would not get onto a connecting flight. Her entourage slept in the airport, waiting for her to agree to continue on to the concert. Finally, when the very last option was leaving, Simone had to be physically restrained and forced onto the plane.

Raymond Gonzalez, who had promoted some Simone dates in Europe, assumed a new role at this point in her life. The first time he met her, backstage after a show at the Palais des Glaces in Paris, he said she was "horrifying," brandishing a bowie knife and attacking one of her fans in the dressing room. He wanted to exit quietly to avoid the raging singer, but when Simone found out that he was the artistic director of a music festival in Pamplona, she insisted he stay. As a fan of the bullfights in Pamplona, she then proceeded to spend months trying to get Gonzalez to put her in his lineup.

She was booked at the festival, and a day before her concert Gonzalez went to Geneva to accompany her to the site. She wasn't home, but he came back early the next morning to get her onto the one flight that would arrive on time.

The door to her hotel room was wide open when he arrived; Nina was inside, wearing black tights and drinking cognac. She informed Gonzalez that she wouldn't be going to Pamplona. "After hassling me for months, you're not gonna go?" he said, and she replied, "No, I don't need the money anymore." She had recently received a payment from Claude Nobs for the rights to her film of her Montreux performance, as she was writing Gonzalez a letter to explain (he noted that the letter was written in different colors and different-size letters). He started to leave, and she said, "You're not a man—if you were a man, you would have called a taxi."

The trip was anarchic; after summoning a cab herself, Simone threatened the driver, disappeared when she saw bootleg Nina Simone albums in an airport record store, and insisted on a wheelchair to get her onto the flight. When they arrived in Pamplona, they found that all of her luggage was lost. The sizes she gave Gonzalez for replacement outfits were long out of date, and when he returned to the hotel with the new clothes that didn't fit her, she was swimming naked in the pool, having drained three bottles of champagne.

Somehow, they made it to the stage, where an inebriated Simone played a terrible set and cursed at the audience. The next morning, city officials showed up and told Gonzalez they had to arrest her. He defused the situation, hustled her out of town, and put her on a train home, assuming he would never hear from her again after such a disaster.

"Needless to say, it wasn't over," he said. "After that I got a phone call from her brother, who asked me if I would book a tour."

Maybe it was easier to just keep moving than to confront her escalating problems. Simone determined again that it was time for another change and moved from Geneva to Paris. She recorded the odd, fascinating album *Fodder on My Wings,* her first new release since *Baltimore* four years earlier. The record featured some of her most personal songs, including the rewritten version of "Alone Again (Naturally)" for her father; "Liberian Calypso," recounting her arrival in Africa; and "La Peuple en Suisse," a farewell to her unhappy years in Switzerland.

The title track was less literal—but just as autobiographical—as the other material. "It's the story of my going to Africa, in the form of a bird who fell to earth and reincarnated from her birth, which is me," she said. "She flitted here and there. She went to Europe; England; Denver, Colorado; Switzerland; and Spain, everywhere, trying to find out if people still knew how to give. And when she didn't find this, she went on to Africa, where, of course, they certainly still know how to give. That's the story of that song."

But the album, released on the obscure Carrere label, wasn't widely distributed, and its failure set the tone for a disappointing period in Paris. "I went back to Paris thinking that I could resume my career," she said. "I did it alone, and I landed in the wrong place and I fell from grace. I didn't know that you had to stay at the George V to be regarded as a star. People didn't come and see me; they didn't believe that I was in this small, small place, and I was working for about $300 a night."

Living in a tiny apartment, Simone would stand on the sidewalk in front of various Latin Quarter nightclubs and invite passersby to come in and see her perform. "She didn't take her medicine, so the concerts were incredible if she did them," said Gerrit De Bruin. "But could you imagine Barbra Streisand outside the venue—'Hey, come in, I'm singing tonight'?"

De Bruin visited Simone and cleaned her filthy apartment. "That was the worst period, but at that moment she was still uncontrollable," he said. "She had to dive deeper in the shit before she realized she had to change something."

One bright spot in Paris was that Simone reconnected with old friend James Baldwin. They spoke at length about their religious families (Baldwin had been a preacher in his youth), and he sometimes joined her onstage. She recalled that Baldwin would often say to her, "Nina Simone, you have made this world you're living in—you're going to have to deal with it."

During a swing through Los Angeles in 1983, Nina met Anthony Sanucci, a businessman who had, among other interests, a video company. The two got on and discussed the possibility of Sanucci managing her. Though he had no real experience, when she got back to Paris and considered her situation she called him and agreed to move forward.

Not surprisingly, she would express mixed feelings about this high roller, sometimes within the same conversation; she was impressed by his style but not always with his results. "Sanucci had twelve cars, and a home in Palm Springs, one in Las Vegas, and one in California," she said. "He's a salesman, but I don't think he was dishonest. He's full of fun, and no matter what you say to him he's always your friend—you can curse him out, and he will say, 'You're cursing me out because I won and you didn't win.' I admire winners, that's all I've got to say."

She was also trying to sort out the right musical direction. When she was asked if she would continue to sing protest songs, she expressed uncertainty. "I stopped singing love songs because my protest songs were needed. So the direction I'll take in the future depends entirely on what happens to my people. If my people go back into hiding, perhaps I'll start singing love songs again. If we continue to make more strides, then I shall go on singing protest songs—protest songs that are acceptable, however, because I don't particularly want everybody to die. I just want everybody to know who we are."

Simone demonstrated her continued involvement with liberation politics when she went to Guinea at the invitation of President Sékou Touré and spent a few weeks visiting with Miriam Makeba and Stokely Carmichael. While she was there, Touré died and she escaped, she claimed, with Carmichael's aid just a day before a military coup.

She said that her periodic returns to Africa were essential for her to maintain her identity. "I have to hide my blackness in order to stay in white Europe and white America," she said, "and then of course I don't hide it when I'm in these black places. I'm in atmospheres that are less black, and therefore I tend to act like the people around me. But I have a secret self that is very black, and I don't get a chance to show that very often anymore. I get more lonely when I can't show it."

In January 1984, Simone started performing at Ronnie Scott's famed jazz room in London; at the same time, she met drummer Paul Robinson. Both the venue and the musicians offered high points (and rare markers of stability) in what had been a difficult decade for Nina. Sam Waymon had scouted Robinson during a big-band gig and asked him to play with Simone. He joined her through two stands at the club, but he had no idea that the third time around he would be playing as half of a duo.

"She had great taste," said Robinson. "She could pick a good tune, or a tune that you would think has been rubbed in the ground, and she would Nina-ize it, put her own angle on it. If she wasn't in the mood she'd be very lazy, and if she's got a guitarist and a bass player and someone else there, they might fill in the holes, which she'd be very happy to let them do. But with me, there was a big hole, and that added to another one of Nina's strengths, which was drama. Sometimes she wasn't musically right on it, but she knew how to handle the audience and the room that you were in by using silence and space."

The drummer recalled that she would arrive at Ronnie Scott's as late as she could, not even stopping in the dressing room but walking directly onstage. Tony Sanucci would take her fur coat, she'd already be wearing a gown underneath, and she would sit down and start. She also tried not to play one minute more than the hour she was contracted to do. "If she could milk the audience," Robinson said, "if the audiences start going crazy and clapping, she'd use that for about four or five minutes, so we could get out of playing something else." But the fact that she could get this kind of reaction shows that whatever the challenges of getting Nina Simone onto a stage in this period, she was still capable of controlling and mesmerizing a room.

Though her live performances were holding steady, Simone had grown increasingly obsessed with what she was convinced was a widespread bootlegging of her recordings. "I don't crave recognition, I crave money," she said. "I want my money. I will never get it. I hate them because of it, and I hate with a consuming rage they ate my music and they gave me nothing. I crave what meant most to them, because I gave them what meant most to me."

She fought for what was rightly owed her and did recover some payments due, but some of her friends felt it wasn't a useful battle. "Every artist feels that, and in most cases they're right," said George Wein. "Because the record companies have their way of keeping books that the artists don't understand. Even if they're not legally ripped off, they *feel* ripped off, and, in a sense, they are. Anything, any angle the record company could find to legally give themselves the money—every time they would come to a club to see their artists they'd sign the check and charge it to the artist's account, something like that. But it is also the fact that maybe she didn't sell as many records as she thought she was selling."

"She thought that everything that was out was illegal because she was not getting any money," said Raymond Gonzalez. "I think she was completely traumatized by the IRS—all of a sudden she found herself [going] from being a superstar to being poor, of course blaming it on everybody else, and maybe she was right."

Out of rage or the sense that she could not rely on anyone else for protection, Simone started taking it upon herself to exact revenge. One time, she witnessed someone badgering her brother, trying to force his name onto a concert contract. She asked the man to step outside the room and started to beat him with her belt.

She told him to take his glasses off, and then hit him three times. "By the third time I saw the fear," she said. "I thought I would stop, but I got a taste of him in my mouth, and I wanted to cut him." She told him to pay the bill and take care of the proper payments, which he did in a matter of minutes. "I will kill anything that moves that's going to make me not get what I deserve in terms of the treatment I get, the respect I get," she said.

Simone was increasingly fascinated by weapons and violence, so much so that others who knew this could read even her innocuous actions as potentially aggressive. Roger Nupie told of one show in England where she asked for half of her fee before she went onstage. The promoter didn't want to give her the amount she requested, and she opened her handbag—and took out a handkerchief. "He was so scared," said Nupie. "He was turning pale because he thought, 'Oh, my God, she's taking a gun or a knife or whatever.' So she had this reputation and she could use it anytime. She got her money."

This all came to a head during yet another strange episode in Casablanca. Convinced that Susan Baumann and Josephine Jones were following her, Simone brought a gun to Morocco, ready to shoot the erstwhile managers in self-defense. When she arrived, she told Al Schackman, "The dykes are after me. They want to kill me. The police took my gun but they said that they would protect me."

Simone and Schackman were in Casablanca to open a new penthouse club in a hotel to be called the Nina Simone Room, with the idea that she would have a regular place to perform and stay in luxury. The space was beautiful—lounge chairs and sofas, surrounded by wraparound windows—and it seemed like an ideal, easy setup for her to make some steady money. But when they started playing, Schackman could tell that something was bugging Simone.

She started snapping at the audience, telling them that they didn't understand her music. A woman with a French accent called out, saying that they loved Nina and just wanted to hear her play. Simone started arguing with her, and the woman said, "I don't have to sit here and listen to this," and walked out.

Nina leaped up to follow her, with Schackman trailing behind. As she was chasing the woman, Simone pulled out a knife; her guitarist grabbed her and held her back as the woman got onto the elevator. Schackman took Simone to her room, put her to bed, and returned to the lounge and played piano, trying to keep the audience distracted from the evening's chaos.

Simone's solitude was also getting the best of her. Leopoldo Fleming and Raymond Gonzalez both resorted to hiring male companions for her on the road. "Nina would always talk about sex," said Gonzalez. "It was a fantasy thing, but she was not obsessed by it physically. I think it was just a conversation piece actually—'I'm not getting enough attention.'"

"Nina was a very shy southern girl, very innocent," Schackman agreed. "She could put on a show, she could come on voracious, but I think that in some ways sexuality scared her."

One happy moment came when Nina became a grandmother. "When [Lisa] had the child, she softened and she became a woman again, and she called me," said Simone. She added that it was too complicated for her to visit Lisa, so she should bring the child to her instead. "I tried to get out there, but because I'm chased by most of the Western world, I never made it. So I told her, 'You come here and bring that baby.'"

But then Lisa called again with more news, this time less

joyous. She had gotten a divorce, and the baby was staying with Andy. Nina told Lisa, "I'm not gonna have that child like I was passed around, like you was passed around." She hired detectives to locate Stroud and find the baby but didn't sustain the efforts.

As she grappled with issues of anger and desire and the arrival of a new generation in the family, her living situation remained unsettled. She lived in Trinidad for a while and then stayed with Amiri Baraka and his wife in New Jersey. Baraka believed that Nina had long been punished simply for standing up for herself. "The fact that many times she was in the right and was trying to do what most of us would do, defend ourselves, seldom got through," he wrote. "She knows, as does any person really clear about American life, that such injustice is rooted in the racism and class bias of the society's history and development."

But Simone was in a downward spiral. Schackman got a call one night from a hospital where Simone had been brought after the police found her lying on a bench in the Newark train station with a jug of wine. Gerrit De Bruin and Raymond Gonzalez decided that it was time to intercede. They determined that, though she was still being managed by the American-based Sanucci, it would be best for her to be close to them and to the European audience that remained her most loyal fans. They found her a home in Nijmegen, near Amsterdam, and moved her there in 1985.

"Gerrit and Raymond worked hand in hand to try to get Nina in a place where she was comfortable," said Fleming. "They did bring Nina out of a financial funk and a spiritual funk, I believe, and they had her working more. She was happy in Nijmegen for a while. Nina was this kind of person that needed to be on the move a lot, but she was there for a good while."

The move also meant that her friends were ever more aware of the severity of her emotional issues, which their new proximity made difficult to hide. They took her to see several doctors in search of an explanation for her condition.

It was around this time that word reached Lisa Simone about her mother's declining mental state. She was stationed in Frankfurt, Germany, and went to visit Nina in Nijmegen. "I still had a lot of unresolved issues," Lisa said. "There was a lot of anger in me when I went to see her, to the point where the way she chewed her food, the way she walked, the way she sat, just made me want to throw up. But at the same time, that's my mother, and I was very concerned because she had a nervous tic—she'd be talking or sitting and her mouth would always be twitching. And when she would walk, it was more of a shuffle."

She knew that Nina was on medication, and heard words like *manic-depressive* and *bipolar,* although those terms stopped short of being an official diagnosis. And Lisa also had doubts about the treatment and its effects. Still, she recognized that having a clinical explanation for Nina's behavior meant reconsidering her mother's life and her actions.

"A lot of things that I had dealt with, where one minute she'd be happy and the next minute I'd be dealing with someone that wasn't in the room five minutes ago, started to make sense," said Lisa. "It also helped me to not take so much on myself, in terms of the fact that I did something wrong or I helped to cause this. But I was also very angry, I just wanted her to die. There was a lot going on in me that I had to make peace with."

Gerrit De Bruin believed that when Simone told people that she was the reincarnation of an Egyptian queen, she was really indicating that she knew she was different. She had always stood out because of her talent, because she was a Waymon, and because she had different priorities than others in her field, but she also realized that she truly was wired unlike other people. Simone was aware, for instance, that most people were able to recognize when something was worth being angry about, but her chemical imbalance wouldn't allow her to make those distinctions.

"She couldn't control herself," he said. "I've always understood that Nina couldn't help it, and that it was not personal, because you can't blame somebody who has fever for shivering, and it's the same with Nina. I had to be careful and take her out of situations that could harm her or the people around her. In the Grand Hôtel in Paris, somebody looked her in the eyes a bit too long and she was already a bit nervous. She made a movement, and I thought, 'She's gonna hit him.' So I threw my arms around her and dragged her out [to] a taxi, and said to the taxi driver, 'Drive!' A few months later she said, 'Gerrit, thank you for getting me out of that situation in the Grand Hôtel.'"

De Bruin understood that Simone's problems were further complicated by being tied up in the ego and persona of a performer—that she also had an image to uphold, even when she knew she had been out of line. When everything lined up and she could still get on a stage in the right mood, and hold a crowd in her hand, she needed to be ready. "She lived a life which often was full of shame the day after," he said. "She had a row with somebody or whatever, and the next day she felt guilty. But she was Nina Simone, so how can you say 'I'm sorry'?"

CHAPTER 14

Nina was never really gone, she just had a very bad reputation as far as promoters were concerned. "My Baby Just Cares for Me" [reached] a younger public, but the halls were always filled anyway—it just meant that instead of two days, we could do three.

—RAYMOND GONZALEZ

Under Anthony Sanucci's management, and despite weathering the harsh effects of emotional stress, Simone had increased her activity. A 1985 studio album, *Nina's Back,* was an odd mix of songs—from as far into her recording past as "Porgy" to as recent as a remake of "Fodder in Her Wings," from the preceding album—but offered an unusually high proportion of original compositions. She also played much more frequently in the United States during these years, including a return to the Village Gate in September of 1985. This performance surge was documented on two live albums recorded at Hollywood's Vine Street Bar & Grill.

"I left this country because I didn't like this country," she said in 1985. "I didn't like what it was doing to my people and I left. I would do it again if I have to. But they have treated me so well, perhaps I won't."

Along with this softening toward her home country, she had grown uncertain about how to utilize her protest material within her current set. "It's hard for me to incorporate those songs anymore, because they are not relevant to the times," she said. "There aren't any civil rights, there is no reason to sing those songs, nothing is happening. . . . There aren't any leaders for the civil rights in 1985. It leaves you in a particularly sad state."

If Simone's affairs seemed relatively steady again, though, the stability didn't last. In early 1986, she returned to Ronnie Scott's in London for another extended engagement. She played two weeks at the club, but when Sanucci booked her for a third week she didn't show up, forcing the management to cancel the shows. By the time the dust settled, her relationship with the manager, always uneasy, had come to an end.

"He wanted me to do more work at Ronnie Scott and I refused to do that, because they were working me overtime there," she said. "He wanted to sell me again for another week there, with the same amount of money and the same amount of hours, and I walked out. I was overworked."

To his credit, Sanucci had been able to create some momentum around Simone, but Raymond Gonzalez felt that he was never the right match for her as a manager. "Sanucci was not into music—he was a car salesman," he said. "He was the type of guy that didn't want to admit he had faults. If you don't know the European market, you go to someone who's worked with her before and she has security with. He might have had some experience in producing records, but producing a record is not touring, it's not booking. He was basically a moneyman, but he was afraid of being around pros because they would see that he didn't have the experience. His problem was his own basic pride."

In the immediate aftermath of Sanucci's departure, Simone's shows were hit-or-miss. She showed up hours late for a concert at Boston's Symphony Hall; trumpeter Freddie Hubbard played the equivalent of two long sets, as the audience waited patiently for Simone. When she finally appeared, the show was so weak that one review said, "The performance indicated [that] she should have stayed at the hotel."

Bouncing between an apartment in Los Angeles and Amiri Baraka's house in Newark, Simone had a vision. Increasingly desperate for one last chance at true love, she decided that there was "still a man in the world for me to marry" and got back in touch with Errol Barrow. She called him, and he said that she could come to Barbados and he would find her a place to stay.

When she arrived, she found a note from Barrow, but he was in the middle of an election and never made the time or effort to see her. She flew back to Paris from the island, then stayed in Amsterdam. One night in 1987, she was performing in Sweden. Backstage, someone informed her that Barrow, who had recently been reelected as prime minister after a decade out of power, had died of a heart attack. "I suddenly felt more alone than I could remember," she said.

While there had been some recent blows, though, Simone was about to experience an unexpected windfall—a once-in-a-lifetime surprise hit that would make her more popular than ever.

Drummer Paul Robinson remembered going out for a rare evening at a nightclub. "At the end of the night, the closing song was 'My Baby Just Cares for Me' and all these kids got up on the dance floor," he said. "I thought it was weird 'cause we played it at Ronnie Scott's, not thinking that it had any significance at all. I didn't understand what it was all about."

Unbeknownst to Nina, an ad for Chanel No. 5 perfume featured the song, as it had been recorded on Simone's very first album back in 1958. A new, young audience had discovered the number for the first time. Some credited its initial boost to the Caribbean community in London, who noticed the island feel to the song's shuffle groove. Charly Records, who had the rights to the album, released the song as a single, and it spent eleven weeks on the UK singles chart—nineteen years after her last appearance—peaking at number 5.

"My Baby Just Cares for Me" also reached the Top 10 in several other European countries and made it all the way to number 1 in Holland. Its popularity was extended by a music video created by the Oscar-winning studio Aardman Animations; in Aardman's signature Claymation style, the clip depicted Simone as a cat, singing in a club, pursued by another feline who ultimately falls through the roof and into her arms.

"It put her career on a new track," said Roger Nupie. "From that moment on she had a complete new audience, brand-new people who just came for one song and who discovered completely different things. Sometimes she started a concert and said, 'Okay, we'll do the inevitable one, so you won't have to beg for the damn song.'"

The ad should have brought Nina a windfall, but back in 1958 she had signed away the rights to the recording, and everything else on *Little Girl Blue,* before she had even left the studio. She was outraged that an ill-informed decision almost thirty years earlier now cost her "over a million dollars" when this song, initially a throwaway added to the album at the last minute, exploded out of nowhere.

With the help of attorney Steven Ames Brown—who told her when they first met that he had read a story about her stabbing a Charly Records executive at a restaurant because she had not been paid for the commercial or the subsequent reissue of her first album—she filed a series of lawsuits that resulted in the largest sum a singer had ever received for a "reuse" fee. (Simone's music would be used in a number of other advertisements over the years, including "Ain't Got No/I Got Life" in a Müller yo-gurt spot that would be one of the most-played commercials in England between 2005 and 2010.)

Simone had enough clarity to see that beyond being profit-able for her in the short term, the hit was also something she needed to capitalize on. "When 'My Baby Just Cares for Me' came along," she said, "I said, 'I have to take this opportunity now to go all over the world and promote my records, whether I make the money or not from the [sales]. I have to go, because this is my last chance.' I worked very hard to take advantage of my second coming, because it was my last time as far as I was concerned."

Raymond Gonzalez stepped up to answer this opportunity. While Brown set about rebuilding Simone's recording portfo-lio, renegotiating her contracts and consolidating her catalogue, Gonzalez began increasing Simone's bookings, starting with eight dates in Holland. As word spread that she was showing up and delivering, other offers came; the summer and fall of 1988 brought her back to London, Paris, Spain. At some point, Gonzalez asked her about expanding his role and moving from booking her shows to taking the reins as her manager.

He quickly determined, though, that turning Simone's ca-reer around was a job for more than one person and that doing so would also require her complete trust and participation. He considered who were the most reliable and consistent figures in her life and homed in on a few men whose help he considered essential.

"I was at my farm in the Berkshires," said Al Schackman, "and I received a call from Raymond in Paris. Leopoldo Fleming was there with him, and they convinced me that she was better. I said, 'I don't know, but okay.' I went back on in and had a re-ally lovely reunion with Nina, who was very nice and calm and cordial."

Next, Gonzalez approached Simone's friend and sometime aide Gerrit De Bruin and asked him to move back to Holland to act as a more full-time assistant. "When Gerrit came into the picture," said Schackman, "I said, 'I guess we'll call it the A Team,' after Mr. T and those guys."

This ragtag group of men, representing different backgrounds and different nationalities, made a commitment to keep Nina on track. They had all had their conflicts with her—only someone who knew exactly what they were up against had any chance of helping her—but they all believed that hers was a unique gift, a contribution to the world that was worth fighting for. And their strengths were perfectly complementary. "Al was the music, Raymond was the money, and I was the heart," said De Bruin.

Having a structure and his own support system enabled Gonzalez to think more strategically and to survive the inevitable moments when Nina became too much. "She would call me at any hour," he said. "She was exhausting, so I needed these guys—I was nowhere without them, and I guess it was vice versa. Maybe I could have done it, but it was much more fun as a team. When you get beat up, then you can go to someone and they go, 'Don't worry about it, do you want me to go in your place right now? You need a half hour?' So it was teamwork and love and music."

Gonzalez put Nina on a monthly allowance paid out of an account in England, while he handled her rent and taxes. She trusted him enough to be comfortable with the arrangement, and she was rebuilding from being extremely cash-poor when they started. As revenue from the concerts and increased royalty payments started coming in, she bought an apartment in Los Angeles, and then rented a condo in Nijmegen, returning to a more stable living situation after many years of impermanence.

De Bruin also reached out to Simone superfan Roger Nupie in Antwerp. The team was attempting to gather a comprehensive list of her copyrights, and Nupie's archive was a useful resource. He came to London to meet with the group and hit it off with Simone, who demanded that he stay on the road with them.

Initially, he served informally as De Bruin's assistant. Nupie took advice from the more experienced De Bruin about how to handle Nina's ever-changing moods. He was told not to react to her or interfere, to just let her rant and scream (that was how she tested people), and then to try to distract her by making funny faces or cracking jokes. Doing something that might make her laugh was the best way to disrupt her internal tension. "Most of the time it worked," he said.

Nupie observed that Gonzalez had to be the bad cop because he was the one who made her work. Even after her "second coming," she didn't enjoy touring any more than she ever had. "I think she did enjoy performing, but not everything connected to it—the traveling, the interviews, and all that," said Nupie. "Being onstage, that was really her thing. That was the real Nina Simone, but everything around it, I think it was too much for her."

Though the A Team claimed absolute allegiance to the cause of Nina Simone, some questioned the scope of their involvement. "I think that the team made a lot of decisions that my mother wasn't aware of," said Lisa Simone. "And there were times when I questioned that—what about her heart? What about her well-being? They saw an opportunity, understandably so. But if it was about well-roundedness, then I think there was more that could have been done."

Nina's lawyer and accountant also didn't reveal her finances to her touring squad. The A Team were never told about her royalty or licensing income, perhaps to prevent them from stepping out of their zones of responsibility or challenging their own fee rates.

One additional key to stabilizing Simone was making a medical change. De Bruin asked a friend who was a doctor to examine her in Nijmegen. He prescribed a medication called Trilafon. He told the team that it would help keep her calm without knocking her out the way a Valium would, but that over time it would affect her motor skills, her speech, her piano playing; he advised that they could deal with those effects or deal with the degenerative effects of her illness.

Eventually, the changes in her dexterity resulting from the medication would lead to widespread rumors that Simone had become an alcoholic or a drug addict. "All of us were asked, for quite a few years until she died, about her being crazy," said Schackman. "We never offered up that part of her being. We protected that until she was gone. It was nobody's business. She started taking the Trilafon and it really helped. When she was on her meds, it was really good."

What helped was that Nina had now understood the need for treatment and its requirements. "They're to keep my stress down," she said. "It's more psychological than anything. I take four tablets a day, two in the morning and two at night. We keep the same level all the time. And even though you're not stressed, take them anyway because they work over a period of time in your system."

Although she had experimented with recreational drugs when she was younger, now Simone required chemical assistance to stay on track. It made a huge difference—though ironically, whereas in the usual celebrity story self-medication or thrill seeking leads to dangerous drug abuse, Simone now needed to keep herself on a regular and disciplined schedule of drug taking; the problems started when she did *not* take her pills.

Which is not to say that she always took them. "When she's

not taking the medicine, no one can do anything," said Gonzalez. "It's complete panic and we look like three chickens without a head running around—'Where is she? Does she have a gun? Does she have a knife?'"

According to De Bruin, Simone lived in extremes, perhaps a remnant of the chaos and abuse she endured in her relationship with Andrew Stroud. Tellingly, her volatility frequently presented itself in violence or the threat of violence toward men with whom she was close. One night in Athens, she decided that she was going to kill Gonzalez—and was insistent on this plan until her team calmed her down in London. Yet on other days she could be charming and pleasant. Her friends never knew which Nina they were going to meet. "She used to sit in my office and help put the faxes in alphabetical order," De Bruin said. "The people who worked for me loved when Nina came to the office and worked with them."

In 1989, she received an offer from an old fan. Pete Townshend was working on an adaptation of *The Iron Man,* a story by England's poet laureate, Ted Hughes, and was casting various singers for the different parts. He sent a note to Gonzalez asking if she might be available to sing a song as the Space Dragon.

"The letter he wrote let me realize what a star she is," said Gonzalez. "It was like a young kid writing to her, saying, 'Dear Nina, I don't even know if you remember me. When I met you in London, I was a starving musician—I don't know if you remember the name of the group, it was called the Who.' It was fantastic. And when I was in the studio with them, he handled her with kid gloves and you could tell he was so pleased that he was doing this album with her."

"When she arrived, she was like the queen," Townshend said. "She said, 'You can all call me Doctor!'—she had just gotten a doctorate. We modified her voice in places, using an old analog vocoder so that she sounded like a dragon. And she was quite happy to do that. I paid her really well, I gave her twenty-five thousand dollars for one song.

"About halfway through one of the days, she started to demand tickets to go and see *Les Misérables*. She would turn to her manager and he would kind of go (shrug), and I said, 'My PA will work it out for you.' But she was a complete delight."

But Simone was getting tired again and attempted to lay down some boundaries about how her touring was going to go. One night in France, Gonzalez, De Bruin, and Schackman all found notes slipped under the doors of their hotel rooms; Simone was calling a meeting. When they gathered, she presented a long list of new rules: she would play only two concerts per week, she wouldn't ride for more than an hour in a car, no more flying on small airplanes.

Her new travel moratoriums had created an immediate problem that night: They were in Toulon, and the next day they had a show in Deauville. The travel would require either a small plane direct to Deauville, or a big plane and then a four-hour drive, both of which she had just prohibited.

De Bruin started to improvise a plan. He told Simone that she deserved a private plane, like Michael Jackson's. Then, to buy himself some time as he worked out his next move, he sat in the bar and had a glass of wine. He came back to her, saying that a jumbo jet would cost $225,000, so would she give him permission to rent a cheaper, smaller plane. Meantime, he told Gonzalez to book the tickets on the Air France flight to Deauville that they intended to take in the first place.

Next, he returned to Simone and said that if she would give him $2,000 he could sell the remaining seats on the flight, trying to fool her into thinking that the small commercial plane they were taking was actually a private plane for her and that he was defraying the cost by filling it with additional passengers.

It was a ploy she likely saw through, but she played along. They arranged for her to sit in the front row, and as soon as the plane took off she got out of her seat and started asking the confused passengers how they liked her plane. When they arrived, she told De Bruin what a good trip it had been.

A few weeks later, De Bruin and Simone had dinner at Simone's home in Holland. De Bruin recalled that she looked at him and said knowingly, "Gerrit, you got me there with that plane, didn't you?" He responded, "Yes, Nina—oh, by the way, here is your $2,000." Returning the money confirmed the scheme. In these cases, it didn't really matter whether she bought the ruse or not—it was more important that she know to what lengths her associates would go to make her happy and comfortable, and that they didn't judge her when she was overly particular.

But even when she put together a productive touring run, her extravagance was becoming expensive. She insisted that she travel first-class and required that someone stay with her. And her impulsiveness meant things could add up quickly. She once took a vacation in Puerto Rico, an all-inclusive package, and then decided she wanted to stay a few days longer—which meant buying another first-class ticket, costing an additional $7,000 or $8,000. The problem wasn't necessarily the money— she was sometimes pulling in as much as $60,000 a night for her performances—but it was indicative of a renewed sense of entitlement that, if some of her friends felt was earned, others found off-putting.

A phone call with Roland Grivelle, her sometime drummer and tour manager, recorded by Stephen Cleary during the sessions for *I Put a Spell on You*, demonstrates how adamant she had become about traveling in a certain style. "You better get this straight," she snapped. "I told you I am not going unless it's first-class. You tell him that Nina refuses to go second-class. There is no but about it. If I tell you that again I'm going to fire you, man. Did you hear me?"

As Simone's touring took several laps through Europe, Gonzalez worked to reconnect her with Lisa, whom she had not seen for years. "I'm very family oriented," he said, "I'm Latin, and I really wanted to get Nina with her daughter, because I thought it was just the right place to be. I wasn't gonna force it, but if I could help it along, why not?"

He suggested that Lisa come to Simone's concert at the Olympia in Paris. "I didn't prepare Lisa at all," he said, "but I did prepare Nina. 'You see how I am with my mother'—little stupid things—'It would be nice to see you together.' You have to start from somewhere."

Roger Nupie said that the Olympia show worked out in the end. "Lisa was there as a surprise for Nina. Nina was moved, and she sang 'Brown Baby' for Lisa—just one verse, and she started to cry and she went into another song."

"Lisa came, and it seemed to be better," said Gonzalez. "After that, I don't get involved in personal relationships, I'm not a psychologist. I can't remedy years of hurt when you don't even know where the wound is."

Simone had grown tired of the residence in Nijmegen; she shuttled back and forth to her home in Los Angeles. In 1992, her touring took her much farther afield—she played in Australia, New Zealand, and Japan and returned to the United States, including stops at Carnegie Hall and the Hollywood Bowl. For a while she stayed in an apartment that De Bruin found for her in Amsterdam, but after a trip with a music publisher to the South of France she bought a new home in Bouc-Bel-Air, near Aix-en-Provence. "She felt comfortable, she felt at home in southern France," said Leopoldo Fleming.

On top of the more extensive touring, there were other shining moments in her professional life. In 1992 *I Put a Spell on You* was published, and a few months later the John Badham film *Point of No Return* was released, with five of Simone's songs featured in the soundtrack—major exposure in a film that opened at number 2 at the box office. Nina's legal counsel used this placement as a chance to renegotiate her deal with RCA, quadrupling her royalty rates.

There were other opportunities that she didn't take advantage of. Elton John asked her to participate in a duets album. In the studio, Simone was being difficult, and rather than sing her part in "Sacrifice" in her own style, she uncharacteristically decided to imitate John's delivery. "Elton doesn't want you to sing like Elton, he wants you to sing like Nina," Gonzalez told her. In the end, John, who was a huge Simone fan, grew too frustrated and Sinéad O'Connor sang the second part on the recording.

But the biggest news was that Simone released *A Single Woman,* her first new studio album in eight years. She was on a new label, Elektra Records, and working with a prominent producer, André Fischer. Formerly the drummer in the funk band Rufus, Fischer had worked with numerous R&B singers and such artists as Tony Bennett and Nancy Wilson; in 1991, he had produced his then-wife Natalie Cole's Grammy-winning *Unforgettable*.

The material on the album was an odd mix—three songs by Rod McKuen and some schmaltzy Broadway ballads ("Papa, Can You Hear Me?," "If I Should Lose You"). One song in particular had a special emotional resonance for her and took her back to a moment when she felt loved and desired. A version of "The Folks Who Live on the Hill" was dedicated to Errol Barrow; it was the song he had sung to Simone after chasing her through a meadow in Barbados soon after they met.

It was a survivor's record. "The songs on this album reflect a life lived with risk and integrity, humor and somber realism," wrote Ntozake Shange in the liner notes to *A Single Woman*. "A woman in the process of defining her life, deciding her fate, accepting, without shame or guilt, her own needs and desires. . . . The rights and responsibilities, thrills and dissolutions of love between friends, paramours, parents and children are explored with legendary Simone dexterity and compassion."

The album reached number 3 on the jazz charts, but reviews were largely indifferent. Though it was inspiring to see Simone back on a major label, with actual arrangements rather than hastily recorded live performances, the material was subpar and the production dull and gloppy. "*A Single Woman* aims to do nothing more than entertain pleasantly," wrote Arion Berger in *Rolling Stone*, "and that's the one thing Nina Simone, effortless when provoking, grousing or despairing, just can't do."

A Single Woman would be Simone's last album. When it was released, she had just turned sixty years old. Asked how she felt about getting older, she had replied, "Don't like it. Does it have a good side? Wisdom, I think, but that's all. I don't like getting fatter, I don't like losing my voice. I like gaining money, that's a good side of it.

"I don't want to be alive after I'm sixty-five," she had said in another interview around that time. "I want to enjoy some of the fruits of my labor now before I get old, before I'm seen as being old. Young people, they're attracted to me and I want to keep it that way. I may change my mind when I get a lover and when I get someone that I'm married to, I may change my mind about when I want to die. But I don't want to be around until I'm sixty-nine or seventy."

CHAPTER 15

To be a Christian, you do certain things, you don't do certain things, and these things are rules that are unbreakable in Mama's eyes. Now, I broke all her rules and still became a preacher. What you going to do with that?

Nina's move to France, against the wishes of the A Team, gave her a measure of independence that challenged her. She was geographically separated from her closest allies and her mood swings required constant attention and management; being on her own carried great risks.

De Bruin had to work in Holland, so he started a business. He came to France as often as he could, but without her advisers nearby, Simone stopped taking her medication. She called him excitedly one day, saying that she was in a restaurant in Aix-en-Provence, reading a copy of the *Herald Tribune,* and that she truly felt alive. He asked if she had taken her pills and she said, "No, the medicine is downing me. I don't want it anymore."

"I took the plane to get there, but it was too late already. The furniture was burning. Accident with the car. She refused to eat her medicine. I mixed it in her food and that calmed her down after two days. But I wasn't able to do that all day, I had my own life."

The Trilafon needed to be taken consistently to be effective, as Nina knew, so her decisions to skip doses when she felt steady could have disastrous consequences. "She would think that she was cured, and then she'd not take it," said Gonzalez. "We'd go through a week of hell, because sometimes we had dates waiting and had to plan how we could keep her. We didn't know what was gonna happen. There was a point that even the A Team couldn't control."

Other than a visit to Tunisia, all her concerts in 1994 took place in France; a date scheduled in August for Lörrach, Germany, was canceled. Meanwhile, Bouc-Bel-Air was proving an uncomfortably isolated spot to settle.

When Roger Nupie came to visit her, he was distraught to see how she was living. Simone had called Nupie and asked him to come because "something bad happened," but she wouldn't tell him what it was over the phone. He flew into Marseilles and got in a taxi; when he gave the driver the address, he initially refused to make the trip, saying that he knew who lived there and that she was too dangerous.

"She was all alone in the house," he said. "There was no water, no electricity because she hadn't paid the bills. The girl working for her had run away. I found her there in a very poor condition. She was sitting there on the porch of her house, and this image I will never forget, she looked so lost and so lonely."

When he arrived, she informed him what had happened: she had shot two boys who lived next door.

She had been making phone calls in her garden, and the neighbor kids were imitating her deep voice. She yelled at them to stop, but when they didn't she fired buckshot into their yard, injuring them both; one boy had to have eleven pieces of shot removed from his leg. ("It's the one time on record she actually shot somebody," said Andy Stroud, "after all those years always threatening that she had a gun and she was gonna shoot you.")

In August, a month after the shooting, Simone was given a

suspended eight-month jail term and was ordered to undergo psychiatric counseling. The following week, she moved back to Los Angeles.

Back Stateside, Nina was again hospitalized for observation after her sister Frances filed a complaint with the LAPD following a particularly nasty fight with a neighbor. There Nina met a young man named Clifton Henderson—he was an orderly, but Simone apparently thought he was a nurse. He was a young, gay fan of hers, and she befriended him quickly. She even stayed a few extra weeks beyond what was required, treating the hospital like a spa retreat, just to be close to Clifton. When she finally left, he was hired to work for her in France, making sure she ate well and rested sufficiently, as her outbursts seemed closely connected to irregular eating and sleeping habits.

"With the sense of humor that we have, we laugh all the time," Henderson said in 2000. "We spend a lot of time together and the relation just grew from there, and it continues to grow. I think by being an artist as she is, and me being just a simple person, our relation just clicked together."

But while Henderson, unlike the A Team members, was easily able to relocate to her remote location, some people felt he was less than an ideal guardian. "Clifton cooked for her and cleaned the mess, and slowly Nina got weaker, and Clifton didn't take very good care of her," said De Bruin. "I hadn't seen Nina for two months. I came to France, and she gained so much weight that I got so angry with Clifton." (Others speculate, however, that her weight gain was the result of cancer medications she was taking, rather than any neglect on the part of Clifton.)

Concerns about Henderson, though, weren't just restricted to his abilities as a caretaker. As Simone became more dependent on his help, he started to push her for greater responsibilities.

"Gradually, he took over managing her," said Schackman. "He said, 'I'm gonna leave if you don't make me your manager.' She bought him a Mercedes, he had a little condo a couple of miles from her house—he made her believe that he was away with his mother somewhere, but he was enjoying quite a life."

And as Henderson moved in, he made sure that Simone's friends and associates were moved out. "It's the old Hollywood story of pushing your close people away," said Schackman. "He pushed us all away."

De Bruin, meanwhile, thought there might be some sketchy maneuvers on Clifton's part around Nina's finances. He confronted her, asking how she—who had always watched his spending like a hawk—could let this happen. She said that she had no choice; he was in Holland, Al was in America, she had no one to help or even to feed her.

"That was not the Nina that I knew," said De Bruin. "I knew a furious lady. If I would have ever stolen a dollar from Nina and she would have found out, she would have killed me. But now she was weak, she could hardly walk, she needed people around her to [take] care of her. So she let go."

But it might not have been as simple and villainous as the A Team, with their limited perspective on her finances, thought. Henderson never handled any of Simone's business affairs—the title he was given was largely ceremonial. And he may have driven the Mercedes that Simone bought, but the car wasn't his own; it belonged to Nina and he chauffeured her from place to place in it. So Gonzalez remained Simone's manager and Henderson was her "personal manager."

Tensions remained high between Henderson and the A Team. For his part, Schackman hit his limit at one show when Henderson removed his daughter from the side of the stage because the young manager felt that she had disrespected him. The guitarist lunged at Henderson and they had to be separated.

After that, Henderson refused to let him speak to Simone and wouldn't put through his telephone calls.

"It became very difficult for any of us to have contact with her," said Nupie. "If we tried to call her, she was never there, she was in hospital. Once I called her during the night, and when she heard me, she said, 'You son of a bitch, you never call me.' I said, 'I call you all the time, but they always tell me you are not there.'"

New to Simone's business was agent Rusty Michael, president of Nashville-based Fat City Artists. A company bio said that Fat City worked with over 135 artists, none of the others especially distinguished, providing "management and booking services for clients as diverse as Nina Simone, Max Weinberg Seven, John Carter Cash, The Amazing Kreskin, and Dallas Cowboys Cheerleaders." A series of undated recordings of Simone's telephone conversations with Michael in the mid-1990s offers a rare and often disturbing glimpse into her mind at the time.

She frequently started from a place of paranoia and hostility—about her business, her health, her family, her neighbors. She claimed that her dogs had been poisoned, that she didn't trust the doctors who wanted to take blood samples. In truth, she didn't trust Michael, her family, or anyone—and she was very much alone, and, she said, "very angry and violent."

Michael repeatedly came to her with offers to perform for fees of $20,000 to $25,000, but she refused to consider anything under $35,000. He described himself as a "turnaround specialist," and practically pled with her to listen to him: "I'm an excellent negotiator. I also used to be a stockbroker. These people don't have anything on me. This is what I do for a living, and if there was a nickel more that I could get, I would get it."

Though money was steadily coming in from record sales

and licensing, Simone insisted that her financial situation was dire, that she "ain't got no more money than what's in [my] fucking pocket" and that she often lived day to day. Yet she also maintained that she needed larger fees because she had major expenses to cover, such as $17,000 to have her car shipped to France if she played there, because she was a big star in that country and couldn't be seen riding in an ordinary Renault. When Michael said this plan was crazy, she upped the ante, saying that she needed a Learjet "like Bill Cosby," complete with a diplomatic passport so that she could breeze through customs and be "given first-class treatment all the way."

Michael tried many times to persuade Simone to get back into the studio and make a new album. She refused, but in conversation she teased out the outline of what could have been a fascinating record—Prince's "Sign o' the Times," Michael Jackson's "Bad," a novelty tune about Jackie Robinson, Bob Marley's "No Woman No Cry," "Love Me Tender," the gospel song "When I See the Blood I Will Pass Over You." (Several of these, including the Prince and Marley songs, she had actually tried for *A Single Woman*, and the mostly uninspiring recordings were included on a 2008 "Deluxe Edition" reissue of the album.)

Michael Jackson was all over the news during this time, and Rusty Michael asked her if she had ever met Jackson. She seemed to identify with aspects of Jackson's plight, especially his wrestling with issues of fame and race.

She said that she had met Jackson once when he was young. "I told him not to change his hair, his face. He was too small to listen then." Michael asked Nina if she understood Jackson's marriage to Lisa Marie Presley, and she said that she had initially thought it was great because he needed to be with someone at his level of fame, but that then she had seen that it could never actually work. "I should have known that being in the United States, people don't let you alone," she said, adding, "I had hoped that he had married somebody black, but of course that's dreaming."

This undying dream of black pride would soon come to symbolic fruition when she participated in a truly historic event. On July 24, 1998, Simone was a special guest at Nelson Mandela's eightieth birthday in Johannesburg. "It was awesome, to meet a man who's been in jail twenty-seven years, and comes out without bitterness," she later told the *Guardian*. "That's incredible! But he had faith in the people and he had the knowledge that they were behind him."

Amid other guests, including Stevie Wonder, Naomi Campbell, and her old friend Miriam Makeba, Simone stood next to Mandela onstage at Ellis Park Stadium; on her other side was Michael Jackson, the only time she appeared with the self-proclaimed King of Pop. She was overweight and appeared a bit shaky—at one point, Jackson seemed to be steadying her—but she stood out in her strapless white blouse, surrounded by the two black-clad legends and dozens of celebrants in African dress. It was a triumphant moment for her, standing in front of an ecstatic crowd, on the continent she loved, at the invitation of a hero who had carried forth the kind of struggle for racial equality to which she had devoted so many years and so much of her soul.

By this time, Simone was collecting honors and tributes for her storied career; in the next few years, she would be named an honorary ambassador of Côte d'Ivoire and an honorary citizen of Atlanta and would receive a Lifetime Achievement Award in Dublin and a Diamond Award for Excellence in Music from the Association of African American Music. Her recording of "I Loves You, Porgy" was inducted into the Grammy Hall of Fame.

Despite such long-awaited recognition, Nina remained unhappy with her personal life. Her primary concern was the fact that she was getting old and that she had never remarried after leaving Andrew Stroud. "My music is first in my life . . . but secondly I would love to be married," she said in 1999. "I'm unlucky at marriages, not so unlucky at love." The stories of her lost loves—Edney Whiteside, Errol Barrow, C.C. Dennis— dominate the pages of *I Put a Spell on You*.

Even after her failed unions with Don Ross and Andy Stroud, the institution of marriage meant something powerful to Nina—unconditional love, absolute acceptance, or the sort of stability and reliability that had always been missing in her life. The final song on *A Single Woman,* and the album's only Simone composition, was titled "Marry Me"—"Marry me, marry me / Come and share my destiny / Pair with me, dare with me / Stand up and declare with me."

Some of Nina's friends thought she might be addressing her longtime confidant Gerrit De Bruin. "Nina was very much into that," he said, "but I explained to her, 'Listen, Nina, friendship is more valuable than love, and we should keep it as a friendship.' That's how we went on, and in the later years she became more and more dependent. She was lonely, and the group around Nina made it a bit less sharp because we were always there.

"She had always those stories about the deep love she felt for somebody. But it was never answered, and that, sad enough, is because of her condition. People weren't strong enough to support Nina's mind being joyful, suddenly being very sad, very angry. She chased people away. She attracted people and then chased them away."

She also asked Roger Nupie if he would marry her. He reminded her that he was gay, and she replied, "That's your problem, darling—I never wanted you to be gay in the first place." She insisted on meeting his boyfriend, as proof that he wasn't just spurning her. When he brought his companion to a concert in London, and she saw that he was black, her tone changed. She asked if he had any brothers who were single, and then played

"To Be Young, Gifted and Black" for them backstage—changing the words to "Young, Gifted, Black and White."

Nina remained loyal to Clifton Henderson. He kept her eating and sleeping regularly in a safe environment, but he also hired a bodyguard/assistant named Javier, an aspiring musician who started joining her onstage. "There was a time Nina Simone never would have let someone like that play with her," said Schackman, "but by that time, she didn't care, and she was very medicated."

Most significant, though, is that sometime during her time in France Nina Simone developed breast cancer. Her physical decline was exacerbated by her isolation, and also by the serious weight gain from her cancer medication.

"To me, Nina was very open with her physical problems," said De Bruin. "I had a friend who was a doctor, and he took care of Nina when she was in Holland. She had her own dentist, her own doctor, and if she phoned they came or she could go there immediately.

"That was not the case in France, plus there was not the intimate ties that Nina and I had, that made it possible for her to be open over her physical things like disease or whatever. She would have shown me, because she had a wound on her breast, which didn't heal. Apparently that had gone on for a long time, and I had no possibility to visit her. They kept me away from her."

Maybe because she knew she wasn't well, Simone's thoughts turned to her own aging mother, who was into her nineties. Aware that time was running out for a reconciliation, she expressed her wish to make peace with the woman who had never seemed to appreciate or recognize her accomplishments.

"I want the opportunity, before she dies, to give her either a trip around the world—by ship, preferably—or that mobile home she's wanted for twenty years, or/and to have her as a guest in my home, with servants and all the high ways I used to be," she had once said. "I want her to see me as Nina Simone, some-one she maybe will never like, but someone who she's compelled to respect."

Late in Mary Kate's life, she was staying in the Sacramento area, in the care of one of the Waymon siblings. Nina came out to spend time with her mother, and afterward described a joyful visit; she felt so at peace following their reunion that she briefly discussed retiring to the Bay Area to be closer to her mother and assist with her care. Although she never relocated to northern California, Nina did establish a trust for Mary Kate Waymon that supported her until her final days.

If Mary Kate—who died in 2001, at the age of ninety-eight—had never supported Nina's entertainment career, Lisa was now making the choice to follow in her mother's footsteps. After she finished her air force service, she began singing professionally, working under the name "Simone." Her stage debut was a na-tional tour of *Jesus Christ Superstar*. In 1996, she took a slot as a swing and female understudy in the original Broadway produc-tion of *Rent,* and later that year she performed the lead role of Mimi Marquez in its first national tour.

Unlike her own mother, Nina showed her support for Lisa; when *Rent* came to Chicago, she had second-row seats, and her daughter's performance moved her to tears. But while she was visiting, the cast had its holiday party and Nina played the star rather than the mother, holding court and treating Lisa like one of her subjects. Though she respected her daughter's accom-plishments, it was still difficult for her to act maternal toward Lisa—or anyone else.

In 1998, Lisa was pregnant—which didn't make things any easier when she was asked to open for her mother at London's Royal Albert Hall. As the concert approached, Simone called her daughter, saying she was in a bad mood and threatening to cancel the show.

But Lisa stood up to her mother. "She started saying all kinds of mean things," said Lisa, "and I said, 'I'm not gonna deal with this, and if you want to be a part of this family you're gonna have to learn to be nice.' I called my father and told him what had happened, and he said to me, 'She has reached the height of her career, you're trying to get there—you do everything short of embarrassing yourself to get on that stage.'"

When Lisa and her husband got to London, they tried to check into the hotel but found out that her mother had given specific instructions that she be put up in a different hotel, out in the country, and that she didn't want Lisa to be in the theater while she was performing.

That afternoon, De Bruin received a panicked call from Clifton Henderson, saying that Nina didn't want to go onstage because she was fighting with Lisa. De Bruin flew to London from Holland and went to Simone's room. He asked her what was wrong, and she said that Lisa had insulted her, so she wouldn't do the show.

"I went to the bar and had a glass of wine," he said. "I went back to Nina, said, 'Nina, I think the main problem for you is that Lisa and you are in the same concert building at the same time. Am I right?' 'Yes, of course,' she said. 'Okay, then it's easy to solve—you come in the building after Lisa has left the building. Then you can play and still get paid for the concert.'"

De Bruin went to Lisa and told her that after her opening set she should take her name off of her dressing room door so that Nina wouldn't see it, and then come with him to sit in the audience. Nina delivered a strong show and afterward proudly asked De Bruin if he had watched. Then she asked if Lisa had been there, and when he told her that she had been, she said, "Good."

Another chance for some kind of redemption came when Lisa gave birth to her daughter, ReAnna, in 1999. "When my daughter was born, it was as if we were given a new lease on our relationship," said Lisa. "She came three days after ReAnna was born and I dumped the baby in her arms, and she was looking at her, just examining her. And I knew that a lot of the mistakes and the pain that she had from our relationship . . . it was almost like, wow, here is another opportunity to get it right."

That same year, rock's postpunk "prince of darkness," Nick Cave, hosted the Meltdown Festival in London and booked Simone as one of the artists. Her backstage rider reportedly asked for three things—champagne, sausages, and cocaine.

Although cocaine was not a drug anyone had previously associated with her, it reflected the new decadence Nina was reveling in. Cave recounted the scene when he was summoned backstage to meet Simone. "She was sitting in a wheelchair, huge, with gold kind of Cleopatra makeup on, and this horrific expression on her face. And sitting around the edge of this room were her flunkies, who were all kind of quaking in fear of this woman. And I asked her, 'What do you want?' And she said, 'I want you to introduce me, I want you to get it right—I am *Doctor* Nina Simone.' She was so terrifying and so belligerent; I'm like okay, fine.

"She sat down at the piano, took the gum she was chewing out of her mouth and stuck it onto the Steinway, and glared at the piano like it was her enemy. And just thundered into this song. As the songs progressed, they got more and more beautiful and she became inflated with the whole thing. It was just an absolutely chilling thing to see, and by the end of it, she'd been kind of transformed and redeemed in some way."

In 2000, Simone moved one last time, to Carry-le-Rouet, about thirty kilometers from the house in Bouc-Bel-Air. She maintained a relatively steady tour schedule as the new century dawned. The first show that she played after her mother's death would be her final appearance in Paris, a city that had seen some of her highest and lowest moments.

"The last concert in Paris, she was in very poor health," said Nupie. "It was a very short concert, and I introduced her to the audience. I saw people crying from the moment she came on-stage. . . . There were many Japanese people—very young, sixteen or seventeen years old—who came for this concert. And they said, 'It's the most emotional thing we've ever seen,' and they were crying. And it wasn't a good concert, so it's something magical, something strange."

But other nights, right up to her final months, she demonstrated that she was still capable of riveting performances. Three weeks later, on June 28, she played her last concert at the venue that had meant so much to her early in her career, the site of her great initial triumph, Carnegie Hall. "That last time was absolutely fantastic," said George Wein. "It was a memorable, beautiful time. Nina was now an icon, somebody that belonged to the ages. And everybody that had seen her over a period of forty years wanted to see her again. I don't know who the manager was, but they asked for $80,000—it was a fortune, but it didn't make any difference, we could have paid her twice that. We sold out every ticket and nobody complained about the prices or anything, so we didn't lose money that day—which is not important, 'cause you weren't doing it for the money, you were doing it to present Nina Simone."

Simone came onstage fifteen minutes late, wearing a white dress and waving a feather duster back and forth. The crowd gave her a five-minute standing ovation. She sang two or three songs, walked around the stage waving the feathers and talking to the audience. After about fifty-five minutes, she said, "Good night—now go home."

"She was happy that night because she knew that she wasn't

gonna sing very much," said Wein. "Her voice was gone, so she just tried a few songs. And she just stood there and accepted that applause—and for five minutes they applauded and cheered, before she opened her mouth. I think she was happy at that moment. I think that she realized that she'd reached people in her life. And it was purely Memory Lane for the people in the audience, and they wanted to show her that she had reached them.

"Nobody complained. These people paid $100 a ticket, and nobody complained that the show was over at 9:15 and she sung four or five tunes. Everybody just laughed, they all knew about Nina's craziness. She had been totally accepted for what she was. And they just walked out, and they were talking and laughing. It was Nina."

Despite her enduring legacy as a civil rights icon, at the end of her life Simone had complicated feelings about her involvement in the movement. "She talked about Martin Luther King, that she marched with him, and that she knew his family and everything," said Roger Nupie. "But apart from that, she never talked too much about the civil rights movement. Sometimes she said, 'Well, it ruined my career'—even though she kept on singing all those songs up to the very last concert. So what she feels about classical music and how she didn't become a classical pianist, and how it was still a trauma, it was the same thing with the civil rights movement. It was important, and at the same time she thought it might have ruined her career."

Still, she took great pride in the visibility her iconic status had given her, and used it to speak out against racism for the benefit of music's younger generation. One of those artists was of course Nina's own daughter, who continued to pursue her singing career. Lisa Simone Kelly toured and recorded two albums with the acid jazz band Liquid Soul and shared in their

Grammy nomination in 2000. She returned to Broadway in 2002 in the title role of the Disney musical *Aida,* and Nina came to see it soon after it opened.

Elton John called Lisa because he wanted Nina to appear at his annual rain forest benefit and she wasn't taking his request seriously. Lisa called her mother and bargained with her, saying that if she did the benefit she could also come see *Aida.*

The cast was excited that Nina Simone was coming to watch them, and she held court backstage. During the performance, at one dramatic moment, Lisa could hear her mother's voice talking back to the actors onstage.

"All of us just froze, we had to keep from laughing," she said. "It must have been maybe ten or twelve seconds, and then we went back into the scene. The gentleman who played my father, that was really his only scene, so he was walking around all puffed up at the end of the night—'Nina Simone commented on my scene!'"

They took pictures, with Lisa holding ReAnna—three generations of Simone women in front of a Broadway marquee. Nina was bald and wearing a wig with straightened hair; Lisa called her on it, saying, "Miss Revolutionary, where is your Afro?"

"She was in good spirits, abnormally good spirits," said Lisa. "It was not lost upon me that she was very peaceful. We didn't have any arguments. I remember seeing her get into the limo in front of the Palace Theater, and having a really weird feeling as she got in and I said goodbye." It was the last time she would see her mother.

Two months later, on June 29, 2002, Simone played her final concert in Sopot, Poland; if it was an unlikely location for such a historic moment, it only served to illustrate how far her music had spread around the world. She had a global tour planned, but those shows were canceled—not because of Nina's antics, but because she was done. Though she still wasn't aware that her condition was terminal, her cancer was too far advanced, her body no longer able to bear the strain of performing.

Attallah Shabazz continued to speak to Simone, perhaps the most tangible connection she still had to the civil rights movement. "When she would feel like a regular lady over there in France, feeling old and left alone, I would say, 'People talk about you all the time.' She said, 'What do you mean they talk about me?' I said to her, 'You're like an adjective—if someone is going through a rough time, they say, "Oh, I feel like singing a Nina Simone song," or if you see a handsome guy somewhere you say, "Whoa, I need to conjure up a Nina Simone song."' I'd say that and she started laughing."

The last time Shabazz communicated with Simone was a few months before she died. "She kind of saw it coming, maybe two years prior, just sort of felt it. I don't know how much of that was based on her health, or when you get to a certain age, you don't know what your next mission is. She wasn't always really good at taking care of herself. But I think if she were here, with those that loved her unconditionally, what she really yearned for was to be cared for, and that would have given value to the remainder of her time."

Lisa was supposed to go visit Simone in May 2003. "She had cancer for a long time," she said. "She was a strong woman, and there was no reason for me to think that she wasn't gonna be here another ten years. I spoke to her and said, 'Have you lost any weight?' And she said, 'Oh, yeah, I've lost a lot of weight.' And that's when my alarm bells went off. I knew my mother was dying.

"I got off the phone and I burst into tears, and I wrote a song called 'Breakdown' that talks about how I feel about her, and how much I love her, and how I never seemed to have time to really make time for us."

Just days before her death, Nina was still actively protecting her work, planning a lawsuit against Skechers for using her performance in a TV commercial without her consent. She remained focused when it came to such matters, determined to always receive fair compensation, up until the very end.

At least one of Simone's longtime issues reached an overdue resolution. Onstage in Philadelphia in 2001, Nina was still lamenting about her rejection, forty-five years earlier, by the Curtis Institute. Unbeknownst to her, Lisa went to Curtis to see if they would consider honoring her mother. They agreed to award Simone a diploma.

"My mother had had two or three strokes already," said Lisa. "She was informed that the Curtis Institute was giving her a diploma, and she smiled. So at least when she passed away, that part of her heart had some closure. Poor Curtis Institute— they're always going to be known as the place that rejected Nina Simone."

On April 19, 2003, the Curtis Institute named Nina Simone an Honorary Doctor in Music and Humanities. Two days later, in Carry-le-Rouet, Simone passed away.

"She managed to die when she was seventy," said De Bruin. "She's been saying for a long time, 'Oh, I'm gonna die when I'm seventy.' And I laughed. I said, 'Come on, Nina, when you're sixty-nine, you'll postpone it for another ten years.' 'No, Gerrit, I'll die when I'm seventy'—and she did it. Easter Day, she was gone."

On her last day, Simone had the chance to say goodbye to the musician she had worked with the closest and the longest. Al Schackman called Nina while she was resting in her French apartment's garden; an aide brought the phone to Nina, holding it to her ear. Al recalled that their final conversation was short, but born of the deepest affection. "'Nina, I love you.' 'I love you, too, forever.' Those were her last words to me. And a few hours later she was gone."

The funeral was held at the Lady of the Assumption Church, attended by five hundred mourners, including her longtime friend and sometime rival Miriam Makeba, who said, "She was a great artist, but she was also someone who fought for liberty." Elton John sent a bouquet of yellow roses.

The service began with a recording of Jacques Brel's "Ne Me Quitte Pas," which Simone often performed onstage. Lisa Simone Kelly sang a gospel song, and several speakers praised her activism and her courage in speaking out. "Nina Simone was a part of history," read a message from the South African government. "She fought for the liberation of black people. It is with much pain that we received the news of her death."

Simone's body was cremated later that day at a private service in Marseilles for immediate family. At her request, her ashes were scattered across several countries in her beloved Africa.

Shortly before her death, an interviewer asked Nina Simone, "Are you still as temperamental?"

"Not as temperamental," she said, "if I get my way."

Discography

"I made thirty-five albums, they bootlegged seventy," said Nina Simone at the 1976 Montreux Jazz Festival. While she may have overstated her case, the fact remains that attempting a definitive Simone discography is tricky business. In addition to numerous releases on illegal or semilegal labels, even most of her authorized albums have slipped in and out of print at various times. Digital and streaming options have only made things more complicated.

With those caveats, this list encompasses the music Nina Simone released during her lifetime. Other collections, live albums, and DVDs have followed in more recent years; the best and most complete introduction to Simone's work is *To Be Free: The Nina Simone Story,* a three-CD, one-DVD box set released by Sony Legacy in 2008, which serves as a comprehensive overview of her career.

1958 *Little Girl Blue,* Bethlehem Records
1959 *Nina Simone and Her Friends,* Bethlehem Records
1959 *The Amazing Nina Simone,* Colpix Records
1959 *Nina Simone at Town Hall,* Colpix Records
1960 *Nina Simone at Newport,* Colpix Records
1961 *Forbidden Fruit,* Colpix Records
1962 *Nina at the Village Gate,* Colpix Records
1962 *Nina Simone Sings Ellington,* Colpix Records
1963 *Nina's Choice,* Colpix Records
1963 *Nina Simone at Carnegie Hall,* Colpix Records
1964 *Folksy Nina,* Colpix Records
1964 *Nina Simone in Concert,* Philips Records

1964 *Broadway-Blues-Ballads,* Philips Records

1965 *I Put a Spell on You,* Philips Records

1965 *Pastel Blues,* Philips Records

1966 *Nina Simone with Strings,* Colpix Records

1966 *Let It All Out,* Philips Records

1966 *Wild Is the Wind,* Philips Records

1967 *High Priestess of Soul,* Philips Records

1967 *Nina Simone Sings the Blues,* RCA

1967 *Silk & Soul,* RCA

1968 *'Nuff Said!,* RCA

1969 *Nina Simone and Piano!,* RCA

1969 *To Love Somebody,* RCA

1969 *A Very Rare Evening,* PM Records

1970 *Black Gold,* RCA

1971 *Here Comes the Sun,* RCA

1971 *Gifted & Black,* Canyon Records

1972 *Emergency Ward!,* RCA

1972 *Nina Simone Sings Billie Holiday,* Stroud

1973 *Live at Berkeley,* Stroud

1973 *Gospel According to Nina Simone,* Stroud

1974 *It Is Finished,* RCA

1978 *Baltimore,* CTI Records

1980 *The Rising Sun Collection,* Enja

1982 *Fodder on My Wings,* Carrere

1985 *Nina's Back,* VPI

1985 *Live and Kickin',* VPI

1987 *Let It Be Me,* Verve

1987 *Live at Ronnie Scott's,* Hendring-Wadham

1993 *A Single Woman,* Elektra Records

Notes

INTRODUCTION

1   **"Are you ready, black people?"**: footage of Harlem Cultural Festival performance, New York, 1969, "Nina Simone—Harlem Festival—part 5," YouTube video, 7:00, posted by Sergio Vásco, August 19, 2007, https://www.youtube.com/watch?v=RHXtB9ssnhw.

1   **"As I look out"**: Richard Morgan, "Black Woodstock," Smithsonian .com, February 1, 2007, http://www.smithsonianmag.com/history/black-woodstock-146793268/?no-ist.

2   **When she took the stage**: "Nina Simone—Harlem Festival—part 5."

4   **"the only singer"**: Nina Simone (NS), interview by Stephen Cleary, November 6, 1989.

4   **"We had no leaders"**: NS, interview by Stephen Cleary, May 30, 1990.

5   **"Most of my love affairs"**: NS, interview by Stephen Cleary, May 23, 1990.

5   **"What I hear about Nina"**: Gerrit De Bruin, interview by Liz Garbus, March 26, 2014.

5   **Simone "was not at odds with the times"**: Attallah Shabazz, interview by Liz Garbus, May 16, 2014.

6   **"She is loved or feared"**: Maya Angelou, "Nina Simone: High Priestess of Soul," *Redbook,* November 1970, 134.

6   **"I've only got four very famous songs"**: NS, interview by Mary Anne Evans, 1984.

6   **"In many ways"**: Daphne Brooks, "Nina Simone's Triple Play," *Callaloo* 34, no. 1 (2011): 177.

7   **"I heard her sing a song in French"**: "100 Greatest Singers of All Time," *Rolling Stone,* November 27, 2008.

7   **"She was hip-hop"**: David Was, "A Posthumous 'Soul of Nina Simone,'" review of *The Soul of Nina Simone* (RCA, 2005, CD), *Day to Day* (radio program, NPR), November 10, 2005.

7   **"I sing from intelligence"**: NS, appearance on Tim Sebastian (host), *Hard Talk* (TV program, BBC), March 25, 1999.

8   **"gave you back experience"**: James Baldwin, "*The Black Scholar* Interviews James Baldwin" [1973], in *Conversations with James Baldwin*, ed. Fred L. Standley and Louis H. Pratt (Jackson: University Press of Mississippi, 1989), 155.

8   **"White people had Judy Garland"**: "100 Greatest Singers of All Time."

8   **"When you saw her in person"**: Stanley Crouch, interview by Liz Garbus, May 16, 2014.

8   **"Anything musical made me quiver"**: liner notes to *Black Gold*, RCA Victor, 1970, LP.

9   **"Actually, what I do"**: NS, interview by Stephen Cleary, October 31, 1989.

9   **"She didn't copy anybody"**: George Wein, interview by Liz Garbus, March 14, 2014.

9   **"To me, she was the quintessential woman"**: Alicia Keys, liner notes to *Nina Simone: Forever Young, Gifted and Black*, RCA/Legacy, 2006, CD.

12   **"Nina Simone, she's sort of like the ghost"**: Zeba Blay, "Gugu Mbatha-Raw on 'Beyond the Lights,' Pressures of Fame, and the Power of Self-Love," Essence.com, November 12, 2014, http://www .essence.com/2014/11/12/gugu-mbatha-raw-beyond-lights-pressures -fame-and-power-self-love.

12   **"Nina Simone, I used to cross paths with her"**: "Read Bob Dylan's Complete, Riveting MusiCares Speech," *Rolling Stone,* February 9, 2015.

12   **"Nina Simone said it's an artist's duty"**: Jessica Goldstein, "How Nina Simone Inspired John Legend's Oscar Speech," Think Progress.org, February 23, 2015, http://thinkprogress.org/culture /2015/02/23/3625855/artists-duty-nina-simone-inspired-john-legend -commons-oscar-speech/.

13   **"Nina [was] great at that"**: Karu F. Daniels, "Bold Soul: Meshell Ndegeocello Rocks On," NBCNews.com, March 26, 2015, http://www .nbcnews.com/news/nbcblk/meshell-ndegeocello-rocks-n329636.

13   **"Fifty years after her prominence"**: Salamishah Tillet, "Nina Simone's Time Is Now, Again," *New York Times,* June 22, 2015.

14   **"at this critical moment"**: Syreeta McFadden, "The Fierce Urgency of Nina Simone Now," *Nation,* July 2, 2015.

14   **"I really thought that this planet"**: NS, interview by Mary Anne Evans, 1984.

14   **"For films or interviews"**: Gerrit De Bruin, interview by Liz Garbus, March 26, 2014.

14   **"Of course, all the time"**: NS, interview by Stephen Cleary, June 12, 1989.

CHAPTER I

17   **"I was born a child prodigy"**: Nina Simone (NS), interview clip, 1984, in *Nina Simone Live at Ronnie Scott's London,* Quantum Leap, 2003, DVD.

17   **"It was not as rigidly segregated"**: Carrol Waymon, interview by Stephen Cleary, February 4, 1990.

17   **"One of my brothers' friends"**: Ibid.

18   **"a wooden house"**: Frances (Waymon) Fox, interview by Stephen Cleary, January 3, 1990.

18   **"You went out"**: Ibid.

18   **"My first conscious memory"**: NS, interview by Mary Martin Niepold, May 7, 1980.

18   **"Momma never seemed to worry"**: Ibid.

19   **"My daddy putting me on his knee"**: NS, interview by Mary Martin Niepold, May 8, 1980.

19   **"His whole life was playing"**: NS, interview by Stephen Cleary, 1990.

19   **"Daddy loved the 'St. Louis Blues'"**: Carrol Waymon, interview by Stephen Cleary, February 4, 1990.

20   **"I would take him for a walk"**: NS, interview by Mary Martin Niepold, May 8, 1980.

20   **"He was energetic"**: Carrol Waymon, interview by Stephen Cleary, February 4, 1990.

21   **"There was a lot of conflict"**: Frances Fox to Stephen Cleary, January 3, 1990.

21   **"He had more blues"**: NS, interview by Mary Martin Niepold, May 8, 1980.

21   **"I loved the way she looked"**: NS, interview by Mary Martin Niepold, August 14, 1980.

22   **"I didn't get enough love"**: Ibid.

22   **"My mother never kissed me"**: NS, interview by Stephen Cleary, May 22, 1990.

22   **"We were expected to be model kids"**: Carrol Waymon, interview by Stephen Cleary, February 4, 1990.

23   **"I never got into any trouble"**: NS, interview by Stephen Cleary, July 4, 1989.

23 **"I didn't get interested in music"**: NS, interview clip in *Nina Simone Live at Ronnie Scott's, London.*

23 **"Music is a gift"**: NS, interview in Arthur R. Taylor, *Notes and Tones: Musician-to-Musician Interviews* (New York: Perigee, 1982).

24 **"There was music every day"**: Carrol Waymon, interview by Stephen Cleary, February 4, 1990.

24 **"We all liked to play"**: NS, interview by Mary Martin Niepold, May 8, 1980.

24 **"I was and still am influenced"**: NS, interview in Arthur R. Taylor, *Notes and Tones: Musician-to-Musician Interviews* (New York: Perigee, 1982).

24 **"He would come running down"**: NS, interview by Mary Martin Niepold, May 8, 1980.

24 **"My mom christened me"**: NS, interview by Mary Martin Niepold, May 7, 1980.

25 **"On Sunday morning"**: Mary Kate Waymon, interview clip, 1991, in *Nina Simone: La Légende,* TV movie (documentary), dir. Frank Lords, prod. La Sept, System TV, and BBC, 1992.

25 **"They were some of the most exciting times"**: NS, interview by Dick Hubert (host), *Celebrity's Choice* (radio program, WABC), November 12, 1967.

25 **"My early joys were mixed"**: Maya Angelou, "Nina Simone: High Priestess of Soul," *Redbook,* November 1970.

26 **"Whatever she did, I would trace it back"**: Dick Gregory, interview by Liz Garbus, March 14, 2014.

CHAPTER 2

27 **"There was a white woman"**: Maya Angelou, "Nina Simone: High Priestess of Soul," *Redbook,* November 1970, 132.

28 **"It was on a Saturday afternoon"**: Nina Simone (NS), interview by Mary Martin Niepold, August 16, 1980.

28 **"She was so elegant"**: NS, interview by Stephen Cleary, July 5, 1989.

28 **"I thought all white people was like that"**: Ibid.

28 **"Mrs. Mazzanovich used to hold out her arms"**: NS, interview by Stephen Cleary, May 22, 1990.

29 **"little colored child"**: NS, interview by Mary Martin Niepold, August 16, 1980.

29 **"Bach is technically perfect"**: NS, interview by Stephen Cleary, May 22, 1990.

29 **"The band suffered"**: Al Schackman, interview by Liz Garbus, March 26, 2014.

30   **"Without willingness"**: Angelou, "Nina Simone."

30   **"first introduction to being black"**: NS, interview by Stephen Cleary, May 22, 1990.

31   **"I ate it outside, standing"**: NS, interview by Mary Martin Niepold, August 16, 1980.

31   **"My mother had bought me a white dress"**: Ibid.

31   **"They were fixing the seats"**: Mary Kate Waymon, interview clip, 1991, in *Nina Simone: La Légende,* TV movie (documentary), dir. Frank Lords, prod. La Sept, System TV, and BBC, 1992.

32   **"Of course I wish they had admitted"**: NS, appearance on Richard Madeley and Judy Finnigan (hosts), *This Morning* (TV program, ITV [UK]), 1991.

32   **"When [my mother] talked about Jim Crow"**: Lisa Simone Kelly, interview by Liz Garbus, April 10, 2014.

33   **"He is the first person who showed me"**: NS, interview by Mary Martin Niepold, May 8, 1980.

33   **"I had no boyfriend"**: NS, interview by Mary Martin Niepold, May 7, 1980.

34   **"It was a black boarding school"**: NS, interview by Mary Martin Niepold, August 16, 1980.

34   **"In high school, all I did"**: NS, interview by Kiilu Nyasha, 1986.

34   **"from the Black town"**: Angelou, "Nina Simone."

35   **"She constantly, constantly"**: NS, interview by Mary Martin Niepold, August 16, 1980.

35   **"I met her girlfriend"**: Al Schackman, interview by Joe Hagan, 2009.

35   **"I cried and cried"**: NS, interview by Mary Martin Niepold, May 7, 1980.

36   **"He told me, 'If we don't get married'"**: Ibid.

36   **"We petted all the time"**: NS, interview by Stephen Cleary, August 21, 1989.

36   **"He tried to rape me"**: NS, interview by Mary Martin Niepold, May 7, 1980.

37   **"How did Eunice Waymon"**: Angelou, "Nina Simone."

CHAPTER 3

38   **"I had been looked down"**: Maureen Cleave, "Daddy and Mama Always Wanted Her to Play at Carnegie Hall," *Evening Standard,* October 7, 1965.

39   **"There was some talk"**: Carrol Waymon, interview by Stephen Cleary, February 4, 1990.

39   **"I went to Curtis"**: Nina Simone (NS), *Live at Ronnie Scott's, London,* 1984, performance and interview segments, Quantum Leap, 2003, DVD.

40   **"'When I was seventeen'"**: Maya Angelou, "Nina Simone: High Priestess of Soul," *Redbook,* November 1970.

40   **"So the [Eunice Waymon Fund] money"**: NS, appearance on Dick Hubert (host), *Celebrity's Choice* (radio program, WABC), November 12, 1967.

40   **"It had nothing to do with her color"**: Vladimir Sokoloff, interview clip, 1991, in *Nina Simone: La Légende,* TV movie (documentary), dir. Frank Lords, prod. La Sept, System TV, and BBC, 1992

40   **"Whatever the truth is"**: Roger Nupie, interview by Liz Garbus, March 26, 2014.

41   **"[She was] not a genius"**: Sokoloff, interview clip, 1991, in *Nina Simone: La Légende.*

41   **"Friedberg was much more gifted"**: NS, interview by Stephen Cleary, May 22, 1990.

42   **"I accompanied students"**: NS, media appearance on Dick Hubert (host), *Celebrity's Choice.*

42   **"I was near my family"**: NS, interview by Stephen Cleary, May 26, 1990.

42   **"I didn't feel like I belonged anywhere"**: NS, interview by Stephen Cleary, May 22, 1980.

43   **"took care of me"**: Ibid.

44   **"The name derived from her childhood"**: Philips Records press bio, n.d.

44   **"a very crummy bar"**: NS, media appearance on Dick Hubert (host), *Celebrity's Choice.*

44   **"I played everything that I could"**: Ibid.

44   **"It was a joint"**: NS, interview by Stephen Cleary, May 26, 1990.

45   **"They knew she was a star"**: Carrol Waymon, interview by Stephen Cleary, February 4, 1990.

45   **"A cult was developed right then"**: NS, interview by Kiilu Nyasha, 1986.

45   **"All the time I was practicing"**: NS, interview by Stephen Cleary, October 31, 1989.

46   **"I felt dirtied by going into the bars"**: NS, interview by Stephen Cleary, May 22, 1990.

47   **"It had been our secret"**: Carrol Waymon, interview by Stephen Cleary, February 4, 1990.

48   **"Our father was real pleased"**: Ibid.

48 **"Mom always said that my grandmother [hid] her albums"**: Lisa Simone Kelly, interview by Liz Garbus, April 10, 2014.

49 **"He was one of the people who came"**: NS, interview by Stephen Cleary, April 4, 1989.

49 **"charlatan"**: Carrol Waymon, interview by Stephen Cleary, February 4, 1990.

49 **"I couldn't stand him"**: Frances (Waymon) Fox, interview by Stephen Cleary, January 3, 1990.

50 **"After about eight bars"**: Al Schackman, interview by Liz Garbus, March 26, 2014.

50 **"Years later"**: Ibid.

50 **"By the way, please bring your guitar"**: Ibid.

50 **"I had never felt such freedom"**: Al Schackman, interview by Stephen Cleary, April 11, 1990.

51 **"The closest person that had a sound"**: Al Schackman, interview by Liz Garbus, March 26, 2014.

51 **"I had sung all these songs"**: NS, interview by Stephen Cleary, May 25, 1990.

52 **"I didn't know any happier love songs"**: Ibid.

52 **"I had an agent named Jerry Fields"**: NS, interview by Stephen Cleary, April 4, 1989.

53 **"Max was very good for her"**: Al Schackman, interview by Liz Garbus, March 26, 2014.

53 **"I met him when I visited"**: Ibid.

53 **"just out of it"**: Frances (Waymon) Fox, interview by Stephen Cleary, January 3, 1990.

53 **"I think she was very innocent"**: Ibid.

54 **"I married him because I was so lonely"**: NS, interview by Stephen Cleary, April 4, 1989.

CHAPTER 4

55 **"My music had such power"**: Nina Simone (NS), interview by Stephen Cleary, July 5, 1989.

56 **"When I heard the real version"**: Stanley Crouch, interview by Liz Garbus, May 16, 2014.

57 **"She did One Fifth Avenue"**: Al Schackman, interview by Stephen Cleary, April 11, 1990.

57 **"My first piano teacher taught me"**: NS, appearance on Tim Sebastian (host), *Hard Talk* (TV program, BBC), March 25, 1999.

57 **"What Nina was doing"**: Al Schackman, interview by Stephen Cleary, April 11, 1990.

58 **"four reigning queens"**: George Wein, interview by Liz Garbus, March 14, 2014.

58 **"But I had a partner"**: Ibid.

58 **"She could bring deeper meanings"**: Stanley Crouch, interview by Liz Garbus, May 16, 2014.

59 **During her first stand at the Gate**: Al Schackman, interview by Joe Hagan, 2009.

59 **"It was almost always electric"**: Art D'Lugoff, interview clip, 1991, in *Nina Simone: La Légende,* TV movie (documentary), dir. Frank Lords, prod. La Sept, System TV, and BBC, 1992.

59 **"to protect the public from her"**: Unnamed "Village Gate bouncer," interview clip, 1991, in *Nina Simone: La Légende*.

59 **"There were lines around the corner"**: Al Schackman, interview by Joe Hagan, 2009.

60 **"I had my music"**: NS, interview by Stephen Cleary, July 5, 1989.

61 **"If I had had a choice"**: NS, interview by Stephen Cleary, December 6, 1989.

62 **"It didn't hit me that I was sensational"**: NS, interview by Stephen Cleary, July 5, 1989.

62 **They would drive down the West Side Highway**: Al Schackman, interview by Liz Garbus, March 26, 2014.

63 **"very much alone"**: Ibid.

63 **"It was great"**: Al Schackman, interview by Joe Hagan, 2009.

64 **"I couldn't believe what I was seeing"**: Al Schackman, interview by Liz Garbus, March 26, 2014.

64 **One night at the Apollo Theater**: Al Schackman, interview by Joe Hagan, 2009.

65 **"We paid attention to her"**: George Wein, interview by Liz Garbus, March 14, 2014.

66 **"We'll get some rhythm started"**: NS quoted by Al Schackman, interview by Liz Garbus, March 26, 2014.

66 **"I don't remember very much about it"**: Carrol Waymon, interview by Stephen Cleary, February 4, 1990.

66 **"When she would leave the club"**: Al Schackman, interview by Joe Hagan, 1990.

67 **"I attracted a lot of gays"**: NS, interview by Stephen Cleary, May 26, 1990.

67 **"Have I been approached by women?"**: NS, interview by Stephen Cleary, November 10, 1989.

67 **Mathias was a downtown "party girl"**: Andrew Stroud, interview by Joe Hagan, 2009.

67   **"Kevin was a very light-skinned black woman"**: Al Schackman, in-
      terview by Joe Hagan, 2009.

68   **"I have envied other women"**: NS, interview by Stephen Cleary,
      May 22, 1990.

CHAPTER 5

69   **"She had her own mind"**: Andrew Stroud, interview by Joe Hagan,
      2009.

69   **"My dad was the fifth son"**: Lisa Simone Kelly, interview by Liz Gar-
      bus, April 10, 2014.

69   **"And that's what attracted my mom to him"**: Ibid.

70   **"We got cute and whatnot"**: Andrew Stroud, interview by Joe Hagan,
      2009.

70   **"Nice to have met you"**: Andrew Stroud, in "Nina Simone: The
      Rebel," *Fader,* no. 38 (May–June 2006), http://www.thefader.com
      /magazine/38.

70   **"By this time"**: Nina Simone (NS), interview by Mary Anne Evans,
      1984.

70   **"He scared me to death"**: NS, appearance on Dick Hubert (host), *Ce-
      lebrity's Choice* (radio program, WABC), November 12, 1967.

70   **"I had met a lot of women"**: Andrew Stroud, interview by Joe Hagan,
      2009.

71   **"His first wife was from the West Indies"**: NS, interview by Mary
      Anne Evans, 1984.

71   **"I'd catch an eleven or twelve o'clock p.m. plane"**: Andrew Stroud,
      interview by Lisa Simone, 2000s.

72   **"got contaminated"**: Andrew Stroud, interview by Joe Hagan, 2009.

72   **"I don't know what their relationship was"**: Ibid.

72   **"I felt that I had been insulted"**: Ibid.

72   **"I couldn't see"**: NS, interview by Mary Anne Evans, 1984.

73   **"He came and he saw me"**: Ibid.

73   **"Darling Andy"**: NS to Andrew Stroud, July 7, 1961.

74   **"He had five brothers and sisters"**: NS, interview by Mary Anne
      Evans, 1984.

74   **"He started raining blows"**: NS, interview by Stephen Cleary, 1990.

75   **"My husband beat me nineteen hours"**: NS, interview by Mary
      Anne Evans, 1984.

75   **"I had a gun"**: Andrew Stroud, interview by Joe Hagan, 2009.

75   **"You think they're gonna help you?"**: NS, interview by Mary Anne
      Evans, 1984.

75   **"After he was exhausted"**: Ibid.

75   **"She needed to hide out"**: Al Schackman, interview by Liz Garbus, March 26, 2014.

76   **"He asked me who had done that to me"**: NS, interview by Mary Anne Evans, 1984.

76   **"I said, 'Who the hell beat you up?'"**: Andrew Stroud, interview by Lisa Simone, 2000s.

76   **"I told him that he had done it"**: NS, interview by Mary Anne Evans, 1984.

76   **"What have you been doing?"**: Andrew Stroud, interview by Joe Hagan, 2009.

76   **"This beating, it was provoked"**: Ibid.

77   **"This is retaliation"**: Ibid.

77   **"I married him because I needed"**: NS, interview by Mary Anne Evans, 1984.

77   **"She was lost"**: Carrol Waymon, interview by Stephen Cleary, February 4, 1990.

77   **"I knew Andy as a decent friend"**: Al Schackman, interview by Liz Garbus, March 25, 2014.

78   **"My father didn't like him"**: NS, interview by Stephen Cleary, July 5, 1989.

78   **"It was like a black who's who"**: Al Schackman, interview by Joe Hagan, 2009.

78   **"Everybody on the plane"**: Ibid.

79   **"Suddenly we realized"**: Al Schackman, interview by Liz Garbus, March 25, 2014.

79   **"i didn't want to write"**: NS to Stroud, Lagos, December 17, 1961.

80   **"Such a short introduction"**: Nina Simone with Stephen Cleary, *I Put a Spell on You: The Autobiography of Nina Simone* (New York: Da Capo Press, 1992), 81.

81   **"It was a gamble"**: Andrew Stroud, interview by Lisa Simone Kelly, 2000s.

81   **"When [Andy] took over"**: NS, appearance on Dick Hubert (host), *Celebrity's Choice*.

82   **"Most of them were treated badly"**: George Wein, interview by Liz Garbus, March 14, 2014.

82   **"Andrew has a degree in business administration"**: NS, interview by Stephen Cleary, November 6, 1989.

82   **"He didn't take no shit"**: Lisa Simone Kelly, interview by Liz Garbus, April 10, 2014.

83   **"I've been scared to be happy"**: NS to Andrew Stroud, July 5, 1962.

84   **"After that beating"**: Andrew Stroud, interview by Joe Hagan, 2009.

86   **"sacrificed it all for my career"**: NS, interview by Mary Anne Evans, 1984.

86   **"You weren't ever supposed to even fuck"**: NS, interview by Mary Martin Niepold, August 16, 1980.

86   **"How's the baby?"**: NS, interview by Stephen Cleary, July 5, 1989.

86   **"The first three hours after Lisa was born"**: NS, interview by Mary Martin Niepold, August 16, 1980.

87   **"I had to show the servant girl"**: NS, interview by Stephen Cleary, July 5, 1989.

87   **"Nina hated her"**: Andrew Stroud, interview by Joe Hagan, 2009.

87   **"Let's face it"**: Andrew Stroud, interview by Lisa Simone Kelly.

88   **"Andrew was funny"**: Frances (Waymon) Fox, interview by Stephen Cleary, January 3, 1990.

88   **"Subsequently, when Nina would visit her family"**: Andrew Stroud, interview by Joe Hagan, 2009.

89   **"I am so proud"**: NS to Andrew Stroud, December 4, 1962.

89   **"Everything happened in that bedroom"**: Andrew Stroud, interview by Lisa Simone, 2000s.

90   **"He used to tell me to put on the blackboard"**: NS, interview by Stephen Cleary, July 5, 1989.

91   **"Andrew loved me like a serpent"**: Ibid.

CHAPTER 6

92   **"There were two things"**: Andrew Young, interview by Stephen Cleary, January 6, 1990.

92   **"Every time a record came out"**: Andrew Stroud, interview by Lisa Simone, 2000s.

92   **"He was the original Puff Daddy"**: Lisa Simone Kelly, interview by Liz Garbus, April 10, 2014.

93   **"especially in the *New York Times*"**: Andrew Stroud, interview by Lisa Simone, 2000s.

93   **"She was nervous"**: Al Schackman, interview by Liz Garbus, March 26, 2014.

95   **"We had a party after"**: Al Schackman, interview by Joe Hagan, 2009.

95   **"It felt glorious"**: Nina Simone (NS), appearance on Tom Schnabel (host), *Morning Becomes Eclectic* (radio program, KCRW), February 20, 1985.

95 **"Nina idolized Lorraine Hansberry"**: Al Schackman, interview by Liz Garbus, March 26, 2014.

96 **"Lorraine was a very staunch activist"**: Andrew Stroud, interview by Lisa Simone, 2000s.

96 **"When you reference political enlightenment"**: Attallah Shabazz, interview by Liz Garbus, May 16, 2014.

96 **"I didn't get political"**: NS, interview by Stephen Cleary, July 4, 1989.

96 **"I never did agree too much"**: NS, interview by Stephen Cleary, May 27, 1990.

96 **"I'm not nonviolent"**: Al Schackman, interview by Joe Hagan, 2009.

97 Nina went **"ballistic"**: Andrew Stroud, interview by Joe Hagan, 2009.

97 **"When they killed those children"**: NS, interview by Stephen Cleary, July 4, 1989.

97 **"It also put in perspective her childhood"**: Carrol Waymon, interview by Stephen Cleary, February 4, 1990.

98 **"all they wanted to get was the words"**: NS, interview by Stephen Cleary, May 22, 1990.

99 **"There is something about a woman"**: Dick Gregory, interview by Liz Garbus, March 14, 2014.

100 **"I think everybody up this late"**: Steve Allen during NS's appearance on *The Steve Allen Show* (TV program, ABC), September 10, 1964.

100 **"Mom said that her voice broke"**: Lisa Simone Kelly, interview by Liz Garbus, April 10, 2014.

100 **"There are people who see injustice"**: Ilyasah Shabazz, interview by Liz Garbus, May 16, 2014.

101 **"I think she felt she could influence people"**: George Wein, interview by Liz Garbus, March 14, 2014.

102 **"Every home I went to"**: Andrew Young, interview by Stephen Cleary, January 6, 1990.

102 **"There was a concert in Chicago"**: Al Schackman, interview by Joe Hagan, 2009.

103 **"here was a black woman"**: Angela Davis, liner notes to *Nina Revisited: A Tribute to Nina Simone,* RCA, 2015, CD.

103 **"She was an actress"**: Stanley Crouch, interview by Liz Garbus, May 16, 2014.

104 **"a very Simone idea"**: Roger Nupie, interview by Liz Garbus, March 26, 2014.

104 **"He was a gigantic man"**: NS, interview by Stephen Cleary, May 23, 1990.

104   **"my real daddy for about ten years"**: Ibid.

105   **"I loved it"**: NS, diary, March 16, 1964.

105   **"Washington D.C. yesterday"**: NS, diary, May 24, 1964.

105   **"rich black bitch"**: Andrew Stroud, interview by Lisa Simone, 2000s.

105   **"side-tracked with the revolution"**: Ibid.

105   **"She was becoming successful"**: Andrew Stroud, interview by Joe Hagan, 2009.

106   **"They don't want to be told"**: Ibid.

106   **"He wanted her to be able to win"**: Lisa Simone Kelly, interview by Liz Garbus, April 10, 2014.

106   **"She wanted everything"**: Andrew Stroud, interview by Lisa Simone, 2000s.

107   **"Dear Andy—I'm sorry"**: NS, diary entry, August 6, 1964.

108   **"Do I want sex?"**: NS, note to self, on record sleeve, September 1964.

108   **"I can sleep when and if I choose"**: NS, diary entry, September 19, 1964.

109   **"It is not at all farfetched"**: James Baldwin, "Sweet Lorraine," introduction to Lorraine Hansberry, *To Be Young, Gifted and Black: An Informal Autobiography* (New York: Signet Paperback, 1970).

109   **"Her creative ability"**: Martin Luther King Jr. quoted in Robert Nemiroff, "Born Black and Female," liner notes to *To Be Young, Gifted and Black*, Caedmon Records, TRS 342, 1971, available online at Lorraine Hansberry Literary Trust, lhlt.org/born-black-and-female.

109   **Stroud, meanwhile, said**: Andrew Stroud, interview by Lisa Simone, 2000s.

109   **"I was always a Malcolm X fan"**: NS, interview by Stephen Cleary, May 27, 1990.

CHAPTER 7

110   **"Music can change your moods"**: Nina Simone (NS), diary entry, June 13, 1966.

110   **"Mount Vernon was perfect"**: Attallah Shabazz, interview by Liz Garbus, May 16, 2014.

111   **"I think of her at home"**: Ilyasah Shabazz, interview by Liz Garbus, May 16, 2014.

111   **"Music, impromptu music"**: Attallah Shabazz, interview by Liz Garbus, May 16, 2014.

111   **"All I know is that we had a new sister"**: Ilyasah Shabazz, interview by Liz Garbus, May 16, 2014.

112   **"When you have a tribe"**: Attallah Shabazz, interview by Liz Garbus, May 16, 2014.

112   **"Andrew says I've been giving him hell"**: NS, diary entry, February 12, 1965.

113   **"The argument today started"**: NS, diary entry, February 24, 1965.

113   **"Well, I don't think we can take off"**: Al Schackman, interview by Liz Garbus, March 26, 2014.

114   **"She sang 'Mississippi Goddam'"**: Andrew Stroud, interview by Lisa Simone, 2000s.

114   **"A number of stars came down"**: Andrew Young, interview clip, 1991, in *Nina Simone: La Légende,* TV movie (documentary), dir. Frank Lords, prod. La Sept, System TV, and BBC, 1992.

114   **"I wanted to stay down and help"**: Al Schackman, interview by Liz Garbus, March 26, 2014.

115   **"a wild Beast of a man"**: NS, diary entry, March 22, 1965.

115   **"Dear Andrew—I resented you"**: NS, diary entry, April 10, 1965.

116   **"I live inside a cave"**: NS, diary entry, April 10, 1965.

116   **"rules to remember"**: NS, diary entry, June 13, 1966.

118   **"The Animals (the rock & roll group . . .)"**: NS, to Sam Waymon, July 15, 1965.

119   **"Because of the lack of respect"**: NS, interview by unnamed French journalist, 1965, quoted in "Nina Simone Sings of Social Injustice in a 1965 Dutch Television Broadcast," Open Culture (website), October 17, 2012, http://www.openculture.com/2012/10/nina_simone_sings_of_social_injustice_in_a_1965_dutch_television_broadcast.html.

119   **"She was towering, formidable"**: Pete Townshend, interview by Alan Light, May 29, 2015.

119   **"really troublesome"**: Ibid.

119   **"Nina Simone terrified me"**: Viv Groskop, "We Weren't Lovers: Dusty Wasn't My Type," *Sunday Express,* August 13, 2000.

119   **"It's not much fun"**: Sharon Davis, "Dusty from the Soul," *Blues and Soul* 564 (1990), http://www.cpinternet.com/-mbayly/article6.htm.

120   **"She is a tall, powerful woman"**: Maureen Cleave, "Daddy and Mama Always Wanted Her to Play at Carnegie Hall," *Evening Standard,* October 7, 1965.

120   **"Ms. Simone believes"**: Ibid.

121   **"When Andrew Came to Paris"**: NS, poem to Andrew Stroud, 1965.

122   **"The first five years"**: Andrew Stroud, interview by Joe Hagan, 2009.

122   **"it leveled off"**: Ibid.

122   **"That's when she started complaining"**: Ibid.

123 **"everything is going to be fine"**: NS, telegram to Andrew Stroud, 1966.

123 **"my frame of mind is the same"**: NS, diary entry, January 27, 1966.

124 **"I'm looking at 'The 3 faces of Eve'"**: NS, diary entry, February 6, 1966.

125 **"It was like a fairy tale"**: Lisa Simone Kelly, interview by Liz Garbus, April 10, 2014.

125 **"I don't want her to ever feel like she's alone"**: NS, appearance on Dick Hubert (host), *Celebrity's Choice* (radio program, WABC), November 12, 1967.

125 **"a shocking revelation"**: NS, diary entry, February 14, 1966.

125 **"A List of Happy Times"**: NS, diary entry, June 13, 1966.

126 **"with Andrew it feels like"**: NS, diary entry, June 6, 1966.

126 **"had a new feeling yesterday"**: NS, diary entry, February 24, 1966.

126 **"Today is Father's Day"**: NS, card to Andrew Stroud, June 19, 1966.

CHAPTER 8

127 **"'Four Women' was a song"**: Nina Simone (NS), interview by Stephen Cleary, May 27, 1990.

127 **"The first time I wore my hair African"**: NS, interview by Stephen Cleary, 1989.

127 **"The 'black beauty' thing"**: Roger Nupie, interview by Liz Garbus, March 26, 2014.

128 **"She would get very depressed"**: Andrew Stroud, interview by Lisa Simone, 2000s.

128 **"I can't be white"**: NS, diary entry, n.d.

128 **"I decided today that I wanted"**: NS, diary entry, February 20, 1966.

129 **"The civil rights movement"**: NS, interview by Stephen Cleary, May 22, 1990.

129 **"I *am* civil rights"**: Al Schackman, interview by Joe Hagan, 2009.

129 **"I didn't educate myself very well"**: NS, interview by Stephen Cleary, May 22, 1990.

129 **"My mind during this time"**: NS, interview by Stephen Cleary, July 5, 1989.

129 **"One of the things she said to me"**: Andrew Young, interview by Stephen Cleary, January 6, 1990.

130 **"Langston Hughes was befriending me"**: NS, interview by Stephen Cleary, May 27, 1990.

130 **"She thought herself the equal"**: Andrew Stroud, interview by Joe Hagan, 2009.

130 **"During the '60s, my people started having riots"**: NS, interview in Arthur R. Taylor, *Notes and Tones: Musician-to-Musician Interviews* (New York: Perigee, 1982).

131 **"She went absolutely crazy"**: Andrew Stroud, interview by Lisa Simone, 2000s.

131 **"The protest stuff . . . created a negative atmosphere"**: Ibid.

131 **"She became embittered"**: Ron Delsener, interview clip, 1991, in *Nina Simone: La Légende,* TV movie (documentary), dir. Frank Lords, prod. La Sept, System TV, and BBC, 1992.

132 **"I have no faith"**: Nina Simone, appearance on Eric Kulberg (host), *Jazz Now* (radio program, WAMU), May 1966.

132 **"'Four Women' is four distinctive descriptions"**: NS, interview by Mary Anne Evans, 1984.

134 **"Dad claims"**: Lisa Simone Kelly, interview by Liz Garbus, April 10, 2014.

134 **"Nina was Peaches"**: Al Schackman, interview by Liz Garbus, March 26, 2014.

135 **"I could feel the emotions"**: Leopoldo Fleming, interview by Liz Garbus, April 10, 2014.

135 **"'Four Women' was an opportunity"**: Attallah Shabazz, interview by Liz Garbus, May 16, 2014.

135 **"I thought it was stupid"**: NS, interview by Stephen Cleary, May 27, 1990.

135 **"very hurt when they giggled"**: NS, diary entry, February 20, 1966.

135 **"Black people thought it was insulting"**: Roger Nupie, interview by Liz Garbus, March 26, 2014.

136 **"I have always admired"**: RCA Victor press bio, n.d.

136 **"the kind of woman who had so much integrity"**: NS, appearance on Kulberg (host), *Jazz Now.*

136 **"I think they do it"**: NS, interview by Stephen Cleary, May 22, 1990.

136 **"I was never influenced by Billie Holiday"**: NS, interview by Stephen Cleary, April 4, 1989.

137 **"I would travel five hundred miles"**: NS, interview by Stephen Cleary, May 27, 1990.

137 **"These were brilliant"**: Attallah Shabazz, interview by Liz Garbus, May 16, 2014.

138 **"I loved her, and she was like an aunt"**: Ilyasah Shabazz, interview by Liz Garbus, May 16, 2014.

138 **"I remember sitting in the car"**: Lisa Simone Kelly, interview by Liz Garbus, April 10, 2014.

139 **"Andrew—Again I say"**: NS, handwritten note to Andrew Stroud on record sleeve.

140 **"Nina Simone has exploded"**: "Nina Simone: Angry Woman of Jazz," *Sepia* 16 (March 1967), quoted in liner notes to *Silk & Soul,* RCA Legacy reissue, 2006, CD.

140 **"I wasn't going to interfere"**: Andrew Stroud, interview by Joe Hagan, 2009.

141 **"My husband discovered me"**: NS, interview by Stephen Cleary, July 4, 1989.

141 **"partly incoherent"**: Andrew Stroud, interview by Joe Hagan, 2009.

141 **"After a few days' rest"**: Ibid.

CHAPTER 9

143 **"I've had a couple of times onstage"**: Nina Simone (NS), interview clip, 1968, from *Nina,* documentary short (24 min.), dir. Joel Gold, prod. Peter Rodis, 1970.

143 **"If you compare the Philips records"**: Gerrit De Bruin, interview by Liz Garbus, March 26, 2014.

144 **"They are songs of the soil"**: Sid McCoy, liner notes for *Nina Simone Sings the Blues,* RCA Victor, 1967, LP.

144 **"I remember Royal Albert Hall"**: Dick Gregory, interview by Liz Garbus, March 14, 2014.

145 **"I climbed up the stage"**: Gerrit De Bruin, interview by Liz Garbus, March 26, 2014.

146 **"My music, I feel, is the same"**: NS, appearance on Sid Mark (host), *The Mark of Jazz* (radio program, WHAT), 1967.

147 **"She will play Las Vegas yet"**: Leonard Feather, "Nina Simone, from Bach to the Blues," *New York World Journal,* February 12, 1967.

147 **"I gave up in two weeks"**: NS, interview by Stephen Cleary, November 10, 1989.

148 **"I've always thought"**: NS, interview clip, 1968, from *Nina* (dir. Gold).

148 **"I don't sleep with [Andrew]"**: NS, diary entry, December 1, 1967.

148 **"I didn't picture it as a problem"**: Andrew Stroud, interview by Joe Hagan, 2009.

149 **"unless I get to you soon"**: NS, to Andrew Stroud, December 25, 1967.

149 **"I don't think I'd ever realized"**: NS, to Andrew Stroud, December 28, 1967.

149 **"This vacation is wonderful"**: Ibid.

149 **"There are nineteen people"**: NS, interview clip, 1968, from *Nina* (dir. Gold).

150 **"As the fame grew"**: Frances (Waymon) Fox, interview by Stephen Cleary, January 3, 1990.

150 **"If a band does a European tour"**: Al Schackman, interview by Liz Garbus, March 26, 2014.

151 **"[Stroud] didn't understand Nina"**: Sam Waymon, interview clip, 1991, in *Nina Simone: La Légende,* TV movie (documentary), dir. Frank Lords, prod. La Sept, System TV, and BBC, 1992.

152 **"It was Nina Simone's voice"**: Angela Davis, liner notes to *Nina Revisited,* RCA, 2015, CD.

152 **"It's very frustrating"**: NS, interview clip, 1968, from *Nina* (dir. Gold).

152 **"How did you feel when Martin Luther King died?"**: exchange between Tim Sebastian (host), *Hard Talk* (TV program, BBC), and NS, March 25, 1999.

153 **"We're glad to see you"**: John Lingan, "How Nina Simone and James Brown Mourned MLK, Jr. Onstage," *Atlantic*, April 4, 2013, http://www.theatlantic.com/entertainment/archive/2013/04/how-nina-simone-and-james-brown-mourned-mlk-jr-onstage/274605/.

153 **"We learned that song that day"**: Sam Waymon, appearance on "'Why?': Remembering Nina Simone's Tribute to the Rev. Martin Luther King, Jr.," Lynn Neary (host), *Weekend Edition* (radio program, NPR), April 6, 2008.

154 **"Participation in activism"**: Attallah Shabazz, interview by Liz Garbus, May 16, 2014.

154 **"I choose to reflect the times"**: NS, interview clip in *Nina Simone Great Performances: College Concerts and Interviews* (DVD), concert and interview footage from the late 1960s, released as a DVD in 2009.

155 **"If you just think about what everybody is looking for"**: NS, interview by Fred Weintraub, transcript, *Live at the Bitter End,* 1967.

156 **"Andy told me that in 1968 something changed"**: Gerrit De Bruin, interview by Liz Garbus, March 26, 2014.

156 **"In her sane moments"**: Andrew Stroud, interview by Lisa Simone, 2000s.

156 **"She was looking for answers"**: Andrew Stroud, interview by Joe Hagan, 2009.

157 **"If you listen to some of those great recordings"**: Paul Robinson, interview by Liz Garbus, March 25, 2014.

157 **"I think that the artists who don't get involved"**: Nina Simone, appearance on Del Shields (host), *Night Call* (radio program, WRVR), May 6, 1969.

158 **"To me, an artist doesn't necessarily have to take a political stand"**: Ibid.

158 **"We go to bed happy"**: Andrew Stroud, interview by Lisa Simone, 2000s.

158 **"I walked out on Andy"**: Nina Simone with Stephen Cleary, *I Put a Spell on You: The Autobiography of Nina Simone* (New York: Da Capo Press, 1992), 119.

159 **"I wanted a rest from him"**: NS, interview by Stephen Cleary, November 6, 1989.

159 **"Had no idea how tired"**: NS, diary entry, August 28, 1969.

159 **"It's nice to to [sic] feel like a queen"**: NS, to Andrew Stroud, August 31, 1969.

159 **"Let's face it—you + I"**: NS, to Andrew Stroud, September 2, 1969.

163 **"Half of it was in jest"**: NS, interview by Stephen Cleary, November 6, 1989.

163 **"The first day she arrived"**: Andrew Stroud, interview by Joe Hagan, 2009.

163 **"Now that she had been by herself"**: Andrew Stroud, interview by Lisa Simone, 2000s.

164 **"Did she have any marks on her?"**: Andrew Stroud, interview by Joe Hagan, 2009.

165 **"The fact that I knew and I saw"**: Ibid.

CHAPTER 10

166 **"People seem to think"**: Lisa Simone Kelly, interview by Liz Garbus, April 10, 2014.

167 **"She now possesses an absolute mastery"**: Don Heckman, "Growth," review of Simone's Fillmore East performance, *Village Voice,* December 18, 1969.

167 **"This picture caught hold of me"**: Nina Simone (NS), interview clip in *Nina Simone Great Performances: College Concerts and Interviews* (DVD), concert and interview footage from the late 1960s, released as a DVD in 2009.

169 **"To me, we are the most beautiful creatures"**: Ibid.

170 **"I'm born of the young, gifted, and black affirmation"**: Attallah Shabazz, interview by Liz Garbus, May 16, 2014.

170 **"She made the transition"**: Angela Davis, liner notes, *Nina Revisited,* RCA, 2015, CD.

171 **"There is a great deal of electricity"**: *Come Together with Nina Simone: Black Gold Interview LP* (interview LP released at the same time as the LP *Black Gold* and sent to select radio stations), 1970.

171 **"If I'm in a good mood"**: Ibid.

171 **"Nina Simone is able to stand"**: Maya Angelou, "Nina Simone: High Priestess of Soul," *Redbook,* November 1970.

171 **"You really could not grab ahold"**: George Wein, interview by Liz Garbus, March 14, 2014.

172 **"I don't know the details"**: Ibid.

172 **"She had a certain kind of regality"**: Stanley Crouch, interview by Liz Garbus, May 16, 2014.

172 **"At the Village Gate"**: Al Schackman, interview by Joe Hagan, 2009.

172 **"Nina, I think you should sing"**: Stanley Crouch, interview by Liz Garbus, May 16, 2014.

172 **"Jimmy was an angel"**: Al Schackman, interview by Joe Hagan, 2009.

172 **"He was a little drunk"**: Stanley Crouch, interview by Liz Garbus, May 16, 2014.

173 **"She is Priestess"**: John L. Wasserman, *San Francisco Chronicle,* April 28, 1971.

173 **"If you're striking at the heart"**: NS, interview by Stephen Cleary, October 31, 1989.

174 **"I didn't know that my mother was famous"**: Lisa Simone Kelly, interview by Liz Garbus, April 10, 2014.

174 **"By the time I started to put things together"**: Ibid.

174 **"They stayed together ten years"**: Ibid.

174 **"I went to the camp"**: Ilyasah Shabazz, interview by Liz Garbus, May 16, 2014.

175 **"The breakup was really sad"**: Al Schackman, interview by Liz Garbus, March 26, 2014.

175 **"He treated me like a horse"**: NS, appearance on Tim Sebastian (host), *Hard Talk* (TV program, BBC), March 25, 1999.

175 **"All contracts were with her approval"**: Andrew Stroud, interview by Joe Hagan, 2009.

176 **"the best husband"**: Gerrit De Bruin, interview by Liz Garbus, March 26, 2014.

176 **"He was a strong guy"**: Roger Nupie, interview by Liz Garbus, March 26, 2014.

176 **"Andy was a son of a bitch"**: Sam Waymon, interview clip, 1991, in

Nina Simone: La Légende, TV movie (documentary), dir. Frank Lords, prod. La Sept, System TV, and BBC, 1992.

176 **"Mom, she's my blood":** Ibid.

176 **"I always had a problem with Sam":** Al Schackman, interview by Liz Garbus, March 26, 2014.

177 **"I've had sexual relationships":** NS, interview by Stephen Cleary, November 10, 1989.

177 **Simone said that she was "stupid":** NS, interview by Stephen Cleary, August 21, 1989.

177 **"unfortunately, neither Nina's *grande dame* intensity":** Timothy Crouse, review of Simone's *Here Comes the Sun* (RCA, 1971, LP), *Rolling Stone,* August 5, 1971.

178 **"All I saw was its beauty":** NS, interview by Mary Martin Niepold, August 14, 1980.

178 **"One day I got mad":** NS, interview by Mary Martin Niepold, August 6, 1980.

178 **"I moved everything down to Barbados":** NS, interview by Stephen Cleary, October 30, 1989.

179 **"He was chasing me all over":** NS, interview by Stephen Cleary, July 10, 1989.

179 **"Out of all her boyfriends":** Lisa Simone Kelly, interview by Liz Garbus, April 10, 2014.

179 **"I think [the Errol affair] was all theater":** Al Schackman, interview by Liz Garbus, March 26, 2014.

180 **"I'm her guitarist":** Al Schackman, interview by Joe Hagan, 2009.

180 **"I meet this ambassador":** Ibid.

CHAPTER 11

181 **"My dad was God to me":** Nina Simone (NS), interview by Mary Martin Niepold, May 8, 1980.

181 **"Mom decided to make me lunch":** Lisa Simone Kelly, interview by Liz Garbus, April 10, 2014.

181 **"She made a vow":** Ibid.

182 **"The best conversation I ever had":** Ibid.

182 **"Early on, I thought":** Al Schackman, interview by Liz Garbus, March 26, 2014.

183 **"We finally realized":** Ibid.

183 **"I said, 'I don't want to sing'":** NS, interview by Stephen Cleary, November 6, 1989.

183 **"It was very strange"**: Ibid.

184 **"undoubtedly her greatest record"**: Stephen Holden, review of Simone's *Emergency Ward!* (RCA Victor, 1972, LP), *Rolling Stone,* November 9, 1972.

184 **"Today, more than ever"**: Ibid.

185 **"As it gradually lost its buoyancy"**: Angela Davis, liner notes, *Nina Revisited,* RCA, 2015, CD.

185 **"I lived apart from them"**: NS, interview by Stephen Cleary, 1990.

185 **"My mother acts like I've never even left"**: Ibid.

186 **"We were brought up to think"**: NS, interview by Stephen Cleary, May 22, 1990.

186 **"an old man being tactful"**: NS, interview by Mary Martin Niepold, May 8, 1980.

186 **"I was determined not to see him"**: NS, interview by Stephen Cleary, May 22, 1990.

187 **"I wanted to see him"**: Ibid.

188 **"Nina's relationship with her father"**: Al Schackman, interview by Liz Garbus, March 26, 2014.

188 **"My father is here tonight"**: Ibid.

189 **"Who is this person on the other side"**: NS, interview by Stephen Cleary, October 30, 1989.

189 **"like stone"**: Al Schackman, interview by Liz Garbus, March 26, 2014.

189 **"I remember Mom saying that I was a robot"**: Lisa Simone Kelly, interview by Liz Garbus, April 10, 2014.

189 **"Nina was berating her"**: Al Schackman, interview by Liz Garbus, March 26, 2014.

190 **"We were in that same dining hall"**: Ibid.

190 **"Those are the two places"**: Lisa Simone Kelly, interview by Liz Garbus, April 10, 2014.

190 **"When my parents divorced"**: Ibid.

191 **"You're just like your father"**: Al Schackman, interview by Liz Garbus, March 26, 2014.

191 **"Whenever she looked at me"**: Lisa Simone Kelly, interview by Liz Garbus, April 10, 2014.

191 **"Nina had an awful lot of anger"**: Al Schackman, interview by Liz Garbus, March 26, 2014.

191 **"I think she was very resentful"**: Lisa Simone Kelly, interview by Liz Garbus, April 10, 2014.

192 **"Nina was ill"**: Leopoldo Fleming, interview by Liz Garbus, April 10, 2014.

192 **"She didn't know"**: NS, interview by Mary Martin Niepold, August 14, 1980.

193 **"[The pictures] captured this anxiety"**: Ibid.

193 **"She acts as though it doesn't exist"**: NS, interview by Stephen Cleary, May 22, 1990.

194 **"Well, this hurt the prime minister"**: NS, interview by Stephen Cleary, October 29–30, 1989.

194 **"After she divorced my dad"**: Lisa Simone Kelly, interview by Liz Garbus, April 10, 2014.

195 **"He said, 'The first thing I want you to know'"**: NS, interview by Mary Martin Niepold, May 14, 1980.

195 **"He looked just like Charlie Chaplin"**: Ibid.

195 **"He's got more sense than anybody"**: Ibid.

196 **"The most prevalent view"**: Andrew Young, interview by Stephen Cleary, January 6, 1990.

196 **"At least with us"**: Ibid.

196 **"It's almost like it just ended one day"**: Lisa Simone Kelly, interview by Liz Garbus, April 10, 2014.

196 **"chased out of this country"**: NS, interview by Stephen Cleary, July 8, 1989.

196 **"I was angry"**: Ibid.

197 **"Through her involvement in civil rights"**: Roger Nupie, interview by Liz Garbus, March 26, 2014.

CHAPTER 12

198 **"They treated me like I was gold"**: Nina Simone (NS), interview by Stephen Cleary, July 9, 1989.

198 **"She said that she had listened to me"**: NS, interview by Stephen Cleary, July 4, 1989.

199 **"Miriam said, 'This is not the coat I gave you!'"**: Leopoldo Fleming, interview by Liz Garbus, April 10, 2014.

199 **"I've always wanted to go to Africa"**: NS, interview by Mary Martin Niepold, 1980.

200 **"I was so happy"**: NS, interview by Stephen Cleary, October 31, 1989.

200 **"I was delighted"**: Andrew Young, interview by Stephen Cleary, January 6, 1990.

201 **"Don't move. I'll be back"**: NS, interview by Stephen Cleary, November 6, 1989.

201 **"You've been sent here to me"**: Ibid.

202 **"I never met a man like that"**: NS, interview by Mary Anne Evans, 1984.

202 **"I know where you're going"**: NS, interview by Stephen Cleary, November 6, 1989.

203 **"She took the opportunity"**: Ibid.

203 **"It was the stupidest move"**: Ibid.

203 **"She always said Africa was the happiest time"**: Roger Nupie, interview by Liz Garbus, March 26, 2014.

204 **"Everyday life was fulfilling"**: NS, interview by Stephen Cleary, October 31, 1989.

204 **"I found Nina to be very, very lonely"**: Leopoldo Fleming, interview by Stephen Cleary, 1990.

204 **"They couldn't stand her in Africa"**: Al Schackman, interview by Joe Hagan, 2009.

204 **"I resented the fact that he said it"**: NS, interview by Stephen Cleary, October 29–30, 1989.

205 **"It's always that"**: Lisa Simone Kelly, interview by Liz Garbus, April 10, 2014.

205 **"When I got to the house"**: Ibid.

205 **"She had grown up too fast"**: NS, interview by Stephen Cleary, October 29–30, 1989.

206 **"For many years"**: Lisa Simone Kelly, interview by Liz Garbus, April 10, 2014.

206 **"I said, 'Well, then, I'm not going'"**: Ibid.

206 **"I let her come back"**: NS, interview by Stephen Cleary, October 29–30, 1989.

206 **"So what the prime minister predicted"**: Ibid.

206 **"Switzerland was the complete opposite"**: Roger Nupie, interview by Liz Garbus, March 26, 2014.

207 **"I explained that she was very difficult"**: Raymond Gonzalez, interview by Stephen Cleary, November 2, 1989.

207 **"I am a genius"**: Spencer Leigh, "Nina Simone: Maverick Singer with Forthright Political Views," *Independent,* April 23, 2003.

207 **"I cursed out the entire music industry"**: NS, interview by Mary Anne Evans, 1984.

208 **"Sometimes she just got fed up"**: Leopoldo Fleming, interview by Liz Garbus.

208 **"For what?"**: Ibid.

208 **"I talked to her"**: George Wein, interview by Liz Garbus, March 14, 2014.

209 **"I said that she was a woman"**: Ibid.

209   **"Israel is the first place"**: NS, interview by Mary Martin Niepold,
       August 14, 1980.

210   **"There's a song I sing called 'Baltimore'"**: NS, interview by Stephen
       Cleary, 1990.

211   **"Man, I'm telling you"**: Al Schackman, interview by Joe Hagan, 2009.

211   **"God bless you"**: Ibid.

CHAPTER 13

212   **I don't want anything to do with her**: Carrol Waymon, interview by
       Stephen Cleary, February 4, 1990.

212   **"She was losing it"**: Ibid.

212   **"He was very smart"**: Ibid.

213   **"visibly shaken by her ordeal"**: "Nina Simone Pleads Guilty to Tax
       Charges in N.Y.," *Jet* magazine, November 30, 1978.

213   **"I had to crawl to the telephone"**: Nina Simone (NS), interview by
       Stephen Cleary, November 10, 1989.

213   **"I had to have my neck straightened out"**: Ibid.

213   **"Everybody was all just full of joy"**: Lisa Simone Kelly, interview by
       Andrew Stroud, 2000s.

214   **"I avoided her as much as I could"**: Andrew Stroud, interview by
       Lisa Simone Kelly, 2000s.

214   **"We went out to eat"**: Ilyasah Shabazz, interview by Liz Garbus,
       May 16, 2014.

215   **"They figured if I got my money"**: NS, interview by Stephen Cleary,
       November 6, 1989.

215   **"By that time she was under medication"**: Carrol Waymon, inter-
       view by Stephen Cleary, February 4, 1990.

216   **"Part of it is that Nina"**: Ibid.

216   **"If we're through with all this shit"**: NS, interview by Mary Martin
       Niepold, 1980.

217   **"I didn't realize until he was dead"**: NS, interview by Stephen
       Cleary, November 6, 1989.

218   **"horrifying"**: Raymond Gonzalez, interview by Liz Garbus,
       March 25, 2014.

218   **"After hassling me for months"**: Ibid.

219   **"Needless to say, it wasn't over"**: Ibid.

219   **"It's the story of my going to Africa"**: Nina Simone, appearance on
       Pauline Black (host), *Black on Black* (TV program, Channel 4, UK), 1984.

220   **"I went back to Paris"**: NS, interview by Stephen Cleary, Novem-
       ber 6, 1989.

220 **"She didn't take her medicine"**: Gerrit De Bruin, interview by Liz Garbus, March 26, 2014.

220 **"That was the worst period"**: Ibid.

220 **"Nina Simone, you have made this world"**: Quoted by NS in interview by Stephen Cleary, November 10, 1989.

221 **"Sanucci had twelve cars"**: NS, interview by Stephen Cleary, May 30, 1990.

221 **"I stopped singing love songs"**: NS, interview in Arthur R. Taylor, *Notes and Tones: Musician-to-Musician Interviews* (New York: Perigee, 1982).

221 **"I have to hide my blackness"**: NS, interview by Stephen Cleary, May 30, 1990.

222 **"She had great taste"**: Paul Robinson, interview by Liz Garbus, March 25, 2014.

222 **"If she could milk the audience"**: Ibid.

223 **"I don't crave recognition"**: NS, interview by Mary Anne Evans, 1984.

223 **"Every artist feels that"**: George Wein, interview by Liz Garbus, March 14, 2014.

223 **"She thought that everything that was out was illegal"**: Raymond Gonzalez, interview by Liz Garbus, March 25, 2014.

224 **"By the third time"**: NS, interview by Mary Anne Evans, 1984.

224 **"He was so scared"**: Roger Nupie, interview by Liz Garbus, March 26, 2014.

224 **"The dykes are after me"**: NS quoted by Al Schackman, interview by Joe Hagan, 2009.

225 **"I don't have to sit here"**: Ibid.

225 **"Nina would always talk about sex"**: Raymond Gonzalez, interview by Liz Garbus, March 25, 2014.

225 **"Nina was a very shy southern girl"**: Al Schackman, interview by Liz Garbus, March 26, 2014.

225 **"When [Lisa] had the child"**: NS, interview by Mary Anne Evans, 1984.

226 **"I'm not gonna have that child"**: Ibid.

226 **"The fact that many times"**: Amiri Baraka, *Digging: The Afro-American Soul of American Classical Music* (Oakland: University of California Press, 2009).

226 **"Gerrit and Raymond worked hand in hand"**: Leopoldo Fleming, interview by Liz Garbus, April 10, 2014.

227 **"I still had a lot of unresolved issues"**: Lisa Simone Kelly, interview by Liz Garbus, April 10, 2014.

227 **"A lot of things that I had dealt with"**: Ibid.

228 **"She couldn't control herself"**: Gerrit De Bruin, interview by Liz Garbus, March 26, 2014.

228 **"She lived a life"**: Ibid.

CHAPTER 14

229 **"Nina was never really gone"**: Raymond Gonzalez, interview by Liz Garbus, March 25, 2014.

229 **"I left this country"**: Nina Simone (NS), appearance on *Ebony/Jet Showcase* (series, KHJ-TV), 1985.

230 **"It's hard for me"**: Ibid.

230 **"He wanted me to do more work"**: NS, interview by Stephen Cleary, November 10, 1989.

230 **"Sanucci was not into music"**: Raymond Gonzalez, interview by Stephen Cleary, November 2, 1989.

231 **"The performance indicated"**: Ernie Santosuosso, "History of the Boston Globe's Jazz & Blues Festival," 1986, http://www.boston.com/jazzfest/history.shtml (no longer available), quoted in Summerwind Production's "Nina Simone: Chronology," http://www.summerwindproductions.com/nina/dramaturgical/chronology.html.

231 **"still a man in the world"**: NS, interview by Stephen Cleary, October 29–30, 1989.

231 **"I suddenly felt more alone"**: Nina Simone with Stephen Cleary, *I Put a Spell on You: The Autobiography of Nina Simone* (New York: Da Capo Press, 1992), p. 169.

231 **"At the end of the night"**: Paul Robinson, interview by Liz Garbus, March 25, 2014.

232 **"It put her career on a new track"**: Roger Nupie, interview by Liz Garbus, March 26, 2014.

232 **"over a million dollars"**: Simone, *I Put a Spell on You*, p. 60.

233 **"When 'My Baby Just Cares for Me' came along"**: NS, interview by Stephen Cleary, November 6, 1989.

233 **"I was at my farm"**: Al Schackman, interview by Liz Garbus, March 26, 2014.

234 **"When Gerrit came into the picture"**: Ibid.

234 **"Al was the music"**: Gerrit De Bruin, interview by Liz Garbus, March 25, 2014.

234 **"She would call me at any hour"**: Raymond Gonzalez, interview by Liz Garbus, March 25, 2014.

235 **"Most of the time it worked"**: Roger Nupie, interview by Liz Garbus, March 26, 2014.

235 **"I think she did enjoy performing"**: Ibid.

235 **"I think that the team made a lot of decisions"**: Lisa Simone Kelly, interview by Liz Garbus, April 10, 2014.

236 **"All of us were asked"**: Al Schackman, interview by Liz Garbus, March 26, 2014.

236 **"They're to keep my stress down"**: NS, interview by Stephen Cleary, November 10, 1989.

236 **"When she's not taking the medicine"**: Raymond Gonzalez, interview by Liz Garbus, March 25, 2014.

237 **"She used to sit in my office"**: Gerrit De Bruin, interview by Liz Garbus, March 25, 2014.

237 **"The letter he wrote"**: Raymond Gonzalez, interview by Stephen Cleary, November 2, 1989.

237 **"When she arrived"**: Pete Townshend, interview by Alan Light, May 29, 2015.

239 **"Gerrit, you got me there"**: Gerrit De Bruin, interview by Liz Garbus, March 26, 2014.

239 **"You better get this straight"**: NS, to Roland Grivelle, phone call recorded by Stephen Cleary, July 8, 1989.

240 **"I'm very family oriented"**: Raymond Gonzalez, interview by Liz Garbus, March 25, 2014.

240 **"I didn't prepare Lisa at all"**: Ibid.

240 **"Lisa was there"**: Roger Nupie, interview by Liz Garbus, March 26, 2014.

240 **"Lisa came"**: Raymond Gonzalez, interview by Liz Garbus, March 25, 2014.

240 **"She felt comfortable"**: Leopoldo Fleming, interview by Liz Garbus, April 10, 2014.

241 **"Elton doesn't want you to sing like Elton"**: Raymond Gonzalez, interview by Liz Garbus, March 25, 2014.

241 **"The songs on this album"**: Ntozake Shange, liner notes to *A Single Woman,* Elektra, 1993, CD.

242 **"*A Single Woman* aims to do nothing more"**: Arion Berger, album review, *Rolling Stone,* November 11, 1993.

242 **"Don't like it"**: NS, interview by Stephen Cleary, May 23, 1990.

242 **"I don't want to be alive"**: NS, interview by Stephen Cleary, November 10, 1989.

CHAPTER 15

243 **"To be a Christian"**: Nina Simone (NS), interview by Mary Martin Niepold, August 14, 1980.

243 **"No, the medicine is downing me"**: Gerrit De Bruin, interview by Liz Garbus, March 26, 2014.

243 **"I took the plane"**: Ibid.

244 **"She would think that she was cured"**: Raymond Gonzalez, interview by Liz Garbus, March 25, 2014.

244 **"something bad happened"**: Roger Nupie, interview by Liz Garbus, March 26, 2014.

244 **"She was all alone in the house"**: Ibid.

244 **"It's the one time on record"**: Andrew Stroud, interview by Joe Hagan, 2009.

245 **"With the sense of humor"**: Clifton Henderson, *Nina Simone Live in Brazil*, transcript, 2000.

245 **"Clifton cooked for her"**: Gerrit De Bruin, interview by Liz Garbus, March 26, 2014.

246 **"Gradually, he took over"**: Al Schackman, interview by Liz Garbus, March 26, 2014.

246 **"It's the old Hollywood story"**: Ibid.

246 **"That was not the Nina that I knew"**: Gerrit De Bruin, interview by Liz Garbus, March 26, 2014.

247 **"It became very difficult"**: Roger Nupie, interview by Liz Garbus, March 26, 2014.

247 **"management and booking services"**: *Songwriter's Market '94* (Cincinnati, OH: Writer's Digest Books, 1993).

247 **"very angry and violent"**: NS in recorded phone call to Rusty Michael, 1990s.

247 **"I'm an excellent negotiator"**: Rusty Michael in recorded phone call with NS, 1990s.

248 **"ain't got no more money"**: NS in recorded phone call to Rusty Michael, 1990s.

248 **"like Bill Cosby"**: Ibid.

248 **"I told him not to change his hair"**: Ibid.

249 **"It was awesome"**: Libby Brooks, "Sole Survivor," *Guardian,* August 6, 2001, http://www.theguardian.com/g2/story/0,3604,532415,00.html.

250 **"My music is first in my life"**: NS, appearance on Tim Sebastian (host), *Hard Talk* (TV program, BBC), March 25, 1999.

250 **"Nina was very much into that"**: Gerrit De Bruin, interview by Liz Garbus, March 26, 2014.

250 **"That's your problem"**: Roger Nupie, interview by Liz Garbus, March 26, 2014.

251 **"There was a time"**: Al Schackman, interview by Joe Hagan, 2009.

251   **"To me, Nina was very open"**: Gerrit De Bruin, interview by Liz Garbus, March 26, 2014.

251   **"I want the opportunity"**: NS, interview by Mary Martin Niepold, August 14, 1980.

253   **"She started saying all kinds of mean things"**: Lisa Simone Kelly, interview by Liz Garbus, April 10, 2014.

253   **"I went to the bar"**: Gerrit De Bruin, interview by Liz Garbus, March 26, 2014.

253   **"When my daughter was born"**: Lisa Simone Kelly, interview by Liz Garbus, April 10, 2014.

254   **"She was sitting in a wheelchair"**: Nick Cave, appearance on Melvyn Bragg (host), *The South Bank Show* (TV program, ITV [UK]), 2003, YouTube video, 2:08, posted by Andy Lynn, July 30, 2012, https://www.youtube.com/watch?v=9zkwj2JwB7w.

255   **"The last concert in Paris"**: Roger Nupie, interview by Liz Garbus, March 26, 2014.

255   **"That last time was absolutely fantastic"**: George Wein, interview by Liz Garbus, March 14, 2014.

255   **"Good night—now go home"**: NS, quoted by Wein, ibid.

255   **"She was happy that night"**: Ibid.

256   **"She talked about Martin Luther King"**: Roger Nupie, interview by Liz Garbus, March 26, 2014.

257   **"All of us just froze"**: Lisa Simone Kelly, interview by Liz Garbus, April 10, 2014.

257   **"Miss Revolutionary"**: Ibid.

257   **"She was in good spirits"**: Ibid.

258   **"When she would feel like a regular lady"**: Attallah Shabazz, interview by Liz Garbus, May 16, 2014.

258   **"She kind of saw it coming"**: Ibid.

258   **"She had cancer for a long time"**: Lisa Simone Kelly, interview by Liz Garbus, April 10, 2014.

259   **"My mother had had two or three strokes"**: Ibid.

259   **"She managed to die"**: Gerrit De Bruin, interview by Liz Garbus, March 26, 2014.

260   **"'Nina, I love you'"**: Al Schackman, interview by Liz Garbus, March 26, 2014.

260   **"She was a great artist"**: "Jazz Great Nina Simone Buried," *Billboard*, April 25, 2003.

260   **"Nina Simone was a part of history"**: Ibid.

260   **"Are you still as temperamental?"**: *Nina Simone: A Tribute* (TV program, BBC), July 17, 2003.

Bibliographical Sources

ARCHIVED LETTERS AND DIARIES
Nina Simone—diaries, 1961–1969; miscellaneous undated entries
Nina Simone—letters to Andrew Stroud, 1961–1969

PRIVATE TRANSCRIPTS OF INTERVIEWS

By Stephen Cleary
Leopoldo Fleming—1990
Frances Fox—January 3, 1990
Raymond Gonzales—November 2, 1989
Jackie (Nina's assistant)—July 7 and 8, 1989
Roger Nupie—December 6, 1989; April 11, 1990
Al Schackman—April 11, 1990; December 21, 1990
Nina Simone
    April 4, 1989
    July 4, 5, 8, 9, and 10, 1989
    August 21, 1989
    October 29, 30, and 31, 1989
    November 6 and 10, 1989
    December 6, 1989
    no exact date, 1989
    May 22, 23, 25, 25, 27, and 30, 1990
    no exact date, 1990
    (with Al Schackman) July 5 and 6, 1989; December 21, 1990
    (with Andrew Young and Stanley Wise) January 6, 1990
Carrol Waymon—February 4, 1990

By Mary Anne Evans
Nina Simone—1984

By Liz Garbus
Stanley Crouch—May 16, 2014
Gerrit De Bruin—March 26, 2014
Leopoldo Fleming—April 10, 2014
Raymond Gonzalez—March 25, 2014
Dick Gregory—March 14, 2014
Lisa Simone Kelly—April 10, 2014
Roger Nupie—March 26, 2014
Paul Robinson—March 25, 2014
Al Schackman—March 26, 2014
Attallah Shabazz—May 16, 2014
Ilyasah Shabazz—May 16, 2014
George Wein—March 14, 2014
Group interview: Gerrit De Bruin, Raymond Gonzalez, Roger
    Nupie, Paul Robinson, and Al Schackman—March 25, 2014

By Joe Hagan
Al Schackman—2009
Andrew Stroud—2009

By Alan Light
John Lydon—May 1, 2015
Pete Townshend—May 29, 2015

By Mary Martin Niepold
Nina Simone
    May 7, 8, and 14, 1980
    August 6, 14, and 16, 1980
    No exact date, 1980

By Kiilu Nyasha
Nina Simone—1986

By Lisa Simone
Andrew Stroud, 2000s

By Rusty Michaels
Nina Simone, telephone conversations, 1990s

TV AND RADIO INTERVIEWS

Nick Cave

Melvyn Bragg (host), *The South Bank Show* (TV program, ITV [UK]), August 10, 2003, YouTube video, 2:08, posted by Andy Lynn, July 30, 2012, https://www.youtube.com/watch?v=9zkwj2JwB7w

Nina Simone

Steve Allen (host), *The Steve Allen Show* (TV program, ABC), September 3 and September 10, 1964

Pauline Black (host), *Black on Black* (TV program, Channel 4, UK), 1984

Come Together with Nina Simone: Black Gold Interview LP (interview LP released at the same time as the LP *Black Gold* and sent to select radio stations to be played as if it were live), 1970

Tim Graham (host), *Wired* (TV program, Channel 4, UK), 1988

Greg Gumbel and Deborah Crable (hosts), *Ebony/Jet Showcase* (series, KHJ-TV), 1985

Dick Hubert (host), *Celebrity's Choice* (radio program, WABC), November 12, 1967

Institut national de l'audiovisuel (INA), *Nina Simone à Paris,* October 23, 1991, concert and TV interview footage, http://www.ina.fr/video/CAC91059386/nina-simone-a-paris-video.html

Eric Kulberg (host), *Jazz Now* (radio program, WAMU), May 1966

Richard Madeley and Judy Finnigan (hosts), *This Morning* (TV program, ITV [UK]), 1991; bonus feature on the DVD of the BBC program *Nina Simone: A Tribute*

Sid Mark (host), *The Mark of Jazz* (radio program, WHAT), 1967

Mavis Nicholson, *An Afternoon with Mavis Nicholson* (TV program, Channel 4, UK), 1984

Ève Ruggiéri (host), "Les voix noires," *Musiques au coeur* (radio program, France 2), October 23, 1991

Tom Schnabel (host), *Morning Becomes Eclectic* (radio program, KCRW), February 20, 1985

Tim Sebastian (host), *Hard Talk* (TV program, BBC), March 25, 1999

Del Shields (host), *Night Call* (radio program, WRVR), May 6, 1969

Sam Waymon

Lynn Neary (host), "'Why?': Remembering Nina Simone's Tribute to the Rev. Martin Luther King Jr.," *Weekend Edition* (radio program, NPR), April 6, 2008

FILMS/DVDS

Nina, documentary short (24 min.), dir. Joel Gold, prod. Peter Rodis, 1970

Nina Simone: A Tribute (TV program, BBC), July 17, 2003, released as DVD, BBC, 2003

Nina Simone Great Performances: College Concerts and Interviews (DVD), dir. and prod. Andy Stroud, concert and interview footage from the late 1960s, released as DVD in 2009

Nina Simone: La légende, TV movie (documentary), dir. Frank Lords, prod. La Sept, System TV, and BBC (1991 interviews with Carrol Waymon, Mary Kate Waymon, Vladimir Sokoloff, Sam Waymon, Art D'Lugoff, Stanley Wise, unnamed Village Gate bouncer, Ron Delsener, Andrew Young, Gerrit De Bruin, Lisa Simone Kelly, and Nina Simone), 1992

Nina Simone Live at Ronnie Scott's, London, 1984 performance and interview segments, Quantum Leap, 2003, DVD

Acknowledgments

The genesis of this book was a bit unconventional. It was conceived as a companion to Liz Garbus's remarkable documentary *What Happened, Miss Simone?* and I was initially approached about writing it after that film had already been completed. The understanding was that I would be given access to the astonishing research that Liz and her team had done—the new interviews, as well as an extensive trove of archival material, including Nina Simone's diaries and letters and the transcripts from her various attempts at a memoir—and as they had made a movie out of all this, I would create a book. The raw files were so powerful and so thorough that it only made me respect the editing and crafting that Liz did even more, and left me with the responsibility of trying to fill in the story and connect the dots beyond what could be done in a 102-minute film.

So thanks must first go to Liz Garbus and the rest of her documentary team for the impressive research from which these pages were drawn. Justin Wilkes, Amy Hobby, Jayson Jackson, Lisa Nishimura, Adam Del Deo, Sidney Beaumont, Jon Kamen, Cindy Holland, Ted Sarantos, Josh Pearson, Joan Aceste, Steven Ames Brown, Talia Gerecitano, Maura Wogan, Adrienne Collatos, and Meghan Schale all contributed immeasurably to this project. And the book only exists because of the original conversations and reporting done by dozens of journalists, but the work of Stephen Cleary, Mary Niepold, Mary Anne Evans, and Joe Hagan was especially crucial.

Kevin Doughten at Crown Archetype has been a friend for a few years, and he was the one who offered me this fantastic opportunity and humbling assignment, and then guided me toward wrestling

Simone's story into coherent shape. Claire Potter provided invaluable assistance shaping and clarifying such a complicated and emotional tale. Thank you to Elisabeth Magnus for thoughtful and deft copyediting.

Thanks always to Sarah Lazin, agent and wise adviser. My gratitude to the New York City Public Library system and to the DTUT coffee shop, where many of these words were written.

Suzanne and Adam, I love you so very much.

Index

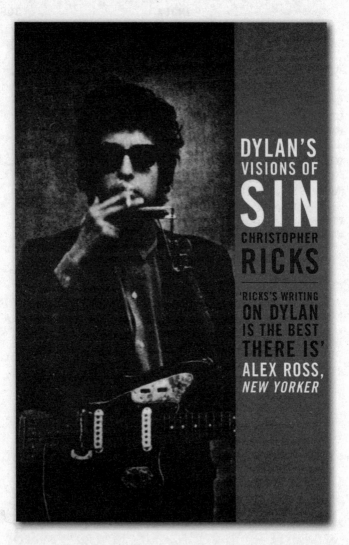

DYLAN'S
VISIONS OF
SIN
CHRISTOPHER
RICKS

'RICKS'S WRITING
ON DYLAN
IS THE BEST
THERE IS'
ALEX ROSS,
NEW YORKER

'A great case has been made by a great critic (Christopher Ricks)

that a great lyricist – Bob Dylan – is, in fact, a poet'

New York Review of Books

CANON‖GATE

JERRY LEE LEWIS
HIS OWN STORY

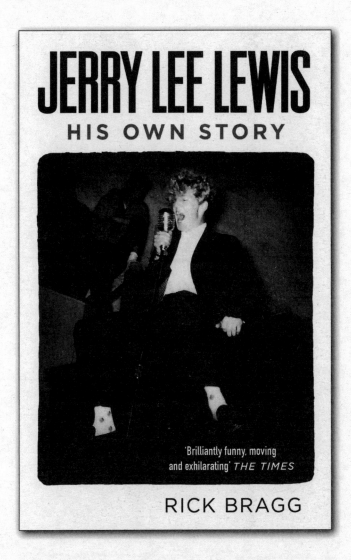

'Brilliantly funny, moving and exhilarating' *THE TIMES*

RICK BRAGG

'The words on the page perfectly match the music and the man' *Roddy Doyle*

CANON‖GATE

The
SICK BAG
Song

Nick Cave

'An epic chronicle'
INDEPENDENT

'As rock'n'roll as you can get . . . shot through with fantasy,
fiction, apocalyptic musings and tall stories' *Sunday Times*

CANON█GATE